GUERRILLA WARFARE AND MARXISM

BOOKS BY THE EDITOR

Half a Century of Socialism: Soviet Life in the Sixties
Guerrilla and Counter-Guerrilla Warfare
*The Forest: A Personal Record of the Huk Guerrilla Struggle
in the Philippines*
Beyond Barriers (poems)

GUERRILLA WARFARE AND MARXISM

A COLLECTION OF WRITINGS FROM KARL MARX
TO THE PRESENT ON ARMED STRUGGLES FOR
LIBERATION AND FOR SOCIALISM

Edited, with an Introduction
by WILLIAM J. POMEROY

INTERNATIONAL PUBLISHERS
New York

Copyright © 1968 by INTERNATIONAL PUBLISHERS CO., INC.
First Edition

Acknowledgments

Excerpts from Ernesto Che Guevara, *Guerrilla Warfare*, copyright by Monthly Review Press, 1961, and from Régis Debray, *Revolution in the Revolution?* copyright by Monthly Review Press, 1967. Excerpt from Kwame Nkrumah, *Handbook of Revolutionary Warfare* (Panaf, London), permission in advance of publication from the author. Excerpt from a forthcoming book by Wilfred G. Burchett by permission of the author. James Connolly, *Revolutionary Warfare*, copyright by New Book Publications, Dublin and Belfast, 1968. Fernand Grenier, *Franc-Tireurs et Partisans Français*, copyright by Cobbett, London, 1943. E. Joannides, *Bloody But Unbound*, copyright by Hermes Press, London, 1949. A number of selections are from articles first appearing in the journals *World Marxist Review,* Prague and Toronto; *The African Communist,* London; *Labour Monthly,* London; and *Political Affairs,* New York.

All Rights Reserved. No part of this book may be reproduced or utilized in any form or by any means without permission in writing from the Publisher, except for brief quotations in reviews.

Library of Congress Catalog Card Number: 68–55606
Manufactured in the United States of America

Contents

INTRODUCTION by WILLIAM J. POMEROY   9

PART ONE: HISTORICAL BACKGROUND   51

1. KARL MARX and FREDERICK ENGELS, The Art of Insurrection, 53
2. KARL MARX, Guerrilla Warfare in Spain, 54
3. FREDERICK ENGELS, On Guerrilla Warfare, 57
4. KARL MARX, The Paris Commune, 61
5. FREDERICK ENGELS, The Force Theory, 63
6. — — —, Barricade Tactics, 68
7. V. I. LENIN, The Revolutionary Army and the Revolutionary Government, 73
8. — — —, Lessons of the Moscow Uprising, 77
9. — — —, Guerrilla Warfare, 84
10. — — —, Lessons of the Commune, 94
11. — — —, Armed Struggle in the 1905 Revolution, 97
12. — — —, The Irish Rebellion of 1916, 102
13. — — —, National Wars Against Imperialism, 107
14. — — —, Marxism and Insurrection, 109
15. — — —, Emancipation of the Peoples of the East, 115

PART TWO: CONTEMPORARY THEORY AND PRACTICE   121

I. THE SOVIET UNION   123

1. I. MINZ, Guerrillas in the Civil War, 124
2. A. FYODOROV, Soviet Partisans in World War II, 127

II. EUROPE   135

1. JAMES CONNOLLY, Street Fighting, 136
2. ENRIQUE LISTER, Guerrilla Warfare in Spain, 1939–51, 139
3. JOSIP BROZ TITO, Specific Features of the Yugoslav Liberation Struggle, 146

4. — — —, The Party and the Liberation Army, 151
5. FERNAND GRENIER, French Partisans in
    World War II, 154
6. E. JOANNIDES, The Greek Resistance Against Nazi
    Occupation, 158
7. ZIZIS ZOGRAFOS, Lessons of the Greek Civil War, 161

III. CHINA 167

1. MAO TSE-TUNG, The Military Problem, 168
2. — — —, On the Purely Military Viewpoint, 174
3. — — —, Characteristics of China's Revolutionary
    War, 177
4. — — —, Base Areas in the Anti-Japanese Guerrilla
    War, 183
5. LIN PIAO, International Significance of Comrade Mao
    Tse-tung's Theory of People's War, 194

IV. SOUTHEAST ASIA 200

1. HO CHI MINH, Instruction to Establish the Vietnam
    Propaganda Unit for National Liberation, 203
2. VO NGUYEN GIAP, The General Insurrection of
    August 1945, 204
3. — — —, The Resistance War Against French
    Imperialism, 208
4. LE DUAN, Political and Military Forces in
    Revolutionary War, 222
5. WILFRED G. BURCHETT, "Self-Defense" Centers in a
    People's War, 225
6. Philippines: Hukbalahap and its Mass Base, 229
7. JORGE MARAVILLA, The Postwar Huk in the
    Philippines, 237
8. Indonesia: Peaceful and Non-Peaceful Ways, 242

V. AFRICA 247

1. Algeria: Features of the Armed Struggle, 249
2. BASHIR HADJ ALI, Lessons of the Algerian Liberation
    Struggle, 254
3. AMILCAR CABRAL, National Liberation and the Social
    Structure, 261
4. South Africa: The Revolutionary Way, 269

5. KWAME NKRUMAH, A Political-Military Strategy for
    African Liberation, 275

VI. LATIN AMERICA 281

1. ERNESTO CHE GUEVARA, Lessons of the Cuban
    Revolution, 287
2. — — —, What Is a Guerrilla? 288
3. OLAS: General Declaration, 291
4. FIDEL CASTRO, Speech to the OLAS Conference, 295
5. RÉGIS DEBRAY, Revolution in the Revolution? 298
6. JUAN RODRÍGUEZ, Venezuela: The Non-Peaceful
    Path, 304
7. Colombia: Theses on the Guerrilla Movement, 308
8. ALBERTO GOMEZ, Criteria of Revolutionary Armed
    Struggle in Colombia, 311
9. JOSÉ MANUEL FORTUNY, Revolutionary Tactics in
    Guatemala, 314
10. JOSÉ CUELLO and ASDRUBAL DOMÍNQUEZ, A Dominican
    View of the Latin American Revolution, 318
11. LUIS CORVALAN, Anti-Imperialist Alliance in
    Latin America, 324

VII. THE UNITED STATES 327

HENRY WINSTON, Revolutionary Struggle for
    Afro-American Freedom, 327

INDEX 332

Introduction

WILLIAM J. POMEROY

In world politics revolutionary armed struggle has occupied the center of the stage for nearly three decades. From the outbreak of World War II to the present time people in no fewer than 50 countries have resorted to guerrilla warfare or to other forms of popular armed struggle, either on an extensive or a limited scale, to achieve national liberation or democratic liberties that have been denied to them. The most outstanding of these episodes have been guided by Marxist concepts of popular armed struggle.

For well over a century, the role of armed struggle in revolutionary change has been a constant subject of discussion among Marxists. Obviously, the problem is complex, having arisen always in the context of specific revolutionary situations, in which particular features of time, place and circumstance have been involved. Nevertheless, certain principles of analysis and approach have been well established in Marxist-Leninist thinking, as tested against actual experience. It would therefore be helpful to know what Marx, Engels and Lenin actually wrote about the employment of armed struggle by revolutionary movements. In addition, an examination is needed into how the revolutionary movements that subscribe to the principles of Marxism-Leninism have sought to apply them in revolutionary situations since World War I and in the contemporary world. This volume endeavors to provide such an insight.

History, it needs to be mentioned at the outset, shows that guerrilla warfare in itself is not necessarily a revolutionary form of struggle. It has occurred in all periods of history as the classic way for less well armed people to fight the organized power of a strong opponent, has often served as an adjunct of regular warfare in the purely military sense, and has at times been employed by reactionary and counter-revolutionary forces as well as by revolutionary movements. Banditry has often had a guerrilla character.

All colonial and imperialist powers, from the days of the *conquistadores,* have met with guerrilla resistance from peoples whom they have sought to subjugate. Furthermore, all classes in society at one time or another have organized, participated in or supported guerrilla struggles. These have been a feature, for example, of many bourgeois democratic revolutions led by a rising national bourgeoisie and supported by workers and peasants. The American Revolution of 1776, the Philippine war for independence against American imperialist conquest at the turn of the century, the Boer War against the British in the same period, or, to cite a recent case, the Algerian war of liberation, have all had these features.

At the present stage of history, with the revolutionary forces in society bringing about the change from capitalism to socialism, guerrilla warfare, as well as all forms of mass struggle, has had its character shaped by Marxist thought, by the ideas and methods of organization brought to it by the Communist movement. The awe-inspiring readiness and ability of peasants and workers, especially in underdeveloped countries, to stand up to the mightiest of military powers and to prevail is most frequently due to the types of revolutionary organization introduced among politicalized mass movements by a leadership with a working class ideology, with the clear-cut goal of replacing a brutal predatory imperialist system with the humanism of socialism.

In all countries with deeply-seated social wrongs there are apt to be, at any given time, some people who can be inspired to take to arms, even when a revolutionary situation does not obtain, in the hope of changing their conditions of life. Such acts, whether spontaneous or conspiratorially planned, are viewed by Marxist-Leninists as isolated cases of desperation or adventurism, and as symptoms, not as solutions, of social problems. Of course, situations do arise where armed defense against punitive violence by a reactionary state or by fascist-type civilian gangs becomes a necessity. This right of armed defense is fully supported by Marxists, who would simultaneously seek to bring into play the widest possible range of legal and civilian mass forces against the reactionary violence. However, a few people taking to arms do not equal a revolution, unless decisive masses of people are already in the motion of struggle toward revolutionary objectives, and the armed action is related to it, as a feature of it.

It would be a grotesque distortion if Marxism-Leninism is equated with violence and armed methods used under all circumstances. Equally serious and erroneous would be a tendency to undertake armed struggle indiscriminately in the name of Marxism-Leninism. Armed means to gain revolutionary ends are employable when masses of people are presented with no other alternative, only in specific, clearly-defined situations where necessary conditions for them exist. This is the basic premise in the Marxist-Leninist attitude toward revolutionary armed struggle, as the selections in this book will indicate.

This collection, it should be kept in mind, has not undertaken to be a history either of guerrilla warfare or of revolutions, nor has it been intended as a vehicle to put forward codes, principles or theories of conducting guerrilla warfare itself. It has not endeavored to encompass all the revolutionary armed struggles in history or even all of those that have occurred since World War II or that are in progress while this is being prepared. For instance, the many instances of guerrilla struggle by Arab liberation movements in the Middle East in the present period are not represented here, mainly due to the unavailability of relevant materials. The central aim is to make clear Marxist-Leninist principles and attitudes in regard to armed struggle, showing how they have emerged in the course of over a century of extremely varied circumstances, and showing how, in the light of new experiences, they may be used to define the issues of controversy that have arisen out of contemporary armed struggles.

1.

There is a risk involved in seeking to examine in isolation any single aspect of Marxist thought or any one practice arising from Marxist theory: the possibility of over-emphasizing the importance of a single factor in situations that are actually complex and many-featured. In no case is this truer than in regard to tactics in a revolutionary situation, which must be based on a careful assessment of social conditions and of forces that have reached a point of instability.

Revolutionary armed struggle tactics, of which guerrilla warfare can be a form, is a particularly delicate area of theory and practice. Its consequences can be more serious and more far-reaching than in any other form of struggle. Success or failure in strikes, in demonstrations, or in other comparatively peaceful political struggles usually do not have the same qualitative effect as a victory or a defeat in armed struggle, which can result in the literal destruction of one of the contending forces.

For this reason, both Karl Marx and Frederick Engels cautioned working class forces repeatedly against being urged or drawn into premature and isolated armed actions. Engels, warning Italian workers against participation in sporadic insurgency called for in the 1890's by Italian bourgeois elements to further their own narrow interests, said:

"If it is our duty to *support* every *real* movement of the people, it is not less our duty to protect the scarcely formed core of our proletarian Party, not to sacrifice it uselessly and not to allow the proletariat to be decimated in fruitless *local* risings. But if, on the contrary, the movement is a really *national* one, our people will not keep themselves hidden and will need no password. . . ."*

Above all, Marx and Engels insisted that any working class action arise out of definite conditions which make the action inevitable and necessary. As early as September 15, 1850, in a discussion in the London Central Committee of the Communist League, Marx opposed a leftist minority that wanted to hurry into uprising:

"The minority substitutes dogmatism for the standpoint of criticism, and idealism for materialism. It treats *pure will* as the motive power of revolution instead of actual conditions. While we say to the workers: 'You have got to go through fifteen, twenty, fifty years of civil wars and national wars not merely in order to change your conditions but in order to change yourselves and become qualified for political power,' you on the contrary tell them, 'We must achieve power immediately, otherwise we may as well lie down and go to sleep.' . . . Just as the democrats turned the word 'people' into a sacred thing, so you have done with the word 'proletariat'. Like the democrats you substitute revolutionary phrases for revolutionary development."†

The first Marxist formulations on revolutionary armed struggle tactics were made in the course of working class struggles in support of the 19th-century bourgeois democratic revolutions in Europe, when the emerging industrial bourgeoisies were engaged in seizing political power from the feudal aristocracies. The much-quoted Marxist definition of "the art of insurrection" dates from that period and was actually a delineation of the tactics that Marx and Engels felt the German bourgeoisie should have followed in 1848 in alliance with the urban workers in meeting

---

* Karl Marx and Frederick Engels, *Selected Correspondence, 1846–1895*, International Publishers, 1935, pp. 522–23.

† *Ibid.*, p. 92.

counter-revolution from the feudalist Junkers and other reactionary forces.

In the struggles of the 1840's a maturing working class was not striving for power for itself but was seeking to enlarge the scope of the revolution in order to gain, in the new regimes, equal representation and benefits. It was in the context of those frustrating experiences that Marx and Engels analyzed the conditions and the role of the working class as the rising force in society, and began to develop the tactics by which it could struggle for its own power and lead the advance from capitalism toward socialism.

From the outset Marx and Engels were positive that the working class must be prepared to employ armed struggle tactics to help realize its historic aims. In the *Communist Manifesto* in 1847 they had declared that the ends of Communists "can be attained only by the forcible overthrow of all existing social conditions." Force, however, in their view—as in the view of outstanding Marxists who have followed them—encompassed the great variety of forms that working class struggles take: mass demonstrations, general strikes, and even the relatively passive boycott, as well as armed uprisings (and in particular, combinations of all of these).

Therefore it would be a distortion of the Marxist approach to seek to isolate one form of struggle and to elevate it to a disproportionate position. Marx and Engels paid the closest attention to all the revolutions and armed uprisings of their epoch, striving to understand the behavior of class forces in revolutionary situations, and hailed every sign of militant action that came from the working class. Their main concern, however, was with the organization and politicalization of the working class, with the transformation of its early spontaneous action into carefully considered, scientific employment of its strength, and with the development of an ideologically-equipped political vanguard to give it leadership.

The need for this was driven home to Marx and Engels precisely because of the failures of armed insurrectionary struggles by workers in the 1840's. Engels, an acknowledged expert in military strategy and tactics, many years later explained in detail the inadequacy of the barricade tactics that were the prime feature of an armed uprising until the mid-century. Prior to the consolidation of bourgeois political power, he observed, barricade tactics were effective chiefly as a moral force. They were essentially a catalytic device by which small determined bodies of revolutionaries who did not rely on mass organization posed a challenge to feudal authority, and they were successful if the urban militia that protected bourgeois property in the cities of the period was persuaded to support the uprising. Even the armed forces of the feudalist state, made up usually of *levees* and hired mercenaries trained for maneuvering in open fields and armed with still primitive firearms, might be won over by revolutionary appeals made from strong points held by even a small body of rebels. However, modern high-caliber weapons in the hands of professional armies, in new circumstances in which the bourgeoisie joined forces with the feudal elements against workers, rendered these early barricade tactics obsolete, and made uprisings by decisive minorities isolated short-lived affairs. (Only a decade after Engels wrote the above, his downgrading of barricade tactics was to be revised in the Russian Revolution of 1905, when changed conditions of struggle restored their effectiveness in a new form.)

It became apparent that the working class would need a relatively prolonged period of preparation, of organization and of experience in struggle, before it could contend with the ramifications of bourgeois power. To lay the basis for this, the First International (1864–1876) encouraged economic struggles by trade unions and the participation of working class parties in political struggles, in elections, and in international solidarity demonstrations. It was understood that the powerful state organization of the bourgeoisie, with its capacity for military suppression, had to be met by a working class movement superior in its organization and power.

Guerrilla warfare, incidentally, did not escape the attention of Marx and Engels in this period; both noted it as a form of popular struggle under conditions of national resistance to foreign invasion or occupation. Marx had stressed its significance in the resistance of the Spanish people to Napoleonic conquest, but in analyzing it he pointed to the degeneration of guerrilla warfare often into banditry or into "praetorianism" (organization of private armies) when individual ambitious military leaders sought to exploit it. Engels pointed to the national response of the French people to German invasion in 1870, calling it a "legitimate form of warfare." He also commented on the failure of guerrilla warfare to develop among the poor whites against the slave-owning Confederacy when the Union armies of Lincoln invaded the South.* Although Marx and Engels approved of guerrilla warfare as a form of popular struggle, neither of them tended to link it with working class tactics of gaining power, which were thought of in terms of insurrection in which the organized masses of the people would be brought into play in decisive action at decisive moments.

The viewpoint of Marx on the use of armed struggle by the working class is perhaps best illustrated by the experience of the Paris Commune in 1871. On the eve of the Commune, Marx warned against a premature revolt by the Parisian workers who lacked a genuine proletarian party at their head and had insufficient mass organization, but were being urged by proponents of *coup d'etat* tactics to take advantage of the chaos following the shattering German victory in the Franco-Prussian War, to seize power from both the counter-revolutionary aristocrats and the capitulationist bourgeoisie. However, when the Paris Commune came into being, Marx unreservedly supported it. He hailed the courage of the Paris workers for daring to "storm heaven." Criticisms he had of the doomed first effort ever to establish workers' power were only made from the standpoint of the workers' failure to observe the cardinal principles of "the art of insurrection," their "too great *honnêteté* [decency]"† in not conducting decisive armed struggle to smash the reactionary government based at Versailles.

While Marx and Engels tried to avoid premature, ill-prepared revolution or inopportune adoption of armed struggle tactics, their support of all genuine revolutionary action, once undertaken by the working class, contrasted sharply with the attitude of the right-wing socialists who deplored all use of violent means by the workers. The Marxist position was developed out of struggle against the terrorist use of violence by the anarchists on the one hand, and against the class-collaborationist denial of all violence by right-wing theorists on the other.

2.

The use by the working class of armed struggle in all its forms and in relation to other forms of struggle emerged clearly in the

---

* Karl Marx and Frederick Engels, *The Civil War in the United States*, International Publishers, 1937, pp. 244–245.

† Marx and Engels, *Selected Correspondence*, p. 307.

Russian Revolution of 1905, in which the working class took the lead in a bourgeois democratic revolution. In this historic period of upsurge that deserves close study by all revolutionary movements, the whole range of tactics and forms of struggle came into play: mass demonstrations, general strikes on a nation-wide scale, barricade fighting, mutiny in the army and navy, peasant revolts, united insurgent action in many cities and towns marked by an alliance of workers and peasants, and, not the least, guerrilla warfare.

In Moscow, in particular, the discarded barricade tactic was re-employed with startling effect, not as an isolated focal point but in the mass, the barricades thickly covering entire districts in which the whole population gave active support to those manning them. The variety and the nation-wide character of the mass struggle testified to the effectiveness of the careful propaganda and organizational work carried out for a period of years by the Russian Social-Democratic Labor Party, particularly by its Bolshevik wing led by Lenin, and by other revolutionary groups. A high degree of worker-peasant unity showed itself, with armed insurrections by the proletariat in the cities coinciding with uprisings of peasants in the countryside, where organized peasant unions had developed.

In the preceding period Lenin had successfully fought against the use of terrorism by small groups of conspiratorial intellectuals who disregarded mass organization. Now, however, in 1905–1906, Lenin wholeheartedly supported the use of guerrilla warfare in the cities by small groups of workers, which took place as *part* of the mass struggle, and the Bolsheviks themselves organized "fighting squads" everywhere.

Of the many significant articles on armed struggle written by Lenin in this period the most important is an essay on "Guerrilla Warfare," published in 1906. This is a basic theoretical work, in which guerrilla warfare is placed in its political context and in its relationship with other forms of struggle, and in which is illustrated Lenin's dynamic awareness of the need to recognize new forms and methods that emerge from new struggles and new revolutions. In defending the use of armed struggle against its right-wing denigrators, he at the same time insisted that it "must be ennobled by the enlightening and organizing influence of socialism." He carried Marx's and Engels's appreciation of guerrilla warfare in national resistance struggles a long step further by showing that it could be a feature of insurrection and civil war as well.

The 1905 experience re-emphasized the need for armed struggle by the proletariat to gain its ends in a revolutionary situation, and made it plain that diverse forms of armed struggle were possible and acceptable. Other lessons could be drawn from the fact that the worker-peasant alliance, although defeated in its revolutionary bid, was able to retreat with its organized forces and its vanguard largely intact, in a position to prepare for the next revolutionary period, a situation made possible precisely because of the variety of forms of struggle employed and tested by the revolutionary movement.

This was the invaluable background to the Russian Revolution in 1917, when once again the whole panoply of agitation and of insurrectionary forms and tactics was put into effect. When Lenin returned from exile in Europe after the March (1917) Revolution which overthrew the tsar, he seriously estimated (in his April Theses) that under given conditions the transformation of the bourgeois democratic revolution into a socialist one could be achieved by peaceful means. But in July, when the Provisional Government under Kerensky used repressive measures against workers' demonstrations calling for transfer of power to the Soviets and sought to suppress Bolshevik and other revolutionary groups, conditions began to change radically. With the workers of Petrograd playing the leading role in defeating the counter-revolutionary uprising led by General Kornilov in August–September, and with the Bolsheviks winning the majority in the Petrograd, Moscow and other Soviets, Lenin urged preparation for the seizure of power before reaction could regather its forces.

Seizure of power on November 7, 1917, is epitomized by the storming of the Winter Palace in Petrograd by armed workers' detachments, followed by the capture of the Kremlin in Moscow in a similar manner. These historic events were the culmination of the revolutionary process and of a vast amount of preparatory work. A recent Marxist-Leninist textbook has emphasized the features of that process and has pointed to their continuing relevance:

"The enemies of communism depict the proletarian revolution as a *coup* carried out by a small group of communist 'conspirators'. That is a deliberate lie. Marxism-Leninism does not recognize the tactics of 'palace revolutions', *putsches,* and the seizure of power by armed minorities. This follows logically from the Marxist conception of social processes. The causes of revolution lie fundamentally in the material conditions of the life of society, in the conflict between the productive forces and the production relations. This conflict finds its expression in a clash between large masses of people, classes, which rise to the struggle under the influence of objective causes that do not depend on the will of separate individuals, groups, or even parties. The Communist Party organizes the actions of the masses, directs the masses, but does not attempt to make a revolution 'for them', with its own forces."

The textbook points out, however, that, "A Party of the Leninist type will never stand by idly, holding aloof and waiting for the 'great hour', the situation which will itself evoke the revolutionary enthusiasm of the working people and weaken the resistance of their enemies. It seeks and finds possibilities for active work among the masses, for an active political struggle, even under the most unfavorable conditions . . . bringing very much closer the hour of the decisive battle, and prepares for this battle not only itself, but also the broadest possible sections of the working people."* Lenin showed in 1917 how the art of political leadership can accentuate or accelerate the revolutionary process. Decisions as to this are not self-evident: Lenin had to overcome opposition by some Bolsheviks who felt that the time was not ripe for insurrection in October. It is in this sense of attunement to the nuances of a developing situation and of readiness to bring prepared forces forward at the critical time that it can be said that a revolutionary "makes" the revolution.

From the time of its socialist revolution, the Soviet Union's experiences in armed struggle have rested on Lenin's strategic and tactical principles. As far as guerrilla warfare is concerned, in two major periods—the Civil War (or War Against Intervention) in 1918–21 and the war against fascist invasion in 1941–45—it was used on a large scale to defend the socialist state. In the earlier case, in fact, the principles of large-scale guerrilla warfare led by Communists were first laid down.

During the Civil War, however, it was made abundantly clear that the guerrilla activities which were very effective when used

---

* *Fundamentals of Marxism-Leninism,* Foreign Languages Publishing House, Moscow, 1963, pp. 168–169; p. 349.

in an organized way under the direction of the revolutionary vanguard could be disastrous when employed haphazardly. Lenin drew attention to the serious setbacks in the Ukraine caused by "guerrillaism" that enabled the invading German army to suppress anarchic resistance:

"In the Ukraine, owing to the low level of proletarian class consciousness, owing to weakness and lack of organization, owing to Petlyura's* disorganizing tactics and the pressures of German imperialism—on these grounds hostility and guerrilla tactics have emerged spontaneously, and in every group the peasants were taking up arms, electing their own ataman, or 'father', to set up an authority, to create it on the spot. They paid no attention to the central authorities and every 'father' thought he was the boss on the spot, that he alone could settle all Ukrainian problems, disregarding what was being done at the center."

This situation was only overcome, Lenin stressed, "when we turned our backs on guerrilla tactics and the scattering of revolutionary phrases—we can do anything!—and began to realize the need for sound, sustained, persistent and difficult organizing activities."† The same problem, however, cropped up in the Siberian regions, in the resistance to invasion by armies headed by the white-guardist, Admiral Kolchak. Here Lenin repeated his criticism: "Fear like the plague the unruly guerrilla spirit, the arbitrary actions of isolated detachments and disobedience to the central authority, for it spells doom as the Urals, Siberia and the Ukraine have demonstrated."‡

It was not against guerrilla warfare as such that Lenin was warning but against its use not led or guided centrally by the party, by organs of the Soviet state, or by the Red Army. He insisted, in the Ukrainian and Siberian instances, that the authority of the party and of the Red Army be observed, that guerrilla activities be coordinated in this manner in accordance with the demands of the overall military and political situation. Guerrilla warfare under Lenin's specifications actually occurred on a mass scale, involving hundreds of thousands of Soviet people, and

---

* Simon Petlyura headed a bourgeois nationalist counter-revolutionary directorate in the Ukraine in 1918 with German sanction.

† V. I. Lenin, "The Present Situation and the Immediate Tasks of Soviet Power," *Collected Works*, Progress Publishers, Moscow, Vol. 29, 1965, p. 462.

‡ V. I. Lenin, "Letter to the Workers and Peasants Apropos of the Victory over Kolchak," *ibid.*, p. 553.

was one of the main factors in the defeat of the White Guard interventionist armies.

These principles were developed to an even higher extent in resistance to Nazi German invasion in World War II, in which hundreds of thousands of guerrillas operated in Soviet territory occupied by the fascists, contributing in a major way to the Soviet victory. This was full-fledged people's warfare. Guerrillas had the closest coordination with Red Army headquarters, were often supplied and equipped by air, and were frequently parachuted into areas where guerrilla organization was required. Furthermore, the guerrilla operations were not limited to the countryside but were also carried on in the cities and towns occupied by the Nazis. The success in this struggle was definitely due to its centralized direction.

In its whole experience with guerrilla warfare, the Russian, and subsequently the Soviet, revolutionary movement has adhered closely to the Leninist principles governing this form of struggle. It has been used at all times in combination with other forms of armed and revolutionary struggle, particularly in closely associating guerrilla with regular warfare. It has been conducted within the framework of the worker-peasant alliance, with the proletariat firmly providing the leadership for it. Furthermore, at all times, the centralized guidance of the party has been maintained, assuring "the enlightening and organizing influence of socialism".

3.

The Russian proletarian revolution, a model of preparation, of timing and of tactical direction, was immediately looked upon as an example to be followed by other working class movements. Its success encouraged the belief that it could be duplicated quite soon in other capitalist countries of Europe. However, although certain revolutionary conditions existed at the end of World War I in parts of Central Europe, the subjective factor of strong, experienced parties of the Bolshevik type was lacking to exploit them successfully, although attempts were made in Germany and Hungary.

In approaching this question, Lenin pointed to the fact that the Russian success "was due simply to a number of historical peculiarities of Russia," and ascribed his party's maturity to its experiences in the 15 years prior to the revolution: "No other country knew anything even approximating to that revolutionary experience, that rapid and varied succession of different forms of the movement—legal and illegal, peaceful and stormy, underground and open, local circles and mass movements, and parliamentary and terrorist forms."*

Warning Communist parties in Europe against the "Left adventurism" of hastening into revolutionary action without necessary conditions or preparations, Lenin stressed that "lengthy, painful and sanguinary experience has taught us the truth that revolutionary tactics cannot be built on a revolutionary mood alone. Tactics must be based on a sober and objective appraisal of *all* the class forces in a particular state (and of the states that surround it, and of all states the world over) as well as of the experience of revolutionary movements."† He then added further substance to the Marxist definitions of revolutionary situations in which uprising or insurrection is feasible:

"The fundamental law of revolution, which has been confirmed by all revolutions and especially by all three Russian revolutions in the twentieth century, is as follows: for a revolution to take place it is not enough for the exploited and oppressed masses to realize the impossibility of living in the old way, and demand changes; for a revolution to take place it is essential that the exploiters should not be able to live and rule in the old way. It is only when the *'lower classes'* do not want to live in the old way and the *'upper classes' cannot carry on in the old way* that the revolution can triumph. This truth can be expressed in other words: revolution is impossible without a nation-wide crisis (affecting both the exploited and the exploiters). It follows that, for a revolution to take place, it is essential, first, that a majority of the workers (or at least a majority of the class-conscious, thinking and politically active workers) should fully realize that revolution is necessary, and that they should be prepared to die for it; second, that the ruling classes should be going through a governmental crisis which draws even the most backward masses into politics."‡

In the period between the two world wars events bore out the accuracy of Lenin's formulations. The working class movements

---

* V. I. Lenin, "Left-Wing Communism, an Infantile Disorder," *Selected Works* (3 vols.), International Publishers, 1967, Vol. 3, pp. 340–41.
† *Ibid*, pp. 373–74.
‡ *Ibid.*, p. 392.

in the capitalist countries passed through a quantitative period of rich experience in every type of struggle, including armed struggles, but mature revolutionary situations of the type described by Lenin did not develop. An Irish republic did win independence in a national liberation struggle in which guerrilla warfare, conducted by the Irish Republican Army, played an important part. Perhaps the most mature revolutionary period occurred in Spain in the 1930's, when a Spanish Republic came into being as a product of the whole range of forms of struggle, culminating in a people's armed struggle to defend the bourgeois democratic republic against fascist counter-revolution. A victory in this civil war, during which the Spanish Communist Party won great prestige, could have smashed the power of the reactionary classes and led toward socialism; this was prevented by foreign fascist intervention. It must be observed that in the course of the popular struggle guerrilla warfare behind the fascist lines was relatively widespread, enjoying support by the peasantry, and that it was combined, as in the case of the Soviet experience, with the regular warfare of the Republican armies.

One other episode in this period deserves attention, as an example from which lessons could be drawn of armed urban insurrection. This was the uprising of the workers in Vienna and in other industrial cities in Austria, in February 1934. A peculiar situation had developed in Austria, with the main political parties obtaining control over sections of the state militia (except the Communist Party, which was small and unable to exert serious influence on events). When the pro-fascist armed body, the *Heimwehr,* attempted to disarm the other units as a prelude to the Hitlerian seizure of power, the armed workers' militia controlled by the Social-Democrats, the *Schutzbund,* fought back, and for three uncertain days an armed struggle took place. The workers were doomed to defeat by the fact that the Social-Democrats ordered only a defensive struggle in which the *Schutzbund* barricaded itself in cooperative housing blocks in Vienna and elsewhere, and were crushed there. At this time the Communist view was that a determined offensive insurrection could have won power for the workers.

In a "Letter to the Austrian Workers," Georgi Dimitrov, general-secretary of the Communist International, commented that "unfortunately your armed struggle was not a struggle for power and thus, as Marx and Lenin have taught, it was not a genuine armed uprising. The fact that your armed struggle lacked the aim—the seizure of power—was the fundamental defect of your heroic action." Dimitrov pointed out that by directing the workers only to defend themselves in their communal houses, "the Social-Democrats caused the initiative in the struggle to slip out of the workers' hands, surrendering it to the fascist enemy."* Even when the armed workers did withdraw from the defended houses "they did not go into the working class districts in order to draw the masses there into the fight, but retreated from the town into the Vienna forest. . . . Without contact with the industrial proletariat, any further fighting by them was useless."† This comment went to the heart of the question of armed insurrection in the developed capitalist countries: the indispensable, decisive, many-sided action of the industrial urban proletariat.

Although circumstances were not favorable for armed proletarian insurrection in this period, the general experiences in Marxist-Leninist principles of mass organization and of struggle, gained by revolutionary movements in the years between the two world wars, accounted for the large and widespread guerrilla resistance movements that played such a big role in the defeat of fascist aggression in 1939–45. In Europe as well as in Asia the large-scale guerrilla movements that arose were based for the most part on mass organizations led by the Communists, on whom even reactionary circles in the wartime anti-Hitler alliance had to rely for such operations.

These guerrilla struggles, it needs to be observed, were mainly in the nature of the national resistance wars noted by Marx and Engels, in which whole populations were aroused against foreign invaders. Even in the Soviet Union the war was termed the Great Patriotic War.

The forms taken by guerrilla movements during World War II varied greatly from country to country, depending on the internal conditions of each, but related in all cases to the main form of overall struggle, regular warfare. In the Asian countries under Japanese occupation they were mainly peasant-based, although activity in the cities and towns was not neglected. In Western Europe, particularly in France and Italy, the reverse was the case, with most guerrilla action striking at German and

---

* Georgi Dimitrov, "Letter to the Austrian Workers," *International Press Correspondence*, Vol. 14, No. 29, May 11, 1934.
† Gruber, "The February Revolt of the Austrian Workers and Its Lessons," *International Press Correspondence*, Vol. 14, No. 14, March 2, 1934.

Italian fascists in the cities and towns (from which, also, the struggle itself was directed by its leaders). Paris was liberated by an insurrection organized by the guerrilla forces.

As a result of the character of the war against fascism, stronger popular movements led by Communists emerged after the war in Western Europe and in Asia; many of these had gained the experience of armed struggle and were in actual possession of arms. In many countries, in varying degrees of seriousness, the question presented itself of whether or not to advance to a higher revolutionary stage of struggle by the use of arms. However, a major difficulty existed in regard to bringing about new class alliances and positions from which the transition from an anti-fascist struggle of a national front character to a socialist revolution could be achieved. In Western Europe this proved insurmountable, while in Eastern Europe, including Yugoslavia where guerrilla warfare reached a peak, the transition to socialism took place with the aid of the protective presence or proximity of the Soviet Red Army as a safeguard against imperialist intervention.

There were two exceptions to these trends in Europe. One was in Spain, where the Spanish Communist Party sought to develop guerrilla warfare against the fascist Franco regime. This had been carried on after the defeat of the Republican government in 1939, throughout World War II, and into the postwar period. In the belief that the defeat of the fascist powers in the war could lead to the overthrow of the Franco regime, guerrilla warfare was intensified, especially between 1945 and 1948, in the hope that a general revolt by the Spanish people could be sparked by this form of struggle. Between 1944 and 1949 there were 5,371 guerrilla operations carried out in Spain.* These failed to stimulate the hoped-for revolt on a mass scale, or even the creation of a broad front of unity behind the struggle. Projection of the armed struggle tended, in fact, to unify reactionary forces behind Franco. In 1948 the Spanish Communist Party decided on a change of tactics, and has since then helped to promote successfully the broad many-sided struggle that has produced a democratic upsurge in Spain, accelerating the process of disintegration of the fascist regime.

The other exception in Europe was Greece, where a large-scale guerrilla armed struggle was launched in 1946 without the neces-

---

* *World Marxist Review*, January 1965, p. 36.

sary favorable conditions or preparations, and by 1949 was disastrously defeated.

4.

Entirely different circumstances prevailed in the colonial countries of Asia.

While warning the Communist parties in the capitalist countries against "Left adventurism," Lenin foresaw that the achievement of Soviet power and the Red Army's revolutionary use of armed struggle would have an enormous impact in the colonial countries. There, he pointed out, "a revolutionary war waged by oppressed peoples, if it really succeeds in arousing the millions of working and exploited people, harbors such potentialities, such miracles, that the emancipation of the peoples of the East is now quite practicable, from the standpoint not only of the prospects of the international revolution, but also of the direct military experience acquired in Asia, in Siberia, the experience of the Soviet Republic, which has suffered the armed invasion of all the powerful imperialist countries."*

This effect of the victory of the Russian working class was greatly increased by the crisis that permeated the world capitalist system after World War I, by its intensified exploitation of colonies, and by the consequent creation of Communist parties throughout the colonial areas. These parties, with the ideological assistance of the Communist International, were encouraged to adopt militant struggle in all its forms, including ("when the revolutionary tide is rising") armed insurrection.

In setting down the conditions for armed struggle in its program, the Communist International insisted: "An absolutely essential condition precedent for this form of action is the organization of the broad masses into militant units, which, by their form, embrace and set into action the largest possible number of toilers." In the course of such action "the party must be guided by the fundamental role of the political tactics of Leninism, which call for ability to lead the masses to revolutionary positions in such a manner that the masses may, by their own experience, convince themselves of the correctness of the party line."

---

* V. I. Lenin, "Address to the Second All-Russian Congress of Communist Organizations of the Peoples of the East (Nov. 22, 1919)," *Selected Works*, Vol. 3, p. 285.

Furthermore, it was declared that each Communist party must adopt the tactics and the form of struggle that fit the specific conditions existing within its own country.*

Probably the clearest demonstration of these principles was the revolutionary armed struggle in China. The Chinese Revolution took its own path, governed by China's peculiar conditions, but its guerrilla warfare was drawn essentially from Marxist-Leninist concepts of armed struggle. In essence, the Chinese Communist Party, acknowledging its debt to the experiences of the Soviet Red Army, adapted to China's conditions principles of struggle that were quite similar to those practiced by Soviet guerrillas. Although it employed guerrilla warfare more extensively and over a longer period of time (1928–1949) than had previously occurred, the guerrilla movement itself was organized along standard Marxist lines: a highly politicalized armed force under the firm direction of the Communist Party. Mao Tse-tung, moreover, in his formulations and directives that added new scope and depth to armed struggle strategy and tactics, condemned "guerrillaism" in the same manner that Lenin had done. Also, the Chinese movement did not rely on guerrilla warfare alone, but combined it with other forms of armed struggle, in particular the regular warfare through which it delivered its decisive blows in the culminating stage of the revolution.

Much attention has been drawn to certain peculiarities of the revolutionary war in China which were shaped by China's own set of conditions. Among these were the strategy of establishing liberated base areas remote from the center of ruling class power, and the strategy of basing the struggle among the peasantry and of surrounding and capturing the cities from the countryside. The establishment of base areas was made possible by the vastness of China and by the relatively undeveloped communication network in the country's hinterland.† The choice of the peasantry for a revolutionary mass base was an alternative choice following the brutal suppression by bourgeois Kuomintang counter-revolution of the original mass base of the Chinese Communists among the urban proletariat.

To be sure, the Chinese proletariat did take the lead in revo-

---

* "Program of the Communist International (1928)," *Handbook of Marxism*, Emile Burns, *ed.*, International Publishers, 1935, pp. 1034–35.

† See "Characteristics of China's Revolutionary War," by Mao Tse-tung, in this volume.

lutionary struggle, in many general strikes and insurrections that were the vanguard actions of the liberation war. However, its revolutionary core was decimated by Kuomintang terror and in ill-conceived, isolated and adventuristic urban uprisings in 1927. These were failures not because the principles of a revolution with urban insurrection playing a key role were not applicable to China, but because of the uneven development of the Chinese Revolution and of its worker-peasant alliance and because of departures from insurrectionary principles (the Canton Commune, for example, had a closer affinity to the Paris Commune than to the October insurrections in Petrograd and Moscow). Moreover, as the revolution developed, the Chinese Communists did pay some attention to revolutionary work in the cities and towns, including armed struggle, while placing the major emphasis on guerrilla war in the countryside. The capture of many of the cities in southern China in the final stages of the war was done from within, in cooperation with the armed forces in the countryside.

The Chinese Revolution was a massive victory of the Chinese people who in a masterly way made use of their own conditions, but it needs to be stated that it was not won in isolation or without the aid of important allies. Its main foreign enemy, Japanese imperialism, was defeated by the alliance of international anti-fascist forces. Then, in 1945, the Soviet Red Army, which had crushed the million-strong Japanese Kwangtung Army in Manchuria, turned over to the Chinese Red Army the Japanese military equipment that it had captured, amounting to over 3,700 artillery pieces, 600 tanks, 861 planes and many naval vessels.* This was a significant factor in the final victorious offensives launched by the Chinese Red Army.

The Chinese Revolution was the most important and most influential of all the colonial liberation struggles, complementing the Russian October Revolution, but there were many other instances of armed uprising or guerrilla warfare in colonial areas in the years between the two world wars, each adding to the revolutionary experience of the peoples involved. Sandino's guerrilla campaign against American marines and monopolies in Nicaragua in the late 1920s and early 1930s was an inspiration to many Latin American revolutionaries. The uprising in Indochina in 1931, when soviets were set up briefly by peasants, was an

---

* V. Vasin, "Loyalty to Internationalist Duty," *Za Rubezhom*, Moscow, No. 52, 1967.

important lesson in the errors of prematurity and of sectarianism for the newly-organized Indochinese Communist Party. Arab national aspirations were stirred by the Riff War led by Abd-el-Krim in Morocco in the 1920s.

In the Philippines a different sort of armed uprising occurred on May 2–3, 1935, the defects of which served to underscore the correctness of Marxist principles for Filipino Communists. This was the abortive Sakdal revolt, organized by the demagogic Sakdalista Party* led by the pro-Japanese, Benigno Ramos. Nearly 65,000 of its almost unarmed poor-peasant followers, who had been aroused on the issue of independence from American rule, suddenly seized control of several Central and Southern Luzon towns, naively expecting the population and even the government troops to join them. They were slaughtered, their revolt suppressed in a day. Filipino Communists opposed this form of action as suicidal and misguided.

5.

Since 1945, Marxist-Leninist theory and practice has been enriched during numerous revolutionary struggles. In each case, the resort to armed struggle was in response to the use of violence by imperialism and its allies. Every liberation movement has preferred to use peaceful, legal means to win freedom. These popular movements, denied such means of expressing themselves and met by an increasing use of violence by a desperate and crumbling imperialist system, have literally been compelled to adopt violent methods to gain popular ends.

The process of world imperialist decline was hastened by the fact that by this time the socialist system had become greatly strengthened and was in a better position to give assistance to revolutionary forces in many countries. As has been pointed out, it was the powerful presence of the Soviet Red Army that enabled anti-fascist resistance movements in Eastern Europe to obtain power. For the same reason, the proletarian insurrection in Czechoslovakia succeeded in February 1948. The assistance and proximity of the Soviet Union and China were also important factors in establishing socialist republics in North Korea and North Vietnam.

* *Sakdal*, a Filipino word meaning "to accuse" or "to strike."

A new factor thus appeared in revolutionary situations after World War II: the active assistance of the socialist part of the world to revolutionary struggles elsewhere. Potentially or to a limited extent, such a factor had existed since 1917, but it had not been strong enough, nor had other conditions matured enough, to make it really effective. To the Marxist formulations regarding internal factors of revolutionary situations and of insurrections could now be added a strong external factor.

Of course, this has not altered the basic Marxist precept that revolutions cannot be exported but must arise and develop from absolutely necessary conditions within a country. Today, as in the case of Vietnam, the external factor has shown itself to be a major factor in the course of a revolutionary struggle, *providing* the revolutionary movement concerned itself requests assistance from outside and it is possible geographically to give it. In addition, the external factor has given protection and active assistance to revolutionary regimes once they have achieved victory and have entered the critical stage of stabilizing themselves against counter-revolution. In numerous cases in the contemporary period the established socialist countries have rendered the economic and military aid that have enabled liberation movements to create strong independent states.

As the breaking up of the imperialist system goes on, outside aid to liberation struggles has come not only from the socialist countries but from other newly independent countries that realize their own security is linked with the elimination of neo-imperialism. In Africa, liberation movements, armed and otherwise, in areas still held in colonial bondage have been provided with bases and active assistance by their newly independent brothers on the continent. The Organization of African Unity, on governmental level, has given formal approval of this policy and has gone to the extent of setting up an African Liberation Committee, although reactionary and neo-imperialist influences within the OAU have prevented it from realizing its potential. As an example, FRELIMO (*Front de Liberation du Mozambique*), has expressed gratitude for aid not only to the OAU, but also to Algeria (an OAU member), India, the Soviet Union, the People's Republic of China, Indonesia and others.

It is unavoidable, in assessing such a phenomenon as the external factor in the revolutions of today, to take account of the thesis advanced by China's Marshal Lin Piao, based on the theories of Mao Tse-tung, that the world-wide struggle against imperialism can be depicted as duplicating on an international scale the guerrilla concept of the surrounding of the cities from the countryside, with the industrialized countries identified as the "cities of the world" and the underdeveloped countries shaking off imperialism identified as the "countryside of the world." This formulation, which dismisses the alliance of the socialist countries and of the working class and revolutionary forces in the capitalist countries with the national liberation movements in the colonial and neo-colonial countries, is in conflict with the fundamental concept of internationalism in Marxist-Leninist theory. The strategic principle that it seeks to advance was based, when applied on a national scale in China, on a profound and detailed analysis of China's conditions, but when expanded into an international principle its lack of any such analysis to substantiate it has emphasized its un-Marxist generalizations. It has been dissipated by the first major liberation struggle that has occurred since it was pronounced—in Vietnam, where the Marxist-Leninist three-way unity of liberation movements, the socialist countries, and the revolutionary and progressive movements in the capitalist countries reached to its greatest heights.

The prominence of armed struggle in liberation movements in many countries should not obscure the fact that independence from imperialist rule has been gained in a large number of cases by other means, including general strikes, mass demonstrations and political organization and agitation that has made popular sentiment undeniably clear. The countries of Tanzania, Mali, Guinea, Ghana, Uganda, Zambia, Congo (Brazzaville), Nigeria and others, large or small, separated themselves from colonial rule in these ways, while armed struggle was only one of the elements in the gaining of independence by such countries as Tunisia, Morocco or Kenya. In these independent states the revolutionary or the liberation process may not have been completed by the act of independence alone, with fresh struggles necessary against neo-colonialism, some of which have progressed successfully, but the same circumstances can also be observed in countries that won their independence principally by armed means (as in the cases of Algeria, Indonesia, Egypt or Cyprus).

In all of these cases, whether the revolutionary goal has been won by armed struggle, by other forms of struggle, or by a combination of them, the fundamental principles stated 40 years ago in the program of the Communist International have prevailed: that the revolutionary movement in each country must base the forms and the conduct of its struggle on the existing set of conditions within the country, and that it must involve the masses before it can succeed.

6.

The spectacular success of guerrilla warfare in a number of liberation struggles—especially in China, Vietnam, Algeria and Cuba—has tended to gloss over the fact that several major guerrilla struggles were defeated in the same period, the most important being in Malaya, the Philippines, Greece, Burma and Kenya, while serious setbacks, at the least, have been given to guerrilla attempts launched in the Congo, Peru, Bolivia and elsewhere. It is quite evident from this that broad and universal generalizations about the efficacy of armed struggle or guerrilla tactics cannot safely be made.

Undoubtedly the only way to a Marxist assessment and understanding of the role of guerrilla warfare and of other armed struggles in the contemporary period is to examine each case in the light of its own conditions and tactics. We can begin by looking beyond the general term "national liberation" that has been used to characterize virtually all of the struggles that have occurred and are occurring in this period (including the struggle of the Negro people for full equality within the United States). "National liberation" has embraced forms of bourgeois democratic revolution, of proletarian revolution, and of revolutions for freedom in countries that have not even reached the stage of bourgeois development, where neither a proletariat nor a Communist-type party exists. It is obvious that the alignment of forces, the nature of leadership, and the manner in which the masses are brought into motion have varied greatly in the struggles that have taken place, and that all of these factors are extremely important in the projection of armed struggle, and in its success or failure. (Also, the nature of leadership and of forces involved have contributed greatly to the degree of readiness of the imperialist countries to come to terms with armed liberation struggles.)

In Southeast Asia armed struggles occurred as a direct consequence of World War II, during which Communist-led guerrilla movements acquired arms and experience in guerrilla warfare. After the end of the war, the movements in Malaya and the Philippines sought to retain some arms in the interests of self-defense (in the Philippines, for example, the guerrillas were subjected to persecution and armed attack by American army elements prior to the war's end), while giving main emphasis to engaging in peaceful forms of organization and struggle. In both cases, the British and American imperialists and their local allies, alarmed at the threat to their control, undertook brutal repressive measures. With arms at hand, the Communist-led forces in both countries responded with guerrilla resistance, developing into bids for power.

Both of these military struggles were crushed, and it is instructive to look into the reasons for defeat. To begin with, in neither case was the guerrilla struggle the result of planned armed action, taken with the initiative of the Communists. Each armed struggle began as a defensive measure against repression and turned into a revolutionary offensive as it strove, through guerrilla warfare, to gain the initiative and to win decisive mass support. The defeats can be measured by the extent to which the Malayan People's Liberation Army (MPLA) and the Philippine Army of National Liberation (popularly known as Huk) failed to overcome the defensive disadvantages with which they started.

The Malayan movement was handicapped by the pattern of the British colonial system which had created a working class for its mines, plantations and docks mainly out of immigrant Chinese and Indian labor, while it maintained a backward semifeudal agrarian society of decentralized sultanates among the native Malays. A militant working class movement, largely of Chinese and Indian origin, took up the banner of national liberation while a stunted Malay middle class and an unorganized peasantry were slow and late in developing as a nationalist force.

Spearheaded by the trade unions, the national liberation movement, although given some impetus by the war against Japanese occupation, was still in its formative stages in the postwar period when British imperialism took steps to nip it in the bud. The suppressive British Emergency Regulations, driving outlawed trade unionists into the jungles, were adopted in June 1948; the first responsive armed actions, taken in self-defense, occurred in July.

The MPLA that came into being on the framework of the anti-Japanese movement thus had an essentially urban working class base instead of a peasant base. It made heroic efforts to overcome its shortcomings: the MPLA armed units eventually had not only Chinese and Indian worker troops (roughly 20 per cent Indian, more or less in proportion to their position in the population) but also at least one regiment of Malays, and some headway was made in gaining support of primitive hill peoples. The main civilian support base, however, was in the towns and cities.

In deciding to undertake an armed struggle, through which they hoped to advance from a defensive to an offensive position, the Malayan Communists were influenced by estimates that British imperialism could not support a long colonial war, that it could not send sufficient numbers of suppression troops to Malaya, and that consequently it would have to resort increasingly to fascist measures that would antagonize all sectors of the population, including not only petty bourgeois elements but even its colonial allies who would be driven to embrace the national liberation movement. Accordingly, the MPLA projected a prolonged guerrilla war, aimed at exhausting British imperialism, during which it hoped to create liberated base areas and to convert guerrilla forces into a revolutionary regular army.*

Contrary to this strategic perspective of the liberation movement, however, British imperialism was able to deploy the means and the troops required for suppression (totalling no less than 400,000, they were perhaps the largest armed force in proportion to population used in a colonial war, testifying both to the support the liberation movement gained and to the degree of the imperialist suppressive effort). This was coupled with tactics of resettling and dividing the population that had an undeniable isolating effect on the guerrilla forces. The most important feature of this was the winning over by the British of significant sections of the Malay petty bourgeoisie through the promise of independence, which was granted (albeit in neo-colonial form) in 1958. The MPLA was unable to overcome these factors of isolation and of the curtailment of potential alliances rather than their expansion.

Certain similarities appear in the Philippine experience, although there the Communist Party had a mass base in both the proletariat and the peasantry. Here, too, however, there were

---

* See "Strategic Problems of the Malayan Revolutionary War," issued by the Malayan Communists, Assault Press, Singapore, December 1948 (to be found in Appendix, Gene Z. Hanrahan, *The Communist Struggle in Malaya*, International Secretariat, Institute of Pacific Relations, 1954).

estimates that American imperialism, caught in crisis, would retreat from Asia rather than commit itself to a determined struggle to retain its positions, and that fascist measures rather than a democratic facade of reforms would be an increasing pattern. As in Malaya, an opposite trend occurred as the guerrilla threat developed.

The Philippine guerrilla struggle also began with a limited base among a relatively small section of the population (chiefly the poor peasantry of the central part of Luzon island), was largely cut away from its base among the urban proletariat, and was unsuccessful, by means of armed expansion, in organizing and building a stable mass base in other regions of the country, although initial successes were made. Filipino petty bourgeois and national bourgeois groupings were won away from actual or potential support of the liberation struggle by terror combined with gestures of imperialist political and economic reform, a trend that was concretized in the coalition around the election of the American presidential protege, Ramon Magsaysay, in 1953.

Basically, the shortcoming in the strategy and tactics of the Malayan and Philippine movements was an overestimation of the maturity of the national liberation struggle in regard to the revolutionary situation. When guerrilla warfare began in both countries revolutionary situations did not exist, but it was hoped that the impact of the guerrilla struggle would help to drive the imperialists and their allies into crisis. This did not materialize. The extent of imperialist crisis was overestimated, forms of struggle were not diversified and developed to bring all sections of the population, including sections of the national bourgeoisie, into the liberation movement, and insufficient masses of the people were led by their own struggle experiences to acceptance of the armed struggle as the only logical alternative. In short, Marxist-Leninist principles of revolutionary situations and of their development were not closely observed.

Although both the Malayan and the Filipino movements were greatly encouraged by the example of the Chinese Revolution (and especially by the failure of serious imperialist intervention to materialize in its latter stages), neither of them actually followed the Chinese pattern of setting up liberated areas and of surrounding the cities from the countryside. (In fact, successfully-conducted guerrilla war has rarely pursued such a pattern, contrary to the belief widely held, and to the claim of the Chinese leaders themselves that it constitutes a model.) In Malaya, the peasant base for such a strategy was literally lacking, however much it may have been desired.

In the Philippines, the guerrilla movement at the beginning of the Japanese occupation in 1942 was influenced to some extent by Chinese Communists in the Philippines who introduced Chinese Red Army ideas into Huk organization. Thenceforth, however, particularly after World War II and the outbreak of civil war in 1946, the movement followed its own path, governed by the Filipino peasant social structure, by Philippine terrain and geographical problems, and by Philippine historical, economic and political conditions. A struggle in the cities, especially in the principal city of Manila where there were Communist-led trade unions, was developed side by side with the war in the countryside. Armed units and armed struggle were maintained in Manila, and a policy of mass organization and of armed operations in towns throughout the country was a central feature of the offensive undertaken in 1950. At that time, a policy document was issued, entitled "Intensify the Struggle in Cities and Towns," which, among other things, defined the proletariat as the leading force which must be developed in urban struggle in coordination with the struggle in the countryside, and called for the setting up of worker committees to take over industry to parallel peasant committees for land distribution. This remained in effect throughout the struggle, during which the concept of liberated areas was rejected (in 1947) as inapplicable in the Philippines, while the concept of surrounding the cities from the countryside was never projected as such.

In only one serious respect was there an attempt to apply in Malaya and the Philippines a formulation derived from the Chinese experience. This was the definition "the new democratic revolution" which was taken up by both the MPLA and the Huk movement in projecting their struggles as national liberation struggles of a bourgeois democratic character led by the proletariat in alliance with the peasantry. In both cases the way in which this was implemented acted to hamper rather than enhance broad liberation movements.

In Malaya, the lack of sufficient peasant support and the appeasement by the imperialists of the bourgeois nationalist issues involved in independence made of this a mechanically applied definition with proletarian features accentuated, tending to foster isolation rather than to broaden the struggle. Philippine

Communists, calling on the people in 1950 to take up arms and overthrow a neo-colonial regime, also declared themselves as having hegemony over a "new democratic revolution" led by the proletariat. This strategic line, with its class struggle features, contributed to the alienation of nationalist-inclined sectors of the Filipino bourgeoisie and petty bourgeoisie, tending to facilitate American imperialist tactics of winning these elements to an alliance against the armed struggle.

7.

Different circumstances prevailed in three major subsequent victories through guerrilla warfare—in Vietnam, in Algeria, and in China.

The Vietnam struggle was unique. Unlike the other anti-Japanese liberation struggles in Asia, the Communist-led movement in Indochina during World War II did not concentrate fully on the military aspect; it devoted its attention throughout the war to organization, to propaganda, and to the building of a broad movement that included all sectors of the population. The rigidly colonial nature of French imperalist policy, which had banned features of self-rule, stimulated national feeling in all strata of the population. Serious military action was not launched until the final stage of the war, and it took the form not of protracted guerrilla warfare but of insurrection. Perfectly timed to coincide with the defeat of Japan, when neither French nor other imperialist forces were on the scene, the insurrection in August 1945, occurring in both cities and countryside, gained immediate power for the Viet Minh, which established an independent republic that had the support of the population. Proletarian leadership was not stressed, the role of the Communist Party was not exclusively projected, and the broad national liberation character of the revolution stood out clearly.

This was a classic in revolutionary strategy and in insurrectionary tactics, and the whole course of the Vietnamese struggle that followed was founded on it. When French imperialism undertook to suppress the functioning republic in 1946, virtually the whole population rallied to its support in a war of national resistance. It was not a question of building up mass bases through guerrilla warfare; the base existed in the whole country. During the struggle, of course, the external factor came into play, with the newly-victorious socialist Republic of China, as well as other socialist countries, able to aid the Vietnamese people. The pattern of a national people's struggle, however, had been set, and it continued into the war of national resistance against American imperialism. It is a striking feature of the war in South Vietnam that the National Liberation Front has involved both the towns and the countryside in the general struggle, in which a variety of forms of armed struggle and of other forms of resistance and protest have been encouraged.

In the case of the Algerian war for liberation (1954–62), a different set of circumstances existed. The national liberation movement was led by Algerian petty-bourgeois elements whose revolutionary temper had been sharpened by antagonism with the French colonists who dominated the country as settlers. Here the Algerian Communist Party, far from being in leadership, actually had to struggle to be accepted as part of the National Liberation Front. However, it effectively supported the nationalist struggle and led the Algerian proletariat, especially in the cities, in support of it. The Algerian people, therefore, were fully united in the war against French imperialism, which could not divide them on class or social lines.

The Algerian struggle started as an uprising that was forced into protracted guerrilla warfare, waged in the cities as well as in the countryside. The external factor was a very important one, with independent Morocco and Tunisia aiding and providing sanctuary for Algerian armed forces, and with the socialist as well as the Arab countries rendering large-scale assistance. In addition, both in the first Vietnamese war of liberation and then in the Algerian war, French workers and intellectuals in the home imperialist country strongly supported the liberation forces. The Algerian liberation war, finally, never had to develop from guerrilla to regular warfare in order to win; the French army was not defeated militarily, the political victory being greatly advanced by mass demonstrations in cities and by the political crisis in France provoked by the protracted and costly imperialist wars first in Indochina and then in Algeria.

The guerrilla liberation war in Cuba also had its own pattern of development, shaped by Cuban conditions. Fidel Castro's 26th of July Movement, which launched the armed struggle in 1956, was in its origins an expression of the revolutionized, nationalist Cuban petty bourgeoisie. It began revolt at a time when a revolutionary tide was rising against a fascist-like regime (it was not directly waged as an anti-imperialist national liberation struggle, a consideration, along with the nature of its leadership, that had much to do with the relatively passive attitude of American imperialism during the struggle). Fidel Castro and his fellow revolutionary leaders correctly grasped the fact that a revolutionary situation was maturing in Cuba, and their armed struggle had a catalytic effect as a revolutionary situation matured. A number of other forces and forms of struggle developed, however, in the cities as well as in the countryside, ranging from the action of conservative bourgeois nationalist groups (even elements of the Catholic Church) to the Cuban Communist Party (known as the Popular Socialist Party) and the trade unions it influenced. General strikes under Communist leadership helped to paralyze the Batista dictatorship in the final stage of the struggle.

One of the features of the Cuban situation, too often overlooked or ignored, was the background of organizational experience and of mass struggle possessed by the Cuban people. In Oriente province, where Fidel Castro's guerrilla force established itself in the Sierra Maestra, and in its city of Santiago de Cuba that served as a supply base, mass organizational work had long existed and people had a familiarity with revolutionary movements.

In defining the revolutionary process in Cuba, it is unavoidable to emphasize its insurrectionary features. All sectors of the population were brought into it, adopting varied forms of struggle as the crisis matured, with the armed struggle playing the decisive role. The existence of a revolutionary situation that matured rapidly to a revolutionary crisis and affected the entire population may account for the fact that a protracted guerrilla war operating from a mass base, as has occurred for example in Asia, was not so essential in Cuban circumstances, particularly since there was no need to cope with serious imperialist intervention. It is for these reasons, no doubt, that the role of the political party and of its mass organizational work in an armed struggle has not been so emphasized by Fidel Castro, Che Guevara and others who view the Cuban experience as the creation of a new pattern for revolutionary guerrilla war.

Of particular significance in the Cuban revolution was the path it took after the seizure of power, when the alliances that had taken shape as the revolution developed were consolidated. Unlike the case of Algeria, where the bourgeois nationalist forces were predominant and sought to exclude the Communist Party as an organization and even compelled its dissolution after power had been won, the revolutionary petty-bourgeois elements in Cuba, after gaining power, combined themselves with the Communists in a leading capacity and, under the pressure of American imperialist counter-revolutionary attempts, advanced the revolution to a proletarian socialist stage.

In the Cuban situation this was a recognition of the working class roots and of the mass influence of the Cuban Communists and of the need for Marxist–Leninist solutions to Cuba's problems of underdevelopment. As a phenomenon, however, the development of Fidel Castro, Che Guevara and the movement they led needs to be related to two important features of the disintegration of the imperialist system. One is the increased radicalization of the colonial petty bourgeoisies as imperialism (especially American imperialism with its all-pervasive character) has expanded its domination and exploitation to all aspects of life—economic, social and cultural—in the colonial and neo-colonial countries. The other related feature is the recognition by some sectors of the nationalist bourgeoisie of the necessity for pursuing non-capitalist paths in order to develop their economies and to overcome the extremely backward conditions they inherit from colonialism.

Whereas the revolutionary upsurge in the colonial areas between the two world wars came chiefly from the workers and peasants, with revolutionary petty-bourgeois intellectuals joining the proletarian movement, in the contemporary period the radicalized petty bourgeoisie often seeks to act with impatience, independently and in advance of the proletarian movement, tending to view student and intellectual sectors as the vanguard of the revolution. They seek armed struggle without waiting for a mass upsurge in its varied forms, in the belief that *action* by a minority will create the mass upheaval. No doubt this outlook has been augmented by the growing importance of the external factor in the revolutionary situations of today, by the knowledge that armed struggles can be supported and their victories protected by the socialist and anti-imperialist countries (as in the case of Cuba).

The growth of revolutionary movements and of revolutionary forces is a development of great satisfaction to Marxists, and the readiness of any sector of a population for the sharpest struggle for national liberation, for non-capitalist paths and for socialism is to be welcomed by them. These may or may not have Marxist-

Leninist leadership. However, Marxists would generally agree that no set of strategy and tactics in a revolution could achieve proletarian goals without observing certain basic factors. Among these are: the agitation and organized activity of the broadest masses of the people, particularly the urban and rural proletariat; the employment of the most varied forms of struggle in order to involve the broadest masses of the people and to attack all possible features of the ruling class state power; the necessity for each revolutionary struggle to arise from and to be shaped by the conditions within each country; and the need for the features of a revolutionary situation to exist before advanced forms of struggle can be employed with any hope of success. Certainly, it would be un-Marxist to contend that such generalizations from past experience cannot be enriched and added to by new experience, including the experience of new forms of struggle and new relationships among them, but this does not mean that basic approaches and concepts can be ignored.

8.

The guerrilla liberation struggles that were begun in the colonies in the southern part of Africa in the 1960's provide some of the best examples of careful, scientific preparation of a party and people for armed struggle. Although there has been Marxist influence in the leadership of all of these national liberation movements, each has been based on a different social structure and a different stage of development, ranging from an extensive working class base that has enabled a Communist Party and a proletarian ideology to play a prominent role in South Africa to the largely pre-capitalist ethnic base in Guinea Bissau, Mozambique and Rhodesia (and an intermediate stage in Angola). These movements have drawn extensively from the experiences of armed struggles led by both Communists and non-Communists and they have had assistance in cadre training from the Soviet Union, China, Vietnam, Cuba and Algeria. Marxist methods of class analysis, of agitation and mass organization, and of political work have influenced these armed struggles considerably.

The following description of the development of the struggle led by the PAIGC (*Partido Africano da Independência da Guiné e Cabo Verde*) in Guinea Bissau indicates the approach that has characterized these movements.

"The six founders of the PAIGC recall that it was September 19, 1956, when, on the basis of the errors committed and the obstacles encountered in the course of militant action, they determined how to go about preparing to set in motion the war of national liberation:

"—on the basis of a sociological analysis of the country and of the relations of forces between the main enemy and the nationalists, the Party determined how to make a dormant people aware of their oppression;

"—with agitation around the interests of the masses, peasantry in the main, the Party asserted itself as the spokesman of the people for Guinea for independence, weeded out opportunist elements, and set up an underground Front;

"—when there were militants in arms, springing out of the people, the Party chose the moment to pass from the political phase to that of the armed struggle.

"Certainly the progress of the political thought of the PAIGC in regard to the creation of the FARP (Revolutionary Armed Force of the People) was inspired partially by the experience of the Viet Minh resistance, but the struggle has its own specific features bestowed upon it by the Guinean conditions and by the African context."*

The founders of PAIGC, headed by Amilcar Cabral, its secretary-general, began to lay the basis for their movement and for an armed liberation struggle in September 1956, but armed action was not actually begun until January 1963, after it was felt that sufficient mass preparation had been made. It was this careful approach that made its base more stable and its successes more evident than in more hastily launched actions in other areas of southern Africa.

Careful steps of a similar kind characterized the establishment of FRELIMO in the Portuguese colony of Mozambique. The liberation front was set up on June 25, 1962, but it did not launch guerrilla military operations until September 1964. According to FRELIMO's president, Eduardo Mondlane, "First, we accepted it as a fact of life that Salazar's Portugal† was unable to accept the idea of self-determination and that there was

---

* "October in Guinea," by Mario de Andrade, *Révolution Africaine* (Organ of the FLN, Algeria), Algiers, December 7, 1967. Andrade is himself coordinator of the secretariat of CONCP (*Conference des Organizations Nationalistes des Colonies Portuguises*), the coordinating body for liberation movements in Portuguese colonies.

† Dr. Antonio de Oliveira Salazar, dictator of Portugal since 1932.

no prospect of negotiating political changes leading toward independence. We had to establish a clandestine political force within Mozambique to prepare the people for the difficult task of liberating the country. Secondly, we decided to establish a clandestine military program. Thirdly, we agreed to establish an educational program that would emphasize leadership training. . . .

"Certainly one of the most important departments is the one responsible for clandestine political work within Mozambique. The executive secretary in charge of this department is assisted by a committee of associate secretaries, one representing each province. They prepare for action everywhere—ahead of the army, with the army and after the army. They are responsible for formulating political lines and transmitting them to local leaders. They establish cells everywhere in Mozambique and make sure that each cell knows what it must do and how its function fits into the party's strategy for the liberation of the whole country. A department of organization within Mozambique has the related task of preparing the people psychologically and politically for the long struggle that we face. We do not make facile promises to people, for it is absolutely essential that they share with us the knowledge that liberation from Portuguese rule may take many years and many lives."*

In South Africa itself the national liberation movement has been equally careful in the steps it has taken toward the development of armed struggle. It was only after exhausting every possible non-violent means that its component groups—the African National Congress, the Communist Party of South Africa, the South African Indian Congress, trade unions and others—decided on armed action. It was initiated on December 16, 1961, with the formation and first attacks by the fighting force *Umkonto We Sizwe* (Spear of the Nation), which declared in a manifesto that "the people prefer peaceful methods of change to achieve their aspirations without the suffering and bitterness of civil war. . . . The government has interpreted the peacefulness of the movement as weakness. . . . We are striking out along a new road for the liberation of the people. The government policy of force, repression and violence *will no longer be met with non-violent resistance only. Umkonto We Sizwe* will be at the front

---

* *Tri-Continental Information Center Bulletin*, New York, Vol. II, No. 1, January 1968, pp. 1, 3.

line of the people's defense, It will be the fighting arm of the people against the government . . ."*

The initial operations of *Umkonto We Sizwe,* which were of a sabotage nature such as the blowing up of electric pylons, were designed to shatter the mold of peaceful methods in which mass action had been set, and immediately brought many volunteers for the armed struggle. A prolonged period of training and preparation for armed struggle itself was needed, however, due in large part to the fact that Africans in South Africa had literally no experience with arms, having been completely excluded from military or police training by ruling class whites and denied possession of arms. It was not until August 1967 that serious armed struggle was begun, when it was felt that cadres and masses were ready. This was the formal launching of guerrilla warfare by forces of the African National Congress in conjunction with the Zimbabwe African People's Union in bordering Rhodesia. Oliver Tambo, acting chairman of the African National Congress, said after the first clashes occurred: "For a long time the ANC has been conducting militant struggles relying on non-violent means. This became particularly intense during the 50s and gradually led to a stage at which the movement switched over from non-violence to the phase of armed struggle. During 1967 the first armed clashes occurred between on the one hand the combined forces of the Smith and Vorster regimes† and on the other the united guerrillas of the ANC and ZAPU. It can be said that for the ANC this is the beginning of the armed struggle for which we have been preparing since the early 60s."‡

9.

Preparations of this kind for armed struggle are to Marxists entirely correct tactics in meeting a situation in which all other doors to legal, peaceful ways of effecting change have been slammed shut. The active world role of US imperialism as the brutal gendarme against revolutions everywhere has proliferated the existence of such situations. The fact that they exist already in so many countries, with violence increasingly used as an in-

* *The African Communist,* No. 9, April–May 1962, pp. 48–49.
† Ian Smith, premier of the illegal white settler regime created in 1965 in Rhodesia, and John Vorster, premier of South Africa.
‡ Press interview, October 1967.

strument of imperialist policy, has, however, fostered the belief on the part of some radical or revolutionary elements that the duty of Marxist-Leninists today is, above all, to make preparations for guerrilla warfare or other types of armed struggle, and either to agitate the people to take up arms or to embark on guerrilla warfare without such a prelude. In a mood of enthusiastic support for the heroic liberation wars of people in many countries, some of these participants or leaders of popular movements have concluded that the imperialist system as a whole can be engulfed and overwhelmed by guerrilla warfare, and that it can and should be undertaken at present in the cities of the United States as well as everywhere in unliberated areas of Asia, Africa and Latin America.

This apocalyptic vision of imperialism and the capitalist system being beseiged and smothered in a mounting crescendo of guerrilla wars is usually based on the view that revolutionary situations exist on whole continents, that they affect underdeveloped and imperialist countries alike, and that this is a permanent situation that can be only further aggravated. Indeed, Marxist-Leninists have long contended that imperialism and the capitalist system as a whole are in a state of crisis and that the present epoch on a world scale is a revolutionary one of transformation from capitalism to socialism. However, within this generalized characterization it is recognized that there exists a wide variety of specific conditions, of levels of revolutionary development, and of intensity of struggle—as between advanced and underdeveloped countries, among countries within a continent, or even among countries within a region. The Marxist-Leninist view of revolutionary situations and of revolutionary struggles, its insistence that revolutions cannot be exported and cannot be willed at random and that they must conform to the specific conditions peculiar to each country, are an integral part of its philosophical concept of the relations between the general and the particular in social development.

An oversimplified estimate of the nature of the imperialist crisis and of the revolutionary situations that flow from it has been reflected in the slogan sometimes raised in connection with this: "The duty of a revolutionary is to make the revolution." This is a slogan with which Marxist-Leninists can be in full agreement, as far as it goes, but it does not become a useful slogan of action unless it is extended to make plain that the duty of a revolutionary with a Marxist outlook is to make the revolution in accordance with scientific concepts of strategy and tactics. It is no contradiction to say that revolutions must be both born and made. There is perhaps no better illustration of the truth of this than the tragic death of the great revolutionary, Che Guevara, in Bolivia in October 1967, which has been traced to over-estimation of the ripeness of the given situation in Bolivia and to insufficient attention having been given to preparation of the people for guerrilla struggle.

Experiences like this point sharply to the need for armed struggle tactics to conform to existing objective and subjective conditions. The question of guerrilla warfare in the United States itself is a case in point, raised in connection with the rebellion of the Afro-Americans against ghetto conditions and the brutal denial of equality, during which some militant black Americans have taken up arms to defend themselves against police violence. The urban guerrilla-like tactics and counter-terror that have occurred in these struggles are popular forms of struggle that, like all such instances historically, can only have genuine revolutionary effect and can gain genuine revolutionary goals when they are controlled and given political content as one form of struggle in a broad mass movement. Marxists participating in these actions would be doing so in the same way that they participate in all popular struggles, in order to help channel desperation and retaliation into scientifically organized efforts and to ensure that inevitably violent measures "be enobled by the enlightening and organizing influence of socialism." In the context of American conditions in the 1960s, however, as Henry Winston, chairman of the Communist Party of the United States, has pointed out, the main task of Marxists is to help develop the most varied forms of action by both white and black people in support of struggles for black liberation, and to help merge these, in all the forms that they take, both violent and non-violent, in the broadest possible movement for freedom, democracy and radical social change.

Affecting attitudes on armed struggle is a frame of mind that tends to the outlook that because armed struggle is defined as representing the highest form of struggle, the true revolutionary must be one who is ready to take to arms at once. In this way of looking at things, a "Left" act can be justified as the expression of "true militancy" while a "Right" act (meaning anything short of the most militant posture) must be condemned as a "betrayal of the revolutionary spirit." The history of Marxist-

Leninist ideas and experience, which is one of struggle against both "Left adventurism" and "Right opportunism" and which is concerned with scientific appraisals of situations and with precisely calculated actions based on them, offers weighty proof that revolutionary attitudes are not merely matters of emotion and temperament. In a revolutionary, prudence and caution can prove to be attributes as important as boldness and daring.

Honest, self-critical Marxists will acknowledge that the experiences of popular struggle in the contemporary period, particularly of armed struggle, have taught many lessons, including the lesson that a revolutionary party must be able to shift with flexibility from one form of struggle to another as warranted by the behavior of reactionary class forces. Events have sometimes indicated that long years of experience in non-violent activities can make it difficult to break a pattern of work and to adopt new and perhaps necessarily violent forms of struggle. In such cases, masses in struggle, acting spontaneously if not led, may force a correction of tactics.

The same principle, however, holds true for those who become overly committed to ideas of armed struggle, to the point where all other forms of struggle that are possible and into which significant masses can be drawn are neglected, and to the point where revolutionary vanguards may become isolated, with the risk of being destroyed or forced into difficult retreats from which it is hard to recuperate. Imperialist counter-insurgency operations have been designed especially to take advantage of this type of error.

It may be worthwhile to cite the experience of the Philippine national liberation movement which, it will be remembered, was totally committed in the 1950s to revolutionary guerrilla warfare virtually to the exclusion of other forms of struggle. Its armed struggle was defeated, and it was forced into the painful process of adjusting to a new situation, out of which, due to particular Philippine conditions, new favorable factors and relationships of forces arose. From a total commitment to one form of struggle, a shift was made over a period of years to varied forms and to other methods of organization, with armed detachments still being retained as one of the forms, but not the main form. In this period, the Communist Party continued to remain outlawed and under the most severe repression.

In 1967 a small "Leftist" group in the Philippines attempted to put forward calls for a return by the national liberation movement to all-out guerrilla warfare, and even issued a false statement in the name of the Communist Party alleging that "the outlawed situation of the Party clearly dictates that there is no path to national and social liberation except armed struggle." This was refuted in the following manner by the Philippine Communist Party:

"By equating the necessity for armed struggle with the outlawed situation of the Party, such a statement displays a very narrow and constricted view of the national situation in the Philippines, and it grossly ignores the ability of the PKP to lead the revolutionary masses in struggle despite its illegal character. Armed struggle is a necessity, as the final step in the overthrow of imperialism, not because of the illegal character of the Party, but because of the nature of imperialism itself. Moreover, the spurious statement creates the impression of a 'call to arms' at this very moment, again ignoring the present state of objective and subjective conditions in the Philippines. The correct position, which is the position of the PKP, is to combine dialectically parliamentary struggle and armed struggle, legal and illegal forms of action."*

In addition, the experience of other liberation movements which have been defeated in an armed struggle illustrates an important political truth: situations are not static and can change in more than one direction, toward or away from revolution. A revolutionary tide may rise or it may ebb, depending on a number of changing conditions. It is not possible to predict precisely what those changes might be. Guerrilla wars might become so widespread as to bring about a qualitative change in which a great variety of forms of struggle could become possible and successful, including *insurrection* rather than protracted people's war. The changes could bring an atomic conflict between socialism and imperialism—a type of armed struggle that the socialist countries and the Communist movement internationally seek to prevent because of the catastrophic effect it would have on mankind in general. Or, it is even in the range of possibility that they might bring a situation, forced on imperialism, in which it would have to recognize the futility and the disastrous effect on itself of its military suppression policies and of other forms of violence against popular movements.

* "Statement of the Philippine Communist Party," *Information Bulletin*, Prague, 1967, Vol. 5, No. 22 (110), p. 35.

French and British imperialism have already been forced in this direction and American imperialism, with divisions in its ranks over the cost of wars of suppression, is not immune from it. The world-wide counter-revolutionary police role that American imperialism has assumed in this period is the central cause of the resort to armed struggles by liberation movements and these will continue to occur, with Marxists-Leninists in their forefront, as long as that role is unaltered. It is unreal, however, to contend that it cannot be altered by mass struggle against it, and it is obvious that in each of the possibilities of changes in the world situation a diversity of forms of struggle would present themselves to revolutionary movements, of which guerrilla warfare would be only one.

Attempts by imperialism in the contemporary period to suppress revolutionary movements by using the most advanced military technology—helicopters, napalm, chemical warfare, electronic devices—bear comparison with the use of then-new military developments to drive revolutionary movements off the streets in the time of Marx and Engels, over 100 years ago. But today superior military technology is offset by the fact that the popular masses have achieved what Marx and Engels set out to do: they have been organized and politically educated for struggle; and also by the fact that effective modern arms are available to national liberation or revolutionary forces.

Furthermore, revolutionary change cannot be viewed in isolation from the dominant fact in international life: the basic conflict between the socialist and capitalist systems, in which the balance of power continues to shift toward the socialist forces, despite the ups and downs inevitable in any historic struggle. The desperate American imperialistic violence in recent years is directly related to this situation, particularly since the Korean War in the 1950s made the balance of power plain. Since then American imperialism has made strenuous efforts to reverse the trend, as in Vietnam where it is again being demonstrated in a major conflict that the historic trend cannot be reversed.

Popular armed struggles of today have been shaped largely by the imperialist tactics of violence, and the forms of struggle in the coming period will be affected to a considerable extent by the degree to which imperialism is forced to recognize the realities in the changed balance of power. Some revolutionaries would contend that American imperialism is rigidly incapable of acknowledging such a fact or of doing anything to meet it other than what it is doing today. However, a Marxist-Leninist, while ready for any form of struggle, must also be prepared for the complexity of change. In any case, one thing is certain: whatever the tactics to which imperialism is driven in the vain hope of survival, these will have been forced upon it to a large extent by revolutionary armed struggles, which will continue to be, whenever conditions make them necessary or feasible, an important means by which the working class and its allies will gain their objectives of national freedom and socialism.

Editor's Note

The selections in Part One are arranged chronologically; in Part Two by regions and countries. The introductions to the various sections and to individual selections are by the editor, who has also supplied the footnotes and the explanations within square brackets in the text. Wherever possible, selections from books have been made from editions most readily available to the general reader; the sources are given at the end of each selection.

PART ONE

Historical Background

1

The Art of Insurrection

KARL MARX and FREDERICK ENGELS

Now, insurrection is an art quite as much as war or any other, and subject to certain rules of proceeding, which, when neglected, will produce the ruin of the party neglecting them. Those rules, logical deductions from the nature of the parties and the circumstances one has to deal with in such a case, are so plain and simple that the short experience of 1848 had made the Germans pretty well acquainted with them. Firstly, never play with insurrection unless you are fully prepared to face the consequences of your play. Insurrection is a calculus with very indefinite magnitudes, the value of which may change every day; the forces opposed to you have all the advantage of organization, discipline, and habitual authority; unless you bring strong odds against them you are defeated and ruined. Secondly, the insurrectionary career once entered upon, act with the greatest determination, and on the offensive. The defensive is the death of every armed rising; it is lost before it measures itself with its enemies. Surprise your antagonists while their forces are scattering, prepare new successes, however small, but daily; keep up the moral ascendency which the first successful rising has given to you; rally those vacillating elements to your side which always follow the strongest impulse, and which always look out for the safer side; force your enemies to a retreat before they can collect their strength against you; in the words of Danton, the greatest master of revolutionary policy yet known, *de l'audace, de l'audace, encore de l'audace!*

—Frederick Engels, *Germany: Revolution and Counter-Revolution*, International Publishers, 1933, p. 100. First published under Marx's name in the *New York Tribune*, September 18, 1852.

2

Guerrilla Warfare in Spain

KARL MARX

... The Spanish standing army, if everwhere defeated, nevertheless presented itself at all points. More than 20 times dispersed, it was always ready again to show front to the enemy, and frequently reappeared with increased strength after a defeat. It was of no use to beat them, because, quick to flee, their loss in men was generally small, and as to the loss of the field they did not care about it. Retiring disorderly to the sierras, they were sure to reassemble and reappear when least expected, strengthened by new reinforcements, and able, if not to resist the French armies, at least to keep them in continual movement, and to oblige them to scatter their forces. More fortunate than the Russians, they did not even need to die in order to rise from the dead.

The disastrous battle at Ocaña, November 19, 1809, was the last great pitched battle which the Spaniards fought; from that time they confined themselves to guerrilla warfare. The mere fact of the abandonment of regular warfare proves the disappearance of the national before the local centers of government. When the disasters of the standing army became regular, the rising of the guerrillas became general, and the body of the people, hardly thinking of the national defeats, exulted in the local successes of their heroes. In this point at least the Central junta shared the popular delusion. "Fuller accounts were given in the *Gaceta* of an affair of guerrillas than of the battle of Ocaña."

As Don Quixote had protested with his lance against gunpowder, so the guerrillas protested against Napoleon, only with different success. "These guerrillas," says the *Austrian Military Journal*, (Vol. I, 1821), "carried their basis in themselves, as it were, and every operation against them terminated in the disappearance of its object."

There are three periods to be distinguished in the history of the guerrilla warfare. In the first period the population of whole provinces took up arms and made partisan warfare, as in Galicia and Asturias. In the second period, guerrilla bands formed of the wrecks of the Spanish armies, of Spanish deserters from the French armies, of smugglers, etc., carried on the war as their own cause, independently of all foreign influence and agreeable to their immediate interest. Fortunate events and circumstances frequently brought whole districts under their colors. As long as the guerrillas were thus constituted, they made no formidable appearance as a body, but were nevertheless extremely dangerous to the French. They formed the basis of an actual armament of the people. As soon as an opportunity for a capture offered itself, or a combined enterprise was meditated, the most active and daring among the people came out and joined the guerrillas. They rushed with the utmost rapidity upon their booty, or placed themselves in order of battle, according to the object of their undertaking. It was not uncommon to see them standing out a whole day in sight of a vigilant enemy, in order to intercept a courier or to capture supplies. It was in this way that the younger Mina captured the Viceroy of Navarra, appointed by Joseph Bonaparte, and that Julian made a prisoner of the Commandante of Ciudad Rodrigo. As soon as the enterprise was completed, everybody went his own way, and armed men were soon scattering in all directions; but the associated peasants quietly returned to their common occupation without "as much as their absence having been noticed." Thus the communication on all the roads was closed. Thousands of enemies were on the spot, though not one could be discovered. No courier could be dispatched without being taken; no supplies could set out without being intercepted; in short, no movement could be effected without being observed by a hundred eyes. At the same time, there existed no means of striking at the root of a combination of this kind. The French were obliged to be constantly armed against an enemy who, continually flying, always reappeared, and was everywhere without being actually seen, the mountains serving as so many curtains. "It was," says the Abbé de Pradt, "neither battles nor engagements which exhausted the French forces, but the incessant molestations of an invisible enemy, who, if pursued, became lost among the people, out of which he reappeared immediately afterward with renewed strength. The lion in the fable tormented to death by a gnat gives a true picture of the French army." In their third period, the guerrillas aped the regularity of the standing army, swelled their corps to the number of from 3,000 to 6,000 men, ceased to be the concern of whole districts, and fell into the hands of a few leaders, who made such use of them as best suited their own purposes. This change in the system of the guerrillas gave the French, in their contests with them, considerable advantage. Rendered incapable by their great numbers to conceal themselves, and to suddenly disappear without being forced into battle, as they had formerly done, the *guerrilleros* were now frequently overtaken, defeated, dispersed, and disabled for a length of time from offering any further molestation.

By comparing the three periods of guerrilla warfare with the political history of Spain, it is found that they represent the respective degrees into which the counter-revolutionary spirit of the government had succeeded in cooling the spirit of the people. Beginning with the rise of whole populations, the partisan war was next carried on by guerrilla bands, of which whole districts formed the reserve and terminated in *corps francs* (commandos) continually on the point of dwindling into *banditti,* or sinking down to the level of standing regiments.

Estrangement from the Supreme Government, relaxed discipline, continual disasters, constant formation, decomposition, and recomposition during six years of the *cadrez* must have necessarily stamped upon the body of the Spanish army the character of praetorianism, making them equally ready to become the tools or the scourges of their chiefs. The generals themselves had necessarily participated in, quarreled with, or conspired against the central government, and always thrown the weight of their sword into the political balance. Thus Cuesta, who afterwards seemed to win the confidence of the Central junta at the same rate that he lost the battles of the country, had begun by conspiring with the *Consejo Real* (Royal Council) and by arresting the Leonese Deputies to the Central junta. General Morla himself, a member of the Central junta, went over to the Bonapartist camp, after he had surrendered Madrid to the French. The coxcombical Marquis de las Romerias, also a member of the junta, conspired with the vainglorious Francisco Palafox, the wretch Montijo, and the turbulent junta of Seville against it. The Generals Castaños, Blake, La Bisbal (an O'Donnell) figured and intrigued successively at the times of the Cortes as Regents, and the Captain-General of Valencia, Don Xavier Elio, surrendered Spain finally to the mercies of Ferdinand VII. The praetorian element was certainly more developed with the generals than with their troops.

On the other hand, the army and *guerrilleros*—which received during the war part of their chiefs, like Porlier, Lacy, Eroles and Villacampa, from the ranks of distinguished officers of the line, while the line in its turn afterward received guerrilla chiefs, like Mina, Empecinado, etc.—were the most revolutionized portion of Spanish society, recruited as they were from all ranks, including the whole of the fiery, aspiring and patriotic youth, inaccessible to the soporific influence of the central government; emancipated from the shackles of the ancient regime; part of them, like Riego, returning after some years' captivity in France. We are, then, not to be surprised at the influence exercised by the Spanish army in subsequent commotions; neither when taking the revolutionary initiative, nor when spoiling the revolution by praetorianism.

As to the guerrillas, it is evident that, having for some years figured upon the theater of sanguinary contests, taken to roving habits, freely indulged all their passions of hatred, revenge and love of plunder, they must, in times of peace, form a most dangerous mob, always ready at a nod in the name of any party or principle, to step forward for him who is able to give them good pay or to afford them a pretext for plundering excursions.

—Karl Marx and Frederick Engels, *Revolution in Spain*, International Publishers, 1939, pp. 51–55. First published in the *New York Tribune*, October 30, 1854.

3

On Guerrilla Warfare

FREDERICK ENGELS

In the course of the last six weeks, the character of the (Franco-Prussian) war has markedly changed. The regular armies of France have disappeared. The struggle is being carried on by recently mobilized troops whose inexperience makes them more or less irregular. Wherever they attempt to mass and fight in the open, they are easily defeated; but when they fight under the cover of villages and towns equipped with barricades and embrasures, it becomes evident that they are capable of offering serious resistance. They are encouraged to carry on this type of struggle, with night surprise attacks and other methods of guerrilla warfare, by proclamations and orders from the government, which also advises the population of the district in which they operate to give them every possible assistance.

If the enemy possessed sufficient troops to occupy the whole of the country, this resistance could be easily broken. But for this, up to the surrender of Metz, he has not had the strength. The ubiquitous "four Uhlans" are no longer able to ride into a village or town outside their own lines, demanding absolute subjection to their orders, without incurring the risk of captivity or death. Requisitioning detachments have to be accompanied by escorting troops, and single companies or squadrons quartering in a village must guard against night attacks, and also, when they are on the march, against attacks from the rear. The German positions are surrounded by a belt of disputed territory, and it is just here that popular resistance makes itself felt most seriously.

In order to break this popular resistance, the Germans are resorting to a type of martial law that is as obsolete as it is barbaric. They act on the principle that any town or village in the defense of which one or more inhabitants have taken part, have fired on German troops or generally assisted the French—any such town or village is to be burnt down. Further, any man found carrying weapons, and not in their eyes a regular soldier, is to be summarily shot. When there is any suspicion that a considerable section of a town has been guilty of such a misdeed, all men capable of bearing arms are to be massacred forthwith. For the past six weeks this policy has been pitilessly carried out, and is still at this moment in full sway. One cannot open a single German newspaper without coming on half a dozen reports of such military executions; these are made to appear as a matter of course, as a simple process of military justice, carried out with salutary firmness by "honest soldiers against cowardly assassins and robbers." There is, of course, no disorder, no looting, no raping of women, no irregularity. Indeed no. Everything is done systematically, and by order. The condemned village is surrounded, the inhabitants driven out, the provisions confiscated, the houses set alight. The real or imaginary culprits are brought before a court martial, where a brief, final confession and half a dozen bullets are their certain lot.

It is no exaggeration to say that wherever the German flying columns march into the heart of France, their path is all too often marked with fire and blood. It is hardly sufficient, in this year of 1870, to claim others not immediately recognizable as soldiers are the equivalent of banditry, and must be put down with fire and sword. Such an argument might have been valid in the day of Louis XIV or Frederick II, when there was no kind of fighting other than that of regular armies. But ever since the American War of Independence and up to the American War of Secession, it has been the rule rather than the exception, for the people to take part in war. Wherever a people has allowed itself to be subjected for no other reason than that its armies have been incapable of offering resistance, it has earned general contempt as a nation of cowards; and wherever a people has energetically waged such irregular warfare, the invader soon found it impossible to carry through the obsolete law of blood and fire. The English in America, the French under Napoleon in Spain, and in 1848, the Austrians in Italy and Hungary, were very soon compelled to treat popular resistance as an entirely legitimate form of warfare. They were compelled to do so from the fear of reprisals against their own prisoners...

Of all the armies in the world, the Prussian army should have been the last to revive these practices. In 1806, Prussia collapsed solely because nowhere in the country was there any sign of such a national spirit of resistance. After 1807, the reorganizers and the administrators of the army did everything in their power to ressurrect this spirit. It was at this time that Spain furnished a glorious example of how a nation can resist an invading army. The military leaders of Prussia all pointed to it as an example worthy of the emulation of their compatriots. Scharnhorst, Gneisenau, Clausewitz—all were of the same opinion. Gneisenau even went to Spain himself to take part in the struggle against Napoleon. The whole military system that was subsequently introduced in Prussia was an attempt to mobilize popular resistance against the enemy, insofar as this was possible at all in an absolute monarchy. Not only had every fit man to join the army and serve in the reserves *(Landwehr)* up to his 40th year; boys between 17 and 20 and men between 40 and 65 were also included in the *levee en masse,* or mass conscription, in the final reserves *(Landsturm)* whose function it was to rise in the rear and on the flanks of the enemy, to interfere with his movements, and to cut off his supplies and his couriers; they were expected to use any weapon they could lay their hands on and to employ without distinction all available measures to harry the invader—"the more effective the measure the better"; nor was "any kind of uniform to be worn," so that the men of the *Landsturm* might at any moment resume their character of civilians, thus remaining unrecognizable to the enemy.

This *Landsturm Order* of 1813, as the document in question was called—its author being no other than Scharnhorst, the organizer of the Prussian army—was drawn up in this spirit of irreconcilable national resistance, according to which all means are valid, and the most effective the best. At that time, however, all this was to be done by the Prussians against the French; when the French chose to behave in precisely the same manner toward the Prussians, it was quite another matter. What had become patriotism in one case became banditry and assassination in the other.

The fact is that the present Prussian government is ashamed of this old semi-revolutionary *Landsturm Order,* and by its actions in France seeks to erase it from memory. But the deliberate atrocities they themselves have committed in France will, instead, call it all the more to mind. The argument brought forward in favor of so despicable a method of waging war serves only as proof that, if the Prussian army has immeasurably improved since Jena,* the Prussian government on the other hand, is ripening for the conditions that made Jena possible.

—*Labour Monthly,* London, August 1943. First published in London, *Pall Mall Gazette,* November 11, 1870.

---

* The battle of Jena, 1806, in which Napoleon defeated the Prussian army.

4

The Paris Commune

KARL MARX

> The bulk of the French army, together with the Emperor, surrendered to the Prussians at Sedan on September 2, 1870. Two days later the republic was proclaimed in France and the so-called Government of National Defense was set up at Versailles, with Thiers at its head, composed largely of landlords and Royalists. In Paris, with the Prussian army at the gates, two unsuccessful attempts (October 31, 1870, and January 22, 1871) were made by the National Guard, composed largely of workers, to overthrow that government to prevent the surrender of the city. After Thiers had sent troops under Vinoy in an unsuccessful attempt to disarm the National Guard, the workers of Paris rose on March 18, 1871, proclaiming the Commune, with the Central Committee of the Paris National Guard as the provisional government. Aided by treachery, Thiers' troops were able to enter Paris on May 21, 1871, and after eight days of heroic resistance by the people of Paris, the Commune was drowned in blood in one of the most brutal massacres in history. In his famous Address on The Civil War in France, written for the International Working Men's Association, Marx gave his classic homage to the Commune. The following excerpts are from two letters to his friend Dr. L. Kugelmann, in which Marx sums up in a few words the significance of the Commune. (For Lenin's estimate see below, "Lessons of the Commune.")

(London) April 12, 1871

... If you look at the last chapter of my *Eighteenth Brumaire** you will find that I say that the next attempt of the French rev-

---
* Karl Marx, *The Eighteenth Brumaire of Louis Bonaparte,* International Publishers, 1963.

olution will be no longer, as before, to transfer the bureaucratic-military machine from one hand to another, but to smash it, and that is essential for every real people's revolution on the Continent. And this is what our heroic party comrades in Paris are attempting. What elasticity, what historical initiative, what a capacity for sacrifice in these Parisians! After six months of hunger and ruin, caused rather by internal treachery than by the external enemy, they rise, beneath the Prussian bayonets, as if there had never been a war between France and Germany and the enemy were not at the gates of Paris. History has no like example of like greatness. If they are defeated only their "good nature" will be to blame. They should have marched at once on Versailles, after first Vinoy and then the reactionary section of the Paris National Guard had themselves retreated. The right moment was lost because of conscientious scruples. They did not want to *start* the *civil war,* as if that mischievous *abortion* Thiers had not already started the civil war with his attempt to disarm Paris. Second mistake: The Central Committee surrendered its power too soon, to make way for the Commune. Again from a too "honorable" scrupulosity! However that may be, the present rising in Paris—even if it be crushed by the wolves, swine, and vile curs of the old society—is the most glorious deed of our party since the June (1848) insurrection in Paris. Compare these Parisians, storming heaven, with the slaves to heaven of the German-Prussian Holy Roman Empire, with its posthumous masquerades, reeking of the barracks, the Church, cabbage-Junkerdom and, above all, of the philistine.

(London) April 17, 1871

... World history would indeed be very easy to make, if the struggle were taken up only on condition of infallibly favorable chances. It would, on the other hand, be of a very mystical nature, if "accidents" played no part. These accidents themselves fall naturally into the general course of development and are compensated again by other accidents. But acceleration and delay are very dependent upon such "accidents," which include the "accident" of the character of those who at first stand at the head of the movement.

The decisive, unfavorable "accident" this time is by no means to be found in the general conditions of French society, but in the presence of the Prussians in France and their position right before Paris. Of this the Parisians were well aware. But of this, the bourgeois *canaille* of Versailles were also well aware. Precisely for that reason they presented the Parisians with the alternative of taking up the fight or succumbing without a struggle. In the latter case, the demoralization of the working class would have been a far greater misfortune than the fall of any number of "leaders." The struggle of the working class against the capitalist class and its state has entered upon a new phase with the struggle in Paris. Whatever the immediate results may be, a new point of departure of world-historic importance has been gained.

—Karl Marx and V. I. Lenin, *The Civil War in France: The Paris Commune*, International Publishers, 1968, pp. 86–87.

5

The Force Theory

FREDERICK ENGELS

Force, nowadays, is the army and navy, and both, as we all know to our cost, are "devilishly expensive." Force, however, cannot make any money; at most it can take away money that has already been made—and even this does not help very much—as we have seen, also to our cost, in the case of the French milliards. In the last analysis, therefore, money must be provided through the medium of economic production; and so once again force is conditioned by the economic order, which furnishes the resources for the equipment and maintenance of the instruments of force. But even that is not all. Nothing is more dependent on economic pre-conditions than precisely the army and navy. Their armaments, composition, organization, tactics and strategy depend above all on the stage reached at the time in production and communications. It is not the "free creations of the mind" of generals of genius that have revolutionized war, but the invention of better weapons and changes in the human material, the soldiers; at the very most, the part played by generals of genius is limited to adapting methods of fighting to the new weapons and combatants.

At the beginning of the 14th century, gunpowder came from the Arabs to Western Europe, and, as every school child knows, completely revolutionized methods of warfare. The introduction of gunpowder and firearms, however, was not all act of force, but a step forward in industry, that is, an economic advance. Industry remains industry, whether it is applied to the production or the destruction of things. And the introduction of firearms had a revolutionizing effect not only on the waging of war itself, but also on the political relationships of domination and subjection. The provision of powder and firearms required industry and money, and both of these were in the hands of the burghers of the towns. From the outset, therefore, firearms were the weapons of the towns, and of the rising monarchy, drawing its support from the towns, against the feudal nobility. The stone walls of the nobleman's castle, hitherto unapproachable, fell before the cannon of the burghers, and the bullets of the burghers' arquebuses pierced the armor of the knights. With the armor-clad cavalry of the feudal lords, the feudal lord's supremacy was also broken; with the development of the bourgeoisie, infantry and guns became more and more the decisive types of weapons; compelled by the development of artillery, the military profession had to add to its organization a new and entirely industrial sub-section, the corps of engineers.

The improvement of firearms was a very slow process. Artillery remained clumsy and the musket, in spite of a number of inventions affecting details, was still a crude weapon. It took over 300 years before a weapon was constructed which was suitable for the equipment of the whole body of infantry. It was not until the early part of the 18th century that the flint-lock musket with a bayonet finally displaced the pike in the equipment of the infantry. The foot soldiers of that period were the mercenaries of princes; they consisted of the most demoralized elements of society, rigorously disciplined but quite unreliable, and only held together by the whip; they were often enemy prisoners of war who had been pressed into service. The only type of fighting in which these soldiers could apply the new weapons was the tactics of the line, which reached its highest perfection under Frederick II. The whole infantry of an army was drawn up in triple ranks in the form of a very long, hollow square, and moved in battle order only as a whole; at very most, one or other of the two wings might move forward or withdraw a little. This cumbrous mass could only move in formation on absolutely level ground, and even then only at a very slow rate (75 paces a minute); a change of formation during a battle was impossible, and once the infantry was engaged, victory or defeat was decided rapidly and at a single blow.

In the American War of Independence, these cumbrous lines came up against bands of insurgents, which although not drilled were all the better able to shoot from their rifled carbines; these rebels were fighting for their own special interests, and therefore did not desert like the mercenaries; nor did they do the English the kindness of advancing against them also in line and across the open plain, but in scattered and rapidly moving troops of sharpshooters, under cover of the woods. In such circumstances the line was powerless and was defeated by its invisible and intangible opponents. Fighting in skirmishing order was re-invented—a new method of warfare which was the result of a change in the human material of war.

In the military sphere also, the French Revolution completed what the American Revolution had begun. Like the American, the French Revolution could oppose to the trained mercenary armies of the coalition only poorly trained but great masses of soldiers, the levy of the whole nation. But these masses had to protect Paris, that is, to hold a definite area, and for this purpose victory in open battle on a mass scale was essential. Mere skirmishes did not suffice: a form had to be invented for use by large bodies of troops, and this form was found in the *column*. Column formation made it possible for even poorly trained troops to move with a fair degree of order, and moreover with greater speed (100 paces and more in a minute); it made it possible to break through the rigid forms of the old line formation; to fight on any ground, and therefore even on ground which was extremely disadvantageous to the line formation; to group the troops in any appropriate way; and, in conjunction with attacks by scattered bands of sharpshooters, to hold up the enemy's lines, keeping them occupied and wearing them out until the moment came for masses held in reserve to break through them at the decisive point in the position. This new method of warfare, based on the combined action of skirmishes and columns and on the partitioning of the army into independent divisions or army corps, composed of all types of arms—a method brought to full perfection by Napoleon in both its tactical and strategical aspects—had become necessary primarily because of the changed personnel: the soldiery of the French Revolution. But it also had two other very important preliminary technical conditions: first, the lighter carriages for field guns constructed by Gribeauval, which alone made possible the more rapid movement now required of them; and secondly, the slanting of the butt, which had hitherto been quite straight, continuing the line of the barrel; introduced in France in 1777, it was copied from hunting weapons and it made it possible to shoot at an individual man without necessarily missing him. But for this improvement it would have been impossible to adopt skirmishing tactics, for which the old weapons were useless.

The revolutionary system of arming the whole people was soon restricted to compulsory conscription (with substitution for the rich, by payment of money) and in this form it was adopted by most of the large states on the Continent. Only Prussia attempted, through its *Landwehr* system, to draw to a still greater extent on the defensive power of the people. After the rifled muzzle-loader, which had been improved between 1830 and 1860 and made suitable for use in war, had played a brief role, Prussia was also the first state to equip its whole infantry with the most up-to-date weapons, the rifled breech-loader. Its successes in 1866 were due to these two factors.

The Franco-Prussian War was the first in which two armies faced each other both equipped with breech-loading rifles, and moreover both fundamentally in the same tactical formations as in the time of the old smooth-bore flintlocks. The only difference was that the Prussians had introduced the company column formation in an attempt to find a form of fighting which was better adapted to the new type of arms. But when, at St. Privat on August 18, the Prussian Guard tried to apply the company column formation seriously, the five regiments which were chiefly engaged lost in less than two hours more than a third of their strength (176 officers and 5,114 men). From that time the company column formation too was condemned, no less than the battalion column and the line; all idea of exposing troops in any kind of close formation to enemy gunfire was abandoned, and on the German side all subsequent fighting was conducted only in those compact bodies of skirmishers into which the columns had so far regularly dissolved of themselves under a deadly hail of bullets, although this had been opposed by the higher officers on the ground that it was contrary to good discipline; and in the same way the only form of movement when under fire from enemy rifles became the *double*. Once again the soldier had been shrewder than the officer; it was he who instinctively found the only way of fighting which has proved of service up to now under the fire of breech-loading rifles, and in spite of opposition from his officers he carried it through successfully.

The Franco-Prussian War marked a turning-point which was of entirely new significance. In the first place the weapons used have reached such a stage of perfection that further progress which would have any revolutionizing influence is no longer possible. Once armies have guns which can hit a battalion at any range at which it can be distinguished, and rifles which are equally effective for hitting individual men, while loading them takes less time than aiming, then all further improvements are more or less unimportant for field warfare. The era of evolution is therefore, in essentials, closed in this direction. And secondly, this war compelled all continental powers to introduce in a stricter form the Prussian *Landwehr* system, and with it a military burden which must bring them to ruin within a few years. The army has become the main purpose of the state, and an end in itself; the peoples are only there in addition in order to provide and feed the soldiers. Militarism dominates and is swallowing Europe. But this militarism also carries in itself the seed of its own destruction. Competition of the individual states with each other forces them, on the one hand, to spend more money each year on the army and navy, artillery, etc., thus more and more hastening financial catastrophe; and on the other hand, to take universal compulsory military service more and more seriously, thus in the long run making the whole people familiar with the use of arms; and therefore making the people more and more able at a given moment to make its will prevail in opposition to the commanding military lords. And this moment comes as soon as the mass of the people—town and country workers and peasants—*has* a will. At this point the armies of princes become transformed into armies of the people; the machine refuses to work, and militarism collapses by the dialectic of its own evolution. What the bourgeois democracy of 1848 could not accomplish, just because it was *bourgeois* and not proletarian, namely, to give the laboring masses a will whose content was in accord with their class position—socialism will infallibly secure. And this will mean the bursting asunder of militarism *from within,* and with it of all standing armies.

That is the first moral of our history of modern infantry. The second moral . . . is that the whole organization and method of fighting of armies, and along with these victory or defeat, proves to be dependent on material, that is, economic conditions; on the human material, and the armaments material, and therefore on the quality and quantity of the population and on technical development. Only a hunting people like the Americans could rediscover skirmishing tactics—and they were hunters as a result of purely economic causes, just as now, as a result of purely economic causes, these same Yankees of the old States have been transformed into farmers, industrialists, seamen and merchants who no longer skirmish in the primeval forest, but instead skirmish all the more effectively in the field of speculation, where they have made progress with it also in its mass application. Only a revolution such as the French, which brought about the economic emancipation of the burghers and especially of the peasantry, could find the method of the mass army and at the same time the free form of movement which shattered the old rigid lines—the military counterparts of the absolutism against which they were fighting. And we have seen in case after case how advances in technique, as soon as they became usable in the military sphere and in fact were so used, immediately and almost violently produced changes in the methods of warfare and indeed revolutionized them, often even against the will of the army command.

—Frederick Engels, *Herr Eugen Dühring's Revolution in Science* (Anti-Dühring), International Publishers, 1939, pp. 184–90. First published as a series of articles in 1877–78 in Leipzig *Vorwärts*, organ of the German Social-Democratic Party.

6

Barricade Tactics

FREDERICK ENGELS

With successful utilization of universal suffrage, an entirely new mode of proletarian struggle came into force, and this quickly developed further. It was found that the state institutions, in which the rule of the bourgeoisie is organized, offer still further opportunities for the working class to fight these very state institutions. They took part in elections to individual diets, to municipal councils and to industrial courts; they contested every post against the bourgeoisie in the occupation of which a sufficient part of the proletariat had its say. And so it happened that the bourgeoisie and the government came to be much more afraid of the legal than of the illegal action of the workers' party, of the results of elections than of those of rebellion.

For here, too, the conditions of the struggle had essentially changed. Rebellion in the old style, the street fight with barricades, which up to 1848 gave everywhere the final decision, was to a considerable extent obsolete.

Let us have no illusions about it: a real victory of an insurrection over the military in street fighting, a victory as between two armies, is one of the rarest exceptions. But the insurgents, also, counted on it just as rarely. For them it was solely a question of making the troops yield to moral influences, which, in a fight between the armies of two warring countries, do not come into play at all, or do so to a much less degree. If they succeed in this, then the troops fail to act, or the commanding officers lose their heads, and the insurrection wins. If they do not succeed in this, then, even where the military are in the minority, the superiority of better equipment and training, of unified leadership, of the planned employment of the military forces and of discipline makes itself felt. The most that the insurrection can achieve in actual tactical practice is the correct construction and defense of a single barricade. Mutual support; the disposition and employment of reserves; in short, the cooperation and harmonious working of the individual detachments, indispensable even for the defense of one quarter of the town, not to speak of the whole of a large town, are at best defective, and mostly not attainable at all; concentration of the military forces at a decisive point is, of course, impossible. Hence the passive defense is the prevailing form of fight: the attack will rise here and there, but only by way of exception, to occasional advances and flank assaults; as a rule, however, it will be limited to occupation of the positions abandoned by the retreating troops. In addition, the military have, on their side, the disposal of artillery and fully equipped corps of skilled engineers, resources of war which, in nearly every case, the insurgents entirely lack. No wonder, then, that even the barricade struggles conducted with the greatest heroism—Paris, June 1848;

Vienna, October 1848; Dresden, May 1849—ended with the defeat of the insurrection, so soon as the leaders of the attack, unhampered by political considerations, acted from the purely military standpoint, and their soldiers remained reliable.

The numerous successes of the insurgents up to 1848 were due to a great variety of causes. In Paris in July 1830 and February 1848, as in most of the Spanish street fights, there stood between the insurgents and the military a civic militia, which either directly took the side of the insurrection, or else by its lukewarm, indecisive attitude caused the troops likewise to vacillate, and supplied the insurrection with arms into the bargain. Where this citizens' guard opposed the insurrection from the outset, as in June 1848 in Paris, the insurrection was vanquished. In Berlin in 1848, the people were victorious partly through a considerable accession of new fighting forces during the night and the morning of the 19th, partly as a result of the exhaustion and bad victualing of the troops, and, finally, partly as a result of the paralyzed command. But in all cases the fight was won because the troops failed to obey, because the officers had lost their power of decision or because their hands were tied.

Even in the classic time of street fighting, therefore, the barricade produced more of a moral than a material effect. It was a means of shaking the steadfastness of the military. If it held out until this was attained, then victory was won; if not, there was defeat. This is the main point, which must be kept in view, likewise when the chances of contingent future street fights are examined.

The chances, however, were in 1849 already pretty poor. Everywhere the bourgeoisie had thrown in its lot with the governments, "culture and property" had hailed and feasted the military moving against the insurrections. The spell of the barricade was broken; the soldier no longer saw behind it "the people," but rebels, agitators, plunderers, levelers, the scum of society; the officer had in the course of time become versed in the tactical forms of street fighting, he no longer marched straight ahead and without cover against the improvised breastwork, but went round it through gardens, yards and houses. And this was now successful, with a little skill, in nine cases out of ten.

But since then there have been very many more changes, and all in favor of the military. If the big towns have become considerably bigger, the armies have become bigger still. Paris and Berlin have, since 1848, grown less than fourfold, but their garrisons have grown more than that. By means of the railways, the garrisons can, in 24 hours, be more than doubled, and in 48 hours they can be increased to huge armies. The arming of this enormously increased number of troops has become incomparably more effective. In 1848 the smooth-bore percussion muzzle-loader, today the small-caliber magazine breechloading rifle, which shoots four times as far, ten times as accurately and ten times as fast as the former. At that time the relatively ineffective round-shot and grape-shot of the artillery; today the percussion shells, of which one is sufficient to demolish the best barricade. At that time the pickaxe of the sapper for breaking through walls; today the dynamite cartridge.

On the other hand, all the conditions on the insurgents' side have grown worse. An insurrection with which all sections of the people sympathize will hardly recur; in the class struggle all the middle sections will never group themselves round the proletariat so exclusively that the reactionary parties gathered round the bourgeoisie well-nigh disappear. The "people," therefore, will always appear divided, and with this a powerful lever, so extraordinarily effective in 1848, is lacking. Even if more soldiers who have seen service were to come over to the insurrectionists, the arming of them becomes so much the more difficult. The hunting and luxury guns of the gun shops—even if not previously made unusable by removal of part of the lock by the police—are far from being a match for the magazine rifle of the soldier, even in close fighting. Up to 1848 it was possible to make the necessary ammunition oneself out of powder and lead; today the cartridges differ for each rifle, and are everywhere alike only in one point, that they are a special product of big industry, and therefore not to be prepared *ex tempore* [on the spur of the moment], with the result that most rifles are useless as long as one does not possess the ammunition specially suited to them. And, finally, since 1848 the newly built quarters of the big towns have been laid out in long, straight, broad streets, as though made to give full effect to the new cannons and rifles. The revolutionary would have to be mad, who himself chose the working-class districts in the North and East of Berlin for a barricade fight. Does that mean that in the future the street fight will play no further role? Certainly not. It only means that the conditions since 1848 have become far more unfavorable for civil fights, far more favorable for the military. A future street fight can therefore only be victorious when this unfavorable situation is compensated by other factors. Accordingly, it will occur more seldom in the beginning of a great revolution than in its further progress, and will have to be undertaken with greater forces. These, however, may then well prefer, as in the whole Great French Revolution or on September 4 and October 31, 1870,* in Paris, the open attack to the passive barricade tactics.

Does the reader now understand why the ruling classes decidedly want to bring us to where the guns shoot and the sabers slash? Why they accuse us today of cowardice, because we do not betake ourselves without more ado into the street, where we are certain of defeat in advance? Why they so earnestly implore us to play for once the part of cannon fodder?

The gentlemen pour out their prayers and their challenges for nothing, for nothing at all. We are not so stupid. They might just as well demand from their enemy in the next war that he should take up his position in the line formation of old Fritz [Frederick the Great of Prussia], or in the columns of whole divisions *a la* Wagram† and Waterloo, and with the flintlock in his hands at that. If the conditions have changed in the case of war between nations, this is no less true in the case of class struggle. The time of surprise attacks, of revolutions carried through by small conscious minorities at the head of the unconscious masses, is past. Where it is a question of a complete transformation of the social organization, the masses themselves must be also in it, must themselves already have grasped what is at stake, what they are going in for with body and soul. The history of the last 50 years has taught us that. But in order that the masses may understand what is to be done, long, persistent work is required, and it is just this work which we are now pursuing, and with a success that drives the enemy to despair.

—Introduction (1895) to Karl Marx, *The Class Struggles in France, 1848–50,* International Publishers, 1964, pp. 21–25.

* Dates of the overthrow of the government of Louis Bonaparte, and of the unsuccessful insurrection against the temporary bourgeois republic that preceded the establishment of the Commune on March 18, 1871.

† The site of the battle in 1809 where Napoleon I defeated the Austrian army.

7

The Revolutionary Army and the Revolutionary Government

V. I. LENIN

The uprising in Odessa and the siding of the armored cruiser *Potemkin* with the revolution marked a further big step forward in the development of the revolutionary movement against the autocracy. Events have confirmed with amazing rapidity the timeliness of the calls to insurrection and to the formation of a provisional revolutionary government, which were addressed to the people by the class-conscious spokesmen of the proletariat as represented by the Third Congress of the Russian Social-Democratic Labor Party.* The new outbreak of the revolutionary conflagration throws light on the practical significance of these calls and makes us determine more precisely the tasks of the revolutionary fighters in the present situation in Russia.

The armed uprising of the people is maturing and is organizing itself before our very eyes under the impact of the spontaneous course of events. It was not so very long ago that the only manifestation of the people's struggle against the autocracy were *revolts*—unconscious, unorganized, spontaneous, sometimes wild outbreaks. But the labor movement, as the movement of the most advanced class, the proletariat, rapidly outgrew this initial stage. The goal-conscious propaganda and agitation carried on by the Social-Democrats had their effect. Disturbances gave way to organized strike struggles and *political demonstrations* against the autocracy. The brutal military reprisals of the past few years have "educated" the proletariat and the common people of the towns, and have prepared them for higher forms of revolutionary struggle. The criminal and ignominious [Russo-

---

* A resolution calling for an armed uprising had been adopted by the Congress.

Japanese] war into which the autocracy has plunged the people filled the cup of their endurance to overflowing. The crowds began to offer armed resistance to the tsarist troops. Real *street fighting, barricade battles,* started between the people and the troops. Quite recently the Caucasus, Lodz, Odessa, and Libau have shown us examples of proletarian heroism and popular enthusiasm. The struggle grew into an insurrection. Even the tsar's troops gradually began to see that they were being made to play the shameful role of executioners of freedom, of henchmen of the police. And the army began to waver. At first isolated cases of insubordination, outbreaks among reservists, protests from officers, propaganda among the soldiers, refusal of some companies and regiments to shoot at their own brothers, the workers. Then—*the siding of part of the army with the uprising.*

The tremendous significance of the recent events in Odessa lies precisely in the fact that, for the first time, an important unit of the armed force of tsarism—a battleship—has openly gone over to the side of the revolution. The government made frantic efforts and resorted to all possible tricks to conceal this event from the people, to stifle the mutiny of the sailors from the outset. But to no avail. The warships sent against the revolutionary armored cruiser *"Potemkin" refused to fight* against their comrades. By spreading throughout Europe the report that the *Potemkin* had surrendered and that the tsar had ordered the revolutionary armored cruiser to be sunk, the autocratic government only completed its disgrace in the eyes of the entire world. The squadron has returned to Sevastopol, and the government is hastening to disband the crews and to disarm the warships; reports are current of wholesale resignations of officers of the Black Sea Fleet; a fresh mutiny broke out on the armored cruiser *Georgi Pobedonosets,* which had surrendered. The sailors are also rising in Libau and in Kronstadt; clashes with the troops are becoming more frequent; sailors and workers are fighting the troops on the barricades (in Libau). The foreign press reports mutinies on a number of other warships (the *Minin,* the *Alexander II,* and others). The tsarist government finds itself *without a navy.* The most that it has been able to achieve so far is to hold back the fleet from actively going over to the side of the revolution. Meanwhile, the armored cruiser *Potemkin* remains an unconquered territory of the revolution, and whatever its fate may be, the undoubted fact and the point of highest significance is that here we have the attempt to form the *nucleus of a revolutionary army*.

No reprisals, no partial victories over the revolution can diminish the importance of this event. The first step has been taken. The Rubicon has been crossed. The siding of the army with the revolution has impressed itself as a fact upon the whole of Russia and the entire world. The events in the Black Sea Fleet will inevitably be followed by further and still more energetic attempts to form a revolutionary army. It is our task now to give the utmost support to these efforts, to explain to the broadest masses of the proletariat and the peasantry the nation-wide significance of a revolutionary army in the struggle for freedom, to assist various units of this army to unfurl the popular *banner of freedom,* the banner capable of attracting the masses and rallying the forces that will crush the tsarist autocracy.

Outbreaks—demonstrations—street fighting—units of a revolutionary army—such are the stages in the development of the popular uprising. Now at last we have reached the final stage. This does not mean, of course, that the movement in its entirety has advanced to this new and higher stage. No, there is still a good deal of backwardness in the movement; in the Odessa events there are unmistakable signs of old-time rioting. But it does mean that the advance waves of the elemental flood have already reached the very threshold of the absolutist "stronghold." It does mean that the advanced representatives of the popular masses have themselves arrived, not as a result of theoretical reasoning, but under the impact of the growing movement, at new and higher tasks of the struggle, the final struggle against the enemy of the Russian people. The autocracy has done *everything* to prepare this struggle. For years it has provoked the people to an armed struggle with its troops, and now it is reaping what it sowed. The units of the revolutionary army are springing up out of the army itself.

The task of these units is to proclaim the insurrection, to give the masses *military leadership,* as essential in civil war as in any other war; to create strong points for the open mass struggle; to spread the uprising to neighboring districts; to establish complete political freedom, if only at first in a small part of the country; to embark on the revolutionary transformation of the decayed absolutist system; and to give full scope to the revolutionary creative activity of the masses, who participate but little in this activity in time of peace, but who come to the forefront in revolutionary epochs. Only by clearly understanding these new tasks, only by posing them boldly and broadly, can the units of the revolutionary army win complete victory and become the strong points of a *revolutionary government*. And a revolutionary government is as vitally essential at the present stage of the popular uprising as a revolutionary army. The revolutionary army is needed for military struggle and for military leadership of the masses against the remnants of the military forces of the autocracy. The revolutionary army is needed because great historical issues can be resolved only *by force,* and, in modern struggle, the *organization of force* means military organization. Besides the remnants of the autocracy's military forces there are the military forces of the neighboring states for whose support the tottering Russian government is already begging. . . .

The revolutionary government is needed for the political leadership of the masses, at first in that part of the country which has been wrested from tsarism by the revolutionary army, and later in the country at large. The revolutionary government is needed for the immediate launching of the political reforms, for the sake of which the revolution is being made—the establishment of a revolutionary self-government of the people, the convocation of a truly popular and truly Constituent Assembly, and the introduction of "liberties" without which there can be no true expression of the people's will. The revolutionary government is necessary for the political unification and the political organization of the insurgent section of the people, which has actually and finally broken away from the autocracy. Of course, that political organization can only be provisional, just as the revolutionary government, which has taken power in the name of the people in order to enforce the will of the people and to act through the instrumentality of the people, can only be provisional. But this work of organization must start *immediately,* and it must be indissolubly combined with every successful step of the uprising; for political consolidation and political leadership cannot be delayed for a single moment. Immediate political leadership of the insurgent people is no less essential for the complete victory of the people over tsarism than the military leadership of its forces.

—V. I. Lenin, *Collected Works*, Vol. 8, Progress Publishers, Moscow, 1962, pp. 560–64. First published in *Proletary* (The Proletarian, underground Bolshevik weekly, edited by Lenin, and at the time published in Geneva), July 10, 1905.

8

Lessons of the Moscow Uprising

V. I. LENIN

The publication of the book *Moscow in December 1905* (Moscow, 1906)* could not have been more timely. It is an urgent task of the workers' party to assimilate the lessons of the December uprising. Unfortunately, this book is like a barrel of honey spoiled by a spoonful of tar: most interesting material—despite its incompleteness—and incredibly slovenly, incredibly trite conclusions. We shall deal with these conclusions on another occasion; at present we shall turn our attention to the burning political question of the day, to the lessons of the Moscow uprising.

The principal forms of the December movement in Moscow were the peaceful strike and demonstrations, and these were the only forms of struggle in which the vast majority of the workers took an active part. Yet, the December action in Moscow vividly demonstrated that the general strike, as an independent and predominant form of struggle, is out of date, that the movement is breaking out of these narrow bounds with elemental and irresistible force and giving rise to the highest form of struggle—an uprising.

In calling the strike, all the revolutionary parties, all the Moscow unions recognized and even intuitively felt that it must inevitably grow into an uprising. On December 6 the Soviet of Workers' Deputies resolved to "strive to transform the strike into an armed uprising." As a matter of fact, however, none of the organizations were prepared for this. Even the Joint Council

* Menshevik version of the 1905 events.

of Volunteer Fighting Squads* spoke (*on December 9!*) of an uprising as of something remote, and it is quite evident that it had no hand in or control of the street fighting that took place. The organizations *failed to keep pace* with the growth and range of the movement.

The strike was growing into an uprising, primarily as a result of the pressure of the objective conditions created after October. A general strike could no longer take the government unawares: it had already organized the forces of counter-revolution, and they were ready for military action. The whole course of the Russian revolution after October, and the sequence of events in Moscow in the December days, strikingly confirmed one of Marx's profound propositions: revolution progresses by giving rise to a strong and united counter-revolution, i.e., it compels the enemy to resort to more and more extreme measures of defense and in this way devises ever more powerful means of attack.

December 7 and 8: a peaceful strike, peaceful mass demonstrations. Evening of the 8th: the siege of the Aquarium. The morning of the 9th: the crowd in Strastnaya Square is attacked by the dragoons. Evening: the Fiedler building is raided. Temper rises. The unorganized street crowds, quite spontaneously and hesitatingly, set up the first barricades.

The 10th: artillery fire is opened on the barricades and the crowds in the streets. Barricades are set up more deliberately, and no longer in isolated cases, but on a really mass scale. The whole population is in the streets; all the main centers of the city are covered by a network of barricades. For several days the volunteer fighting units wage a stubborn guerrilla battle against the troops, which exhausts the troops and compels Dubasov [Military Governor-General of Moscow] to beg for reinforcements. Only on December 15 did the superiority of the government forces become complete, and on December 17 the Semyonovsky Regiment crushed Presnya District, the last stronghold of the uprising.

From a strike and demonstrations to isolated barricades. From isolated barricades to the mass erection of barricades and street fighting against the troops. Over the heads of the organizations, the mass proletarian struggle developed from a strike to an up-

---

* Formed in Moscow in November 1905, originally in order to avert the menace of pogroms by the Black Hundreds—gangs organized by the police to fight the revolutionary movements by attacks, assassinations and anti-Jewish pogroms.

rising. This is the greatest historic gain the Russian revolution achieved in December 1905; and like all preceding gains it was purchased at the price of enormous sacrifices. The movement was raised from a general political strike to a higher stage. It compelled the reaction to go *to the limit* in its resistance, and so brought vastly nearer the moment when the revolution will also go to the limit in applying the means of attack. The reaction *cannot* go further than the shelling of barricades, buildings and crowds. But the revolution can go very much further than the Moscow volunteer fighting units; it can go very, very much further in breadth and depth. And the revolution has advanced far since December. The base of the revolutionary crisis has become immeasurably broader—the blade must now be sharpened to a keener edge.

The proletariat sensed sooner than its leaders the change in the objective conditions of the struggle and the need for a transition from the strike to an uprising. As is always the case, practice marched ahead of theory. A peaceful strike and demonstrations immediately ceased to satisfy the workers; they asked: What is to be done next? And they demanded more resolute action. The instructions to set up barricades reached the districts exceedingly late, when barricades were aready being erected in the center of the city. The workers set to work in large numbers, but *even this did not satisfy them;* they wanted to know: what is to be done next?—they demanded active measures. In December, we, the leaders of the Social-Democratic proletariat, were like a commander-in-chief who has deployed his troops in such an absurd way that most of them took no active part in the battle. The masses of the workers demanded, but failed to receive, instructions for resolute mass action.

Thus, nothing could be more short-sighted than Plekhanov's view, seized upon by all the opportunists, that the strike was untimely and should not have been started, and that "they should not have taken to arms." On the contrary, we should have taken to arms more resolutely, energetically and aggressively; we should have explained to the masses that it was impossible to confine things to a peaceful strike and that a fearless and relentless armed fight was necessary. And now we must at last openly and publicly admit that political strikes are inadequate; we must carry on the widest agitation among the masses in favor of an armed uprising and make no attempt to obscure this question by talk about "preliminary stages," or to befog it in any way.

We would be deceiving both ourselves and the people if we concealed from the masses the necessity of a deperate, bloody war of extermination, as the immediate task of the coming revolutionary action.

Such is the first lesson of the December events. Another lesson concerns the character of the uprising, the methods by which it is conducted, and the conditions which lead to the troops coming over to the side of the people. An extremely biased view on this latter point prevails in the right wing of our party. It is alleged that there is no possibility of fighting modern troops; the troops must become revolutionary. Of course, unless the revolution assumes a mass character and affects the troops, there can be no question of serious struggle. That we must work among the troops goes without saying. But we must not imagine that they will come over to our side at one stroke, as a result of persuasion or their own convictions. The Moscow uprising clearly demonstrated how stereotyped and lifeless this view is. As a matter of fact, the wavering of the troops, which is inevitable in every truly popular movement, leads to a real *fight for the troops* whenever the revolutionary struggle becomes acute. The Moscow uprising was precisely an example of the desperate, frantic struggle for the troops that takes place between the reaction and the revolution. Dubasov himself declared that of the 15,000 men of the Moscow garrison, only 5,000 were reliable. The government restrained the waverers by the most diverse and desperate measures: they appealed to them, flattered them, bribed them, presented them with watches, money, etc.: they doped them with vodka, they lied to them, threatened them, confined them to barracks and disarmed them, and those who were suspected of being least reliable were removed by treachery and violence. And we must have the courage to confess, openly and unreservedly, that in this respect we lagged behind the government. We failed to utilize the forces at our disposal for such an active, bold, resourceful and aggressive fight for the wavering troops as that which the government waged and won. We have carried on work in the army and we will redouble our efforts in the future ideologically to "win over" the troops. But we shall prove to be miserable pedants if we forget that at a time of uprising there must also be a physical struggle for the troops.

In the December days, the Moscow proletariat taught us magnificent lessons in ideologically "winning over" the troops, as, for example, on December 8 in Strastnaya Square, when the crowd surrounded the Cossacks, mingled and fraternized with them, and persuaded them to turn back. Or on December 10, in Presnya District, when two working girls, carrying a red flag in a crowd of 10,000 people, rushed out to meet the Cossacks crying: "Kill us! We shall not surrender the flag alive!" And the Cossacks were disconcerted and galloped away, amidst the shouts from the crowd: "Hurrah for the Cossacks!" These examples of courage and heroism should be impressed forever on the mind of the proletariat.

But here are examples of how we lagged behind Dubasov. On December 9, soldiers were marching down Bolshaya Serpukhovskaya Street singing the *Marseillaise,* on their way to join the insurgents. The workers sent delegates to meet them. Malakhov [Chief of Staff of the Moscow Military Area] himself galloped at breakneck speed toward them. The workers were too late, Malakhov reached them first. He delivered a passionate speech, caused the soldiers to waver, surrounded them with dragoons, marched them off to barracks and locked them in. Malakhov reached the soldiers in time and we did not, although within two days 150,000 people had risen at our call, and these could and should have organized the patrolling of the streets. Malakhov surrounded the soldiers with dragoons, whereas we failed to surround the Malakhovs with bomb-throwers. We could and should have done this; and long ago the Social-Democratic press (the old *Iskra*) pointed out that ruthless extermination of civil and military chiefs was our duty during an uprising. What took place in Bolshaya Serpukhovskaya Street was apparently repeated in its main features in front of the Nesvizhskiye Barracks and the Krutitskiye Barracks, and also when the workers attempted to "withdraw" the Ekaterinoslav Regiment, and when delegates were sent to the sappers in Alexandrov, and when the Rostov artillery on its way to Moscow was turned back, and when the sappers were disarmed in Kolomna, and so on. During the uprising we proved unequal to our task in the fight for the wavering troops.

The December events confirmed another of Marx's profound propositions, which the opportunists have forgotten, namely, that insurrection is an art and that the principal rule of this art is the waging of a desperately bold and irrevocably determined *offensive.* We have not sufficiently assimilated this truth. We ourselves have not sufficiently learned, nor have we taught the masses, this art, this rule to attack at all costs. We must make up for this omission with all our energy. It is not enough to take sides on the question of political slogans; it is also necessary to take sides on the question of an armed uprising. Those who are opposed to it, those who do not prepare for it, must be ruthlessly dismissed from the ranks of the supporters of the revolution, sent packing to its enemies, to the traitors or cowards; for the day is approaching when the force of events and the conditions of the struggle will compel us to distinguish between enemies and friends according to this principle. It is not passivity that we should preach, not mere "waiting" until the troops "come over." No! We must proclaim from the housetops the need for a bold offensive and armed attack, the necessity at such times of exterminating the persons in command of the enemy, and of a most energetic fight for the wavering troops.

The third great lesson taught by Moscow concerns the tactics and organization of the forces for an uprising. Military tactics depend on the level of military technique. This plain truth Engels demonstrated and brought home to all Marxists. Military technique today is not what it was in the middle of the 19th century. It would be folly to contend against artillery in crowds and defend barricades with revolvers. Kautsky was right when he wrote that it is high time now, after Moscow, to review Engel's conclusions, and that Moscow had inaugurated *"new barricade tactics."* These tactics are the tactics of guerrilla warfare. The organization required for such tactics is that of mobile and exceedingly small units, units of ten, three or even two persons. We often meet Social-Democrats now who scoff whenever units of five or three are mentioned. But scoffing is only a cheap way of ignoring the *new* question of tactics and organization raised by street fighting under the conditions imposed by modern military technique. Study carefully the story of the Moscow uprising, gentlemen, and you will understand what connection exists between "units of five" and the question of "new barricade tactics."

Moscow advanced these tactics, but failed to develop them far enough, to apply them to any considerable extent, to a really mass extent. There were too few volunteer fighting squads, the slogan of bold attack was not issued to the masses of the workers and they did not apply it; the guerrilla detachments were too uniform in character, their arms and methods were inadequate, their abilty to lead the crowd was almost undeveloped. We must make up for all this and we shall do so by learning from the experience of Moscow, by spreading this experience among the masses and by stimulating their creative efforts to develop it still further. And the guerrilla warfare and mass terror that have been taking place throughout Russia practically without a break since December, will undoubtedly help the masses to learn the correct tactics of an uprising. Social-Democracy must recognize this mass terror and incorporate it into its tactics, organizing and controlling it of course, subordinating it to the interests and conditions of the working-class movement and the general revolutionary struggle, while eliminating and ruthlessly lopping off the "hooligan" perversion of this guerrilla warfare which was so splendidly and ruthlessly dealt with by our Moscow comrades during the uprising and by the Letts during the days of the famous Lettish republics.*

There have been new advances in military technique in the very recent period. The Japanese War produced the hand grenade. The small-arms factories have placed automatic rifles on the market. Both these weapons are already being successfully used in the Russian revolution, but to a degree that is far from adequate. We can and must take advantage of improvements in technique, teach the workers' detachments to make bombs in large quantities, help them and our fighting squads to obtain supplies of explosives, fuses and automatic rifles. If the mass of workers takes part in uprisings in the towns, if mass attacks are launched on the enemy, if a determined and skillful fight is waged for the troops who, after the Duma, after Sveaborg and Kronstadt, are wavering more than ever—and if we ensure participation of the rural areas in the general struggle—victory will be ours in the next all-Russian armed uprising.

Let us, then, develop our work more extensively and set our tasks more boldly, while mastering the lessons of the great days of the Russian revolution. The basis of our work is a correct estimate of class interests and of the requirements of the nation's development at the present juncture. We are rallying, and shall continue to rally, an increasing section of the proletariat, the peasantry and the army under the slogan of overthrowing the tsarist regime and convening a constituent assembly by a revolutionary government. As hitherto, the basis and chief content

---

* In December 1905 various Lettish towns were seized by armed detachments of insurgent workers, farm laborers and peasants, starting a guerrilla war against the tsarist troops. In January 1906 the uprisings in Latvia were suppressed by punitive expeditions under tsarist generals.

of our work is to develop the political understanding of the masses. But let us not forget that, in addition to this general, constant and fundamental task, times like the present in Russia impose other, particular and special tasks. Let us not become pedants and philistines, let us not evade these special tasks of the moment, these special tasks of the given forms of struggle, by meaningless references to our permanent duties, which remain unchanged at all times and in all circumstances.

Let us remember that a great mass struggle is approaching. It will be an armed uprising. It must, as far as possible, be simultaneous. The masses must know that they are entering upon an armed, bloody and desperate struggle. Contempt for death must become widespread among them and will ensure victory. The onslaught on the enemy must be pressed with the greatest vigor; attack, not defense, must be the slogan of the masses; the ruthless extermination of the enemy will be their task; the organization of the struggle will become mobile and flexible; the wavering elements among the troops will be drawn into active participation. And in this momentous struggle, the party of the class-conscious proletariat must discharge its duty to the full.

—V. I. Lenin, *Selected Works* (3 vols.), International Publishers, 1967, Vol. 1, pp. 577–83. First published in *Proletary,* August 29, 1906.

9

Guerrilla Warfare

V. I. LENIN

The question of guerrilla action is one that greatly interests our party and the mass of the workers. We have dealt with this question in passing several times, and now we propose to give the more complete statement of our views we have promised.

I.

Let us begin from the beginning. What are the fundamental demands which every Marxist should make of an examination of the question of forms of struggle? In the first place, Marxism differs from all primitive forms of socialism by not binding the movement to any one particular form of struggle. It recognizes the most varied forms of struggle; and it does not "concoct" them, but only generalizes, organizes, gives conscious expression to those forms of struggle of the revolutionary classes which arise of themselves in the course of the movement. Absolutely hostile to all abstract formulas and to all doctrinaire recipes, Marxism demands an attentive attitude to the *mass* struggle in progress, which, as the movement develops, as the class-consciousness of the masses grows, as economic and political crises become acute, continually gives rise to new and more varied methods of defense and attack. Marxism, therefore, positively does not reject any form of struggle. Under no circumstances does Marxism confine itself to the forms of struggle possible and in existence at the given moment only, recognizing as it does that new forms of struggle, unknown to the participants of the given period, *inevitably* arise as the given social situation changes. In this respect Marxism *learns,* if we may so express it, from mass practice, and makes no claim whatever to *teach* the masses forms of struggle invented by "systematizers" in the seclusion of their studies. We know—said Kautsky, for instance, when examining the forms of social revolution—that the coming crisis will introduce new forms of struggle that we are now unable to foresee.

In the second place, Marxism demands an absolutely *historical* examination of the question of the forms of struggle. To treat this question apart from the concrete historical situation betrays a failure to understand the rudiments of dialectical materialism. At different stages of economic evolution, depending on differences in political, national-cultural, living and other conditions, different forms of struggle come to the fore and become the principal forms of struggle; and in connection with this, the secondary, auxiliary forms of struggle undergo change in their turn. To attempt to answer yes or no to the question whether any particular means of struggle should be used, without making a detailed examination of the concrete situation of the given movement at the given stage of its development, means completely to abandon the Marxist position.

These are the two principal theoretical propositions by which we must be guided. The history of Marxism in Western Europe provides an infinite number of examples corroborating what has been said. European Social-Democracy at the present time regards parliamentarism and the trade union movement as the principal forms of struggle; it recognized insurrection in the past, and is quite prepared to recognize it, should conditions change, in the future—despite the opinion of bourgeois liberals like the Russian Cadets and the *Bezzaglavtsi*.* Social-Democracy recognized street barricade fighting in the 40's, rejected it for definite reasons at the end of the 19th century, and expressed complete readiness to revise the latter view and to admit the expediency of barricade fighting, after the experience of Moscow, which, in the words of K. Kautsky, initiated new tactics of barricade fighting.

II.

Having established the general Marxist propositions, let us turn to the Russian revolution. Let us recall the historical development of the forms of struggle it produced. First there were the economic strikes of workers (1896–1900), then the political demonstrations of workers and students (1901–02), peasant revolts (1902), the beginning of mass political strikes variously combined with demonstrations (Rostov 1902, the strikes in the summer of 1903, January 9, 1905), the all-Russian political strike accompanied by local cases of barricade fighting and armed uprising (December, 1905), the peaceful parliamentary struggle (April–June 1906), partial military revolts (June 1905–July 1906) and partial peasant revolts (autumn 1905–autumn 1906).

Such is the state of affairs in the autumn of 1906 as concerns forms of struggle in general. The "retaliatory" form of struggle adopted by the autocracy is the Black-Hundred pogrom, from Kishinev in the spring of 1903 to Sedlets in the autumn of 1906. All through this period the organization of Black-Hundred

---

* Cadets, short term for Constitutional Democratic Party; the *Bezzaglavsti* were a semi-Cadet, semi-Menshevik group of the Russian bourgeois intellectuals.

pogroms and the beating up of Jews, students, revolutionaries and class-conscious workers continued to progress and perfect itself, combining the violence of Black-Hundred troops with the violence of hired ruffians, going as far as the use of artillery in villages and towns and merging with punitive expeditions, punitive trains and so forth.

Such is the principal background of the picture. Against this background there stands out—unquestionably as something partial, secondary and auxiliary—the phenomenon to the study and assessment of which the present article is devoted. What is this phenomenon? What are its forms? What are its causes? When did it arise and how far has it spread? What is its significance in the general course of the revolution? What is its relation to the struggle of the working class organized and led by Social-Democracy? Such are the questions which we must now proceed to examine after having sketched the general background of the picture.

The phenomenon in which we are interested is the *armed* struggle. It is conducted by individuals and by small groups. Some belong to revolutionary organizations, while others (the *majority* in certain parts of Russia) do not belong to any revolutionary organization. Armed struggle pursues two *different* aims, which must be *strictly* distinguished: in the first place, this struggle aims at assassinating individuals, chiefs and subordinates in the army and police; in the second place, it aims at the confiscation of monetary funds both from the government and from private persons. The confiscated funds go partly into the treasury of the party, partly for the special purpose of arming and preparing for an uprising, and partly for the maintenance of persons engaged in the struggle we are describing. The big expropriations go mostly, and sometimes entirely, to the maintenance of the "expropriators." This form of struggle undoubtedly became widely developed and extensive only in 1906, i.e., after the December uprising. The intensification of the political crisis to the point of an armed struggle and, in particular, the intensification of poverty, hunger and unemployment in town and country was one of the important causes of the struggle we are describing. This form of struggle was adopted as the preferable and even *exclusive* form of social struggle by the vagabond elements of the population, the *lumpen* proletariat and anarchist groups. Declaration of martial law, mobilization of fresh troops, Black-Hundred pogroms (Sedlets), and military courts must be regarded as the "retaliatory" form of struggle adopted by the autocracy.

III.

The usual appraisal of the struggle we are describing is that it is anarchism, Blanquism,* the old terrorism, the acts of individuals isolated from the masses, which demoralize the workers, repel wide strata of the population, disorganize the movement and injure the revolution. Examples in support of this appraisal can easily be found in the events reported every day in the newspapers.

But are such examples convincing? In order to test this, let us take a locality where the form of struggle we are examining is *most* developed—the Lettish Territory. This is the way *Novoye Vremya*† (in its issues of September 9 and 12) complains of the activities of the Lettish Social-Democrats. The Lettish Social-Democratic Labor Party (a section of the Russian Social-Democratic Labor Party) regularly issues its paper in 30,000 copies. The announcement columns publish lists of spies whom it is the duty of every decent person to exterminate. People who assist the police are proclaimed "enemies of the revolution," liable to execution and, moreover, to confiscation of property. The public is instructed to give money to the Social-Democratic Party only against signed and stamped receipts. In the party's latest report, showing a total income of 48,000 rubles for the year, there figures a sum of 5,600 rubles contributed by the Libau branch for arms which was obtained by expropriation. Naturally, *Novoye Vremya* rages and fumes against this "revolutionary law," against this "terror government."

Nobody will be so bold as to call these activities of the Lettish Social-Democrats anarchism, Blanquism or terrorism. But why? Because here we have a clear connection between the new form of struggle and the uprising which broke out in December and which is again brewing. This connection is not so perceptible in the case of Russia as a whole, but it exists. The fact that "guerrilla" warfare became widespread precisely after December, and its connection with the accentuation not only of the economic

---

* The teachings of the French revolutionist, Louis Auguste Blanqui (1805–81), a utopian communist, favoring the overthrow of the ruling power through secret plots of a few revolutionists rather than through preparation and organization of the masses led by a revolutionary party.

† *New Times*, a reactionary newspaper published in St. Petersburg.

crisis but also of the political crisis is beyond dispute. The old Russian terrorism was an affair of the intellectual conspirator; today as a general rule guerrilla warfare is waged by the worker combatant, or simply by the unemployed worker. Blanquism and anarchism easily occur to the minds of people who have a weakness for stereotype; but under the circumstances of an uprising, which are so apparent in the Lettish Territory, the inappropriateness of such trite labels is only too obvious.

The example of the Letts clearly demonstrates how incorrect, unscientific and unhistorical is the practice so very common among us of analyzing guerrilla warfare without reference to the circumstances of an uprising. These circumstances must be borne in mind, we must reflect on the peculiar features of an intermediate period between big acts of insurrection, we must realize what forms of struggle inevitably arise under such circumstances, and not try to shirk the issue by a collection of words learned by rote, such as are used equally by the Cadets and the *Novoye Vremya*-ites: anarchism, robbery, hooliganism!

It is said that guerrilla acts disorganize our work. Let us apply this argument to the situation that has existed since December 1905, to the period of Black-Hundred pogroms and martial law. What disorganizes the movement more in *such* a period: the absence of resistance or organized guerrilla warfare? Compare the center of Russia with her western borders, with Poland and the Lettish Territory. It is unquestionable that guerrilla warfare is far more widespread and far more developed in the western border regions. And it is equally unquestionable that the revolutionary movement in general, and the Social-Democratic movement in particular, are *more disorganized* in central Russia than in the western border region. Of course, it would not enter our heads to conclude from this that the Polish and Lettish Social-Democratic movement are less disorganized *thanks* to guerrilla warfare. No. The only conclusion that can be drawn is that guerrilla warfare is not to blame for the state of disorganization of the Social-Democratic working-class movement in Russia in 1906.

Allusion is often made in this respect to the peculiarities of national conditions. But this allusion very clearly betrays the weakness of the current argument. If it is a matter of national conditions then it is not a matter of anarchism, Blanquism or terrorism—sins that are common to Russia as a whole and even to the Russian especially—but of something else. Analyze this something else *concretely,* gentlemen! You will then find that national oppression or antagonism explain nothing, because they have always existed in the western border regions, whereas guerrilla warfare has been engendered only by the present historical period. There are many places where there is national oppression and antagonism, but no guerrilla struggle, which sometimes develops where there is no national oppression whatever. A concrete analysis of the question will show that it is not a matter of national oppression, but of conditions of insurrection. Guerrilla warfare is an inevitable form of struggle at a time when the mass movement has actually reached the point of an uprising and when fairly large intervals occur between the big "engagements" in the civil war.

It is not guerrilla actions which disorganize the movement, but the weakness of a party which is incapable of taking such actions *under its control.* That is why the anathemas which we Russians usually hurl against guerrilla actions go hand in hand with secret, casual, unorganized guerrilla actions which really do disorganize the party. Being incapable of understanding what historical conditions give rise to this struggle, we are incapable of neutralizing its deleterious aspects. Yet the struggle is going on. It is engendered by powerful economic and political causes. It is not in our power to eliminate these causes or to eliminate this struggle. Our complaints against guerrilla warfare are complaints against our party weakness in the matter of an uprising.

What we have said about disorganization also applies to demoralization. It is not guerrilla warfare which demoralizes, but *unorganized* irregular, non-party guerrilla acts. We shall not rid ourselves one least bit of this *most unquestionable* demoralization by condemning and cursing guerrilla actions, for condemnation and curses are absolutely incapable of putting a stop to a phenomenon which has been engendered by profound economic and political causes. It may be objected that if we are incapable of putting a stop to an abnormal and demoralizing phenomenon, this is no reason why the *party* should adopt abnormal and demoralizing methods of struggle. But such an objection would be a purely bourgeois-liberal and not a Marxist objection, because a Marxist cannot regard civil war, or guerrilla warfare, which is one of its forms, as abnormal and demoralizing *in general.* A Marxist bases himself on the class struggle, and not social peace. In certain periods of acute economic and political crisis the class struggle ripens into a direct civil war, i.e., into an armed struggle between two sections of the people. In such periods a Marxist is *obliged* to take the stand of civil war. Any moral condemnation of civil war would be absolutely impermissible from the standpoint of Marxism.

In a period of civil war the ideal party of the proletariat is a *fighting party*. This is absolutely incontrovertible. We are quite prepared to grant that it is possible to argue and prove the *inexpediency* from the standpoint of civil war of particular forms of civil war at any particular moment. We fully admit criticism of diverse forms of civil war from the standpoint of *military expediency* and absolutely agree that in *this* question it is the Social-Democratic practical workers in each particular locality who must have the final say. But we absolutely demand in the name of the principles of Marxism that an analysis of the conditions of civil war should not be evaded by hackneyed and stereotyped talk about anarchism, Blanquism and terrorism, and that senseless methods of guerrilla activity adopted by some organization or other of the Polish Socialist Party at some moment or other should not be used as a bogey when discussing the question of the participation of the Social-Democratic Party as such in guerrilla warfare in general.

The argument that guerrilla warfare disorganizes the movement must be regarded critically. *Every* new form of struggle, accompanied as it is by new dangers and new sacrifices, inevitably "disorganizes" organizations which are unprepared for this new form of struggle. Our old propagandist circles were disorganized by recourse to methods of agitation. Our committees were subsequently disorganized by recourse to demonstrations. Every military action in any war to a certain extent disorganizes the ranks of the fighters. But this does not mean that one must not fight. It means that one must *learn* to fight. That is all.

When I see Social-Democrats proudly and smugly declaring, "we are not anarchists, thieves, robbers, we are superior to all this, we reject guerrilla warfare"—I ask myself: Do these people realize what they are saying? Armed clashes and conflicts between the Black-Hundred government and the population are taking place all over the country. This is an absolutely inevitable phenomenon at the present stage of development of the revolution. The population is spontaneously and in an unorganized way— and for that very reason often in unfortunate and *undesirable* forms—reacting to this phenomenon also by armed conflicts and attacks. I can understand us refraining from party leadership of *this* spontaneous struggle in a particular place or at a particular time because of the weakness and unpreparedness of our organization. I realize that this question must be settled by the local practical workers, and that the remolding of weak and unprepared organizations is no easy matter. But when I see a Social-Democratic theoretician or publicist not displaying regret over this unpreparedness, but rather a proud smugness and a self-exalted tendency to repeat phrases learned by rote in early youth about anarchism, Blanquism and terrorism, I am hurt by this degradation of the most revolutionary doctrine in the world.

It is said that guerrilla warfare brings the class-conscious proletarians into close association with degraded, drunken riff-raff. That is true. But it only means that the party of the proletariat can never regard guerrilla warfare as the only, or even as the chief, method of struggle; it means that this method must be subordinated to other methods, that this method must be commensurate with the chief methods of warfare, and must be ennobled by the enlightening and organizing influence of socialism. And without this *latter* condition, *all*, positively all, methods of struggle in bourgeois society bring the proletariat into close association with the various non-proletarian strata above and below it and, if left to the spontaneous course of events, become frayed, corrupted and prostituted. Strikes, if left to the spontaneous course of events, become corrupted into "alliances"—agreements between the workers and the masters *against* the consumers. Parliament becomes corrupted into a brothel, where a gang of bourgeois politicians barter wholesale and retail "national freedom," "liberalism," "democracy," republicanism, anti-clericalism, socialism and all other wares in demand. A newspaper becomes corrupted into a public pimp, into a means of corrupting the masses, of pandering to the low instincts of the mob, and so on and so forth. Social-Democracy knows of no universal methods of struggle, such as would shut off the proletariat by a Chinese wall from the strata standing slightly above or slightly below it. At different periods Social-Democracy applies different methods, *always* qualifying the choice of them by *strictly* defined ideological and organizational conditions.

IV.

The forms of struggle in the Russian revolution are distinguished by their colossal variety compared with the bourgeois revolutions in Europe. Kautsky partly foretold this in 1902 when he said that the future revolution (with the exception *perhaps* of Russia, he added) might be not so much a struggle of the people against the government as a struggle between two sections of the people. In Russia we undoubtedly see a wider development of this *latter* struggle than in the bourgeois revolutions in the West. The enemies of our revolution among the people are few in number, but as the struggle grows more acute they become more and more organized and receive the support of the reactionary strata of the bourgeoisie. It is therefore absolutely natural and inevitable that in *such* a period, a period of nation-wide political strikes, an *uprising* cannot assume the old form of individual acts restricted to a very short time and to a very small area. It is absolutely natural and inevitable that the uprising should assume the higher and more complex form of a prolonged civil war embracing the whole country, i.e., an armed struggle between two sections of the people. Such a war cannot be conceived otherwise than as a series of a few big engagements at comparatively long intervals and a large number of small encounters during these intervals. That being so—and it is undoubtedly so—the Social-Democrats must absolutely make it their duty to create organizations best adapted to lead the masses in these big engagements and, as far as possible, in these small encounters as well. In a period when the class struggle has become accentuated to the point of civil war, Social-Democrats must make it their duty not only to participate but also to play the leading role in *this civil war*. The Social-Democrats must train and prepare their organizations to be really able to act as a *belligerent side* which does not miss a single opportunity of inflicting damage on the enemy's forces.

This is a difficult task, there is no denying. It cannot be accomplished at once. Just as the whole people are being retrained and are learning to fight in the course of the civil war, so our organizations must be trained, must be reconstructed in conformity with the lessons of experience to be equal to this task.

We have not the slightest intention of foisting on practical workers any artificial form of struggle, or even of deciding from our armchair what part any particular form of guerrilla warfare should play in the general course of the civil war in Russia. We are far from the thought of regarding a concrete assessment of particular guerrilla actions as indicative of a *trend* in Social-Democracy. But we do regard it as our duty to help as far as possible to arrive at a correct *theoretical* assessment of the new forms of struggle engendered by practical life. We do regard it as our duty relentlessly to combat stereotypes and prejudices which hamper the class-conscious workers in correctly presenting a new and difficult problem and in correctly approaching its solution.

—V. I. Lenin, *Collected Works*, Vol. 11, 1962, pp. 213–23. First published in *Proletary*, September, 30, 1906.

10

Lessons of the Commune

V. I. LENIN

After the *coup d'état,* which marked the end of the revolution of 1848, France fell under the yoke of the Napoleonic regime for a period of 18 years. This regime brought upon the country not only economic ruin but national humiliation. In rising against the old regime the proletariat undertook two tasks—one of them national and the other of a class character—the liberation of France from the German invasion and the socialist emancipation of the workers from capitalism. This union of two tasks forms a unique feature of the Commune.

The bourgeoisie had formed a "government of national defense" and the proletariat had to fight for national independence under its leadership. Actually, it was a government of "national betrayal" which saw its mission in fighting the Paris proletariat. But the proletariat, blinded by patriotic illusions, did not perceive this. The patriotic idea had its origin in the Great Revolution of the 18th century; it swayed the minds of the socialists of the Commune; and Blanqui, for example, undoubtedly a revolutionary and an ardent supporter of socialism, could find no better title for his newspaper than the bourgeois cry: *"The country is in danger!"*

Combining contradictory tasks—patriotism and socialism—was the fatal mistake of the French socialists. In the Manifesto of the

International, issued in September 1870, Marx had warned the French proletariat against being misled by a false national idea; profound changes had taken place since the Great Revolution, class antagonisms had sharpened, and whereas at that time the struggle against the whole of European reaction united the entire revolutionary nation, now the proletariat could no longer combine its interests with the interests of other classes hostile to it; let the bourgeoisie bear the responsibility for the national humiliation—the task of the proletariat was to fight for the socialist emancipation of labor from the yoke of the bourgeoisie.

And indeed the true nature of bourgeois "patriotism" was not long in revealing itself. Having concluded an ignominious peace with the Prussians, the Versailles government proceeded to its immediate task—it launched an attack to wrest the arms that terrified it from the hands of the Paris proletariat. The workers replied by proclaiming the Commune and civil war.

Although the socialist proletariat was split up into numerous sects, the Commune was a splendid example of the unanimity with which the proletariat was able to accomplish the democratic tasks which the bourgeoisie could only proclaim. Without any particularly complex legislation, in a simple, straightforward manner, the proletariat, which had seized power, carried out the democratization of the social system, abolished the bureaucracy, and made all official posts elective.

But two mistakes destroyed the fruits of the splendid victory. The proletariat stopped half-way: instead of setting about "expropriating the expropriators," it allowed itself to be led astray by dreams of establishing a higher justice in the country united by a common national task; such institutions as the banks, for example, were not taken over, and Proudhonist theories about a "just exchange," etc., still prevailed among the socialists. The second mistake was excessive magnanimity on the part of the proletariat: instead of destroying its enemies it sought to exert moral influence on them; it underestimated the significance of direct military operations in civil war, and instead of launching a resolute offensive against Versailles that would have crowned its victory in Paris, it tarried and gave the Versailles government time to gather the dark forces and prepare for the blood-soaked week of May.

But despite all its mistakes the Commune was a superb example of the great proletarian movement of the 19th century. Marx set a high value on the historic significance of the Commune—if, during the treacherous attempt by the Versailles gang to seize the arms of the Paris proletariat, the workers had allowed themselves to be disarmed without a fight, the disastrous effect of the demoralization that this weakness would have caused in the proletarian movement, would have been far, far greater than the losses suffered by the working class in the battle to defend its arms. The sacrifices of the Commune, heavy as they were, are made up for by its significance for the general struggle of the proletariat: it stirred the socialist movement throughout Europe, it demonstrated the strength of civil war, it dispelled patriotic illusions, and destroyed the naive belief in any efforts of the bourgeoisie for common national aims. The Commune taught the European proletariat to pose concretely the tasks of the socialist revolution.

The lesson learned by the proletariat will not be forgotten. The working class will make use of it, as it has already done in Russia during the December uprising.

The period that preceded the Russian revolution and prepared it bears a certain resemblance to the period of the Napoleonic yoke in France. In Russia, too, the autocratic clique has brought upon the country economic ruin and national humiliation. But the outbreak of revolution was held back for a long time, since social development had not yet created the conditions for a mass movement and, notwithstanding all the courage displayed, the isolated actions against the government in the pre-revolutionary period broke against the apathy of the masses. Only the Social-Democrats, by strenuous and systematic work, educated the masses to the level of the higher forms of struggle—mass actions and armed civil war.

The Social-Democrats were able to shatter the "common national" and "patriotic" delusions of the young proletariat and later, when the Manifesto of October 17 [1905]* had been wrested from the tsar due to their direct intervention, the proletariat began vigorous preparation for the next, inevitable phase of the revolution—the armed uprising. Having shed "common national" illusions, it concentrated its class forces in its own mass organizations—the Soviets of Workers' and Soldiers' Deputies, etc. And notwithstanding all the differences in the aims and tasks of the Russian revolution, compared with the French

---

* In the Manifesto, the tsar, frightened by the revolution, promised the people civil liberties and a constitution.

revolution of 1871, the Russian proletariat had to resort to the same method of struggle as that first used by the Paris Commune—civil war. Mindful of the lessons of the Commune, it knew that the proletariat should not ignore peaceful methods of struggle—they serve its ordinary, day-to-day interests, they are necessary in periods of preparation for revolution—but it must never forget that in certain conditions the class struggle assumes the form of armed conflict and civil war; there are times when the interests of the proletariat call for ruthless extermination of its enemies in open armed clashes. This was first demonstrated by the French proletariat in the Commune and brilliantly confirmed by the Russian proletariat in the December uprising.

And although these magnificent uprisings of the working class were crushed, there will be another uprising, in face of which the forces of the enemies of the proletariat will prove ineffective, and from which the socialist proletariat will emerge completely victorious.

—Karl Marx and V. I. Lenin, *The Civil War in France: The Paris Commune,* International Publishers, 1968, pp. 96–99. First published in *Zagranichnaya Gazeta* (Foreign Gazette), March 23, 1908.

11

Armed Struggle in the 1905 Revolution

V. I. LENIN

> *In the wake of the unsuccessful Russian Revolution of 1905, bourgeois liberal and Menshevik circles adopted a defeatist attitude, contending that the revolutionary Marxist tactics that had been employed by the proletariat had proved incorrect and that "no one in Russia would now dream of making a revolution according to Marx." They reacted in particular against the armed struggle tactics brought into use by the Russian workers and peasants.*

> Lenin wrote the article from which this is taken for a Polish Social-Democratic journal to make it plain that the Bolsheviks fully supported the whole range of revolutionary tactics.

Just wait, 1905 will come again. That is how the workers look at things. For them that year of struggle provided a model of *what has to be done*. For the intellectuals and the renegading petty-bourgeois it was the "insane year," a model of *what should not be done*. For the proletariat, the working over and critical acceptance of the experience of the revolution must consist in learning how to apply the *then* methods of struggle *more successfully*, so as to make the same October strike struggle and December armed struggle more massive, more concentrated and more conscious....

Karl Kautsky has approached this question in its fundamental theoretical aspect. In the second edition of his well-known work *The Social Revolution*, which has been translated into all the principal European languages, he made a number of additions and amendments touching on the experience of the Russian revolution....

What problems in the experience of the Russian revolution, then, did Kautsky consider sufficiently outstanding and basic, or at least sufficiently important to provide *new* material for a Marxist studying *in general* "the forms and weapons of the social revolution"...?

The author has taken two questions.

First, the question of the class composition of the forces which are *capable* of winning victory in the Russian revolution, making it a really victorious revolution.

Secondly, the question of the importance of those higher forms of mass struggle—higher in the direction of their revolutionary energy and in their aggressive character—which the Russian revolution brought forth, namely, the struggle in December, i.e., the armed uprising.

Any socialist (and especially a Marxist) studying at all attentively the events of the Russian revolution is bound to recognize that these really are the root and fundamental questions in assessing the Russian revolution, and also in assessing the line of tactics dictated to a workers' party by the present state of affairs. Unless we fully and clearly realize what classes are *capable,* in the light of objective economic conditions, of making the Russian bourgeois revolution victorious, all our words about seeking to make that revolution victorious will be empty phrases, mere democratic declamation, while our tactics in the bourgeois revolution will inevitably be unprincipled and wavering.

On the other hand, in order concretely to determine the tactics of a revolutionary party at the stormiest moments of the general crisis which the country is living through, it is obviously insufficient merely to indicate the classes capable of *acting* in the spirit of a victorious completion of the revolution. Revolutionary periods are distinguished from periods of so-called peaceful development, periods when economic conditions do not give rise to profound crisis or powerful mass movements, precisely in this: that the *forms* of struggle in the periods of the first type inevitably are *much more varied,* and the direct revolutionary struggle of the masses predominates rather than the propaganda and agitation activities conducted by leaders in parliament, in the press, etc. Therefore if, in assessing revolutionary periods, we confine ourselves to defining the *line* of activity of the various classes, without analyzing the *forms* of their struggle, our discussion in the scientific sense will be incomplete and undialectical, while from the standpoint of practical politics it will degenerate into the *dead letter of the raisoneur (*with which, we may say in parenthesis, comrade Plekhanov contents himself in nine-tenths of his writings on Social-Democratic tactics in the Russian revolution).

In order to make a genuinely Marxist assessment of the revolution, from the standpoint of dialectical materialism, it has to be assessed as the struggle of live social forces, placed in particular objective conditions, acting in a particular way and applying with greater or less success particular forms of struggle. It is on the basis of such an analysis, and only on that basis of course, that it is appropriate and indeed essential for a Marxist to assess the *technical* side of the struggle, the technical questions which arise in its course. To recognize a definite form of struggle and not to recognize the necessity for studying its technique, is like recognizing the necessity of taking part in *particular* elections while ignoring the law which lays down the technique of *these* elections . . . .

Kautsky discusses . . . the assessment of the insurrection of December 1905, in the preface to the second edition of his booklet. He writes: "I can now no longer assert as definitely as I did in 1902 that armed uprisings and barricade fighting will not play the decisive part in the coming revolutions. Too clear evidence to the contrary is provided by the experience of the street battles in Moscow, when a handful of men held up a whole army for a week in barricade fighting, and would have almost gained the victory, had not the failure of the revolutionary movement in other cities made it possible to dispatch such reinforcements to the army that in the end a monstrously superior force was concentrated against the insurgents. Of course, this relative success of the struggle on the barricades was possible only because the city population energetically supported the revolutionaries, while the troops were completely demoralized. But who can affirm with certainty that something similar is impossible in Western Europe?"

And so nearly a year after the insurrection, when there could be no question of any desire to cheer the spirits of the fighting men, such a careful investigator as Kautsky firmly recognizes that the Moscow insurrection represents a "relative success" of struggle on the barricades, and thinks it necessary to amend his previous general conclusion that the role of street battles in future revolutions cannot be a great one.

The struggle of December 1905 *proved* that armed uprising *can* be victorious in modern conditions of military technique and military organization. As a result of the December struggle the whole international labor movement must henceforth reckon with the probability of similar forms of fighting in the coming proletarian revolutions. These are the conclusions which really follow from the experience of our revolution; these are the lessons which the broadest masses of the people should assimilate. How remote are these conclusions and these lessons from that *line* of argument which Plekhanov opened up by his famous Herostratean comment on the December insurrection: "They should not have taken to arms." What an ocean of renegade comment was called forth by that assessment! What an endless number of dirty liberal hands seized upon it, in order to carry demoralization and a spirit of petty-bourgeois compromise into the ranks of the workers!

There is not a grain of historical truth in Plekhanov's assessment. If Marx, who had said six months before the Commune that an insurrection would be madness, nevertheless was able to sum up that "madness" as the greatest mass movement of the proletariat in the 19th century, then with a thousand times more justification must the Russian Social-Democrats inspire the masses with the conviction that the December struggle was the most essential, the most legitimate, the greatest proletarian movement since the Commune. And the working class of Russia will be trained up in such views, whatever individual intellectuals in the ranks of Social-Democracy may say, and however loudly they may lament.

Here perhaps one remark is necessary, bearing in mind that this article is being written for the Polish comrades. Not being familiar, to my regret, with the Polish language, I know Polish conditions only by hearsay. And it may be easy to retort that it is precisely in Poland that a whole party strangled itself by impotent guerrilla warfare, terrorism and "fireworky" outbreaks, and those precisely in the name of rebel traditions and a joint struggle of the proletariat and the peasantry (the so-called Right wing in the Polish Socialist Party). It may very well be that from this standpoint Polish conditions do in fact radically differ from conditions in the rest of the Russian Empire. I cannot judge of this. I must say, however, that nowhere except in Poland have we seen such a senseless departure from revolutionary tactics, one that has aroused justified resistance and opposition. And here the thought arises unbidden: why, it was precisely in Poland that there was no mass armed struggle in December 1905! And is it not for this very reason that in Poland, and only in Poland, the distorted and senseless tactics of revolution-"making" anarchism have found their home, and that conditions did not permit of the development there of mass armed struggle, were it only for a short time? Is it not the tradition of just *such* a struggle, the tradition of the December armed uprising, that is at times the only serious means of overcoming anarchist tendencies within the workers' party—not by means of hackneyed, philistine, petty-bourgeois moralizing, but by turning from aimless, senseless, sporadic acts of violence to purposeful mass violence, linked with the broad movement and the sharpening of the direct proletarian struggle? . . .

—"The Assessment of the Russian Revolution," V. I. Lenin, *Collected Works*, Vol. 15, 1963, pp. 53–55, 59–61. First published in the Polish Social-Democratic journal, *Przeglad Socjaldemokratyezny*, Cracow, No. 2, April 1908.

12

The Irish Rebellion of 1916

V. I. LENIN

. . .The views of the opponents of self-determination lead to the conclusion that the vitality of small nations oppressed by imperialism has already been sapped, that they cannot play any role against imperialism, that support of their purely national aspirations will lead to nothing, etc. The imperialist war of 1914–16 has provided *facts* which refute such conclusions.

The war proved to be an epoch of crisis for the West-European nations, and for imperialism as a whole. Every crisis discards the conventionalities, tears away the outer wrappings, sweeps away the obsolete and reveals the underlying springs and forces. What has it revealed from the standpoint of the movement of oppressed nations? In the colonies there have been a number of attempts at rebellion, which the oppressor nations, naturally, did all they could to hide by means of the military censorship. Nevertheless, it is known that in Singapore the British brutally suppressed a mutiny among their Indian troops; that there were attempts at rebellion in French Annam [Vietnam] . . . and in the German Cameroons . . . that in Europe, on the one hand, there was a rebellion in Ireland, which the "freedom-loving" English, who did not dare to extend conscription to Ireland, suppressed by executions, and, on the other, the Austrian government passed the death sentence on the deputies of the Czech Diet "for treason," and shot whole Czech regiments for the same "crime."

This list is, of course, far from complete. Nevertheless, it proves that, *owing* to the crisis of imperialism, the flames of national revolt have flared up *both* in the colonies and in Europe, and that national sympathies and antipathies have manifested themselves in spite of the Draconian threats and measures of repression. All this before the crisis of imperialism hit its peak: the power of the imperialist bourgeoisie was yet to be undermined (this may be brought about by a war of "attrition" but has not yet happened) and the proletarian movements in the imperialist countries were still very feeble. What will happen when the war has caused complete exhaustion, or when, in one state at least, the power of the bourgeoisie has been shaken under the blows of proletarian struggle, as that of tsarism in 1905?

On May 9, 1916, there appeared in *Berner Tagwacht*, the organ of the Zimmerwald group, including some of the Leftists, an article on the Irish rebellion entitled "Their Song is Over," and signed with the initials K.R. [Karl Radek]. It described the Irish rebellion as being nothing more nor less than a "putsch," for, as the author argued, "the Irish question was an agrarian one," the peasants had been pacified by reforms, and the nationalist movement remained only a "purely urban, petty-bourgeois movement, which, notwithstanding the sensation it caused, had not much social backing."

It is not surprising that his monstrously doctrinaire and pedantic opinion coincided with that of a Russian national-liberal Cadet, Mr. A. Kulisher . . . who also labeled the rebellion "the Dublin putsch."

It is to be hoped that, in accordance with the adage, "it's an ill wind that blows nobody any good," many comrades, who were not aware of the morass they were sinking into by repudiating "self-determination" and by treating the national movements of small nations with disdain, will have their eyes opened by the "accidental" coincidence of opinion held by a Social-Democrat and a representative of the imperialist bourgeoisie!!

The term "putsch," in its scientific sense, may be employed only when the attempt at insurrection has revealed nothing but a circle of conspirators or stupid maniacs, and has aroused no sympathy among the masses. The centuries-old Irish national movement, having passed through various stages and combinations of class interest, manifested itself, in particular, in a mass Irish National Congress in America . . . which called for Irish independence; it also manifested itself in street fighting conducted by a section of the urban petty bourgeoisie *and a section of the workers* after a long period of mass agitation, demonstrations, suppression of newspapers, etc. Whoever calls *such* an uprising a "putsch" is either a hardened reactionary, or a doctrinaire hopelessly incapable of envisaging a social revolution as a living phenomenon.

To imagine that social revolution is *conceivable* without revolts by small nations in the colonies and in Europe, without revolutionary outbursts by a section of the petty bourgeoisie *with all its prejudices,* without a movement of the politically non-conscious proletarian and semi-proletarian masses against oppression by the landlords, the church and the monarchy, against national oppression, etc.—to imagine all this is to *repudiate social revolution.* So that one army lines up in one place and says, "We are for socialism," and another, somewhere else and says, "We are for imperialism," and that will be the social revolution! Only those who hold such a ridiculously pedantic view could vilify the Irish rebellion by calling it a "putsch."

Whoever expects a "pure" social revolution will *never* live to see it. Such a person pays lip service to revolution without understanding what revolution is.

The Russian revolution of 1905 was a bourgeois-democratic revolution. It consisted of a series of battles in which *all* the discontented classes, groups and elements of the population participated. Among these there were masses imbued with the crudest prejudices, with the vaguest and most fantastic aims of struggle; there were small groups which accepted Japanese money, there were speculators and adventurers, etc. But *objectively,* the mass movement was breaking the back of tsarism and paving the way for democracy; for this reason the class-conscious workers led it.

The socialist revolution in Europe *cannot* be anything other than an outburst of mass struggle on the part of all and sundry oppressed and discontented elements. Inevitably, sections of the petty bourgeoisie and of the backward workers will participate in it—without such participation, *mass* struggle is *impossible,* without it *no* revolution is possible—and just as inevitably will they bring into the movement their prejudices, their reactionary fantasies, their weaknesses and errors. But *objectively* they will attack *capital,* and the class-conscious vanguard of the revolution, the advanced proletariat, expressing this objective truth of a variegated and discordant, motley and outwardly fragmented, mass struggle, will be able to unite and direct it, capture power, seize the banks, expropriate the trusts which all hate (though for different reasons!), and introduce other dictatorial measures which in their totality will amount to the overthrow of the bourgeoisie and the victory of socialism, which, however, will by no means immediately "purge" itself of petty-bourgeois slag.

Social-Democracy, we read in the Polish theses (I,4), "must utilize the struggle of the young colonial bourgeoisie against European imperialism *in order to sharpen the revolutionary crisis in Europe.*" (Authors' italics.)

Is it not clear that it is least of all permissible to contrast Europe to the colonies in *this* respect? The struggle of the oppressed nations *in Europe,* a struggle capable of going all the way to insurrection and street fighting, capable of breaking down the iron discipline of the army and martial law, will "sharpen the revolutionary crisis in Europe" to an infinitely greater degree than a much more developed rebellion in a remote colony. A blow delivered against the power of the English imperialist bourgeoisie by a rebellion in Ireland is a hundred times more significant politically than a blow of equal force delivered in Asia or in Africa.

The French chauvinist press recently reported the publication in Belgium of the 80th issue of an illegal journal, *Free Belgium.* Of course, the chauvinist press of France very often lies, but this piece of news seems to be true. Whereas chauvinist and Kautskyite German Social-Democracy has failed to establish a free press for itself during the two years of war, and has meekly borne the yoke of military censorship (only the Left Radical elements, to their credit be it said, have published pamphlets and manifestos, in spite of the censorship)—an oppressed civilized nation has reacted to a military oppression unparalleled in ferocity by establishing an organ of revolutionary protest! The dialectics of history are such that small nations, powerless as an *independent* factor in the struggle against imperialism, play a part as one of the ferments, one of the bacilli, which help the *real* anti-imperialist power, the socialist proletariat, to make its appearance on the scene.

The general staffs in the current war are doing their utmost to utilize any national and revolutionary movement in the enemy camp: the Germans utilize the Irish rebellion, the French, the Czech movement, etc. They are acting quite correctly from their own point of view. A serious war would not be treated seriously if advantage were not taken of the enemy's slightest weakness and if every opportunity that presented itself were not seized upon, the more so since it is impossible to know beforehand at what moment, where, and with what force a powder magazine will "explode." We would be very poor revolutionaries if, in the proletariat's great war of liberation for socialism, we did not know how to utilize *every* popular movement against *every single* disaster imperialism brings in order to intensify and extend the crisis. If we were, on the one hand, to repeat in a thousand keys the declaration that we are "opposed" to all national oppression and, on the other, to describe the heroic revolt of the most mobile and enlightened section of certain classes in an oppressed nation against its oppressors as a "putsch," we should be sinking to the same level of stupidity as the Kautskyites.

It is the misfortune of the Irish that they rose prematurely, before the European revolt of the proletariat had had time to mature. Capitalism is not so harmoniously built that the various sources of rebellion can immediately merge of their own accord, without reverses and defeats. On the other hand, the very fact that revolts do break out at different times, in different places, and are of different kinds, guarantees wide scope and depth to the general movement; but it is only in premature, individual, sporadic and therefore unsuccessful revolutionary movements that masses gain experience, acquire knowledge, gather strength, and get to know their real leaders, the socialist proletarians, and in this way prepare for the general onslaught, just as certain strikes, demonstrations, local and national, mutinies in the army, outbreaks among the peasantry, etc., prepared the way for the general onslaught in 1905.

—"Discussion on Self-Determination Summed Up," V. I. Lenin, *National Liberation, Socialism and Imperialism,* International Publishers, 1968, pp. 158–62. Written in July 1916, this article was first published in October 1916.

13

National Wars Against Imperialism

V. I. LENIN

The first of Junius's* erroneous propositions is embodied in the fifth thesis of the International Group. "National wars are no longer possible in the epoch of this unbridled imperialism. National interests serve only as an instrument of deception, in order to place the working masses at the service of their mortal enemy: imperialism." The beginning of the fifth thesis, which concludes with the above statement, discusses the nature of the *present* war as an imperialist war. It may be that this negation of national wars generally is either an oversight, or an accidental overstatement in emphasizing the perfectly correct idea that the *present* war [World War I] is an imperialist war, not a national war. This is a mistake that must be examined, for various Social-Democrats, in view of the false assertions that the *present* war is a national war, have likewise mistakenly denied the possibility of *any* national war....

The sole argument in defense of the thesis "national wars are no longer possible," is that the world has been divided among a small group of "great" imperialist powers and for that reason any war, even if it starts as a national war, is *transformed* into an imperialist war involving the interest of one of the imperialist powers or coalitions (Junius, p. 81).

The fallacy in this argument is obvious. That all dividing lines, both in nature and society, are conventional and dynamic, and that *every* phenomenon might, under certain conditions, be transformed into its opposite, is, of course, a basic proposition of

---

* The *Junius Pamphlet*, which is here discussed by Lenin, was produced by the International Group of German Left Social-Democrats, which included Rosa Luxemburg, Karl Liebknecht, Franz Mehring, Clara Zetkin and others. In January 1916 it was renamed the Spartacus Group, and later the Spartacus League, the forerunner of the Communist Party of Germany.

Marxist dialectics. A national war *might* be transformed into an imperialist war *and vice versa*. Here is an example: the wars of the Great French Revolution began as national wars and indeed were such. They were revolutionary wars—the defense of the great revolution against a coalition of counter-revolutionary monarchies. But when Napoleon founded the French Empire and subjugated a number of big, viable and long-established national European states, these national wars of the French became imperialist wars and *in turn* led to wars of national liberation against Napoleonic imperialism....

Further. National wars waged by colonies and semi-colonies in the imperialist era are not only probable but *inevitable*. About 1,000 million people, or *over half* of the world's population, live in the colonies and semi-colonies (China, Turkey, Persia). The national liberation movements there are either already very strong, or are growing and maturing. Every war is the continuation of politics by other means. The continuation of national liberation politics in the colonies will *inevitably* take the form of national wars *against* imperialism. Such wars *might* lead to an imperialist war of the present "great" imperialist powers, but on the other hand they might not. It will depend on many factors....

And if the "great" powers are altogether exhausted in the present war, or if the revolution in Russia triumphs, national wars and even victorious national wars, are quite possible. Practical intervention by the imperialist powers is *not* always feasible. That is one point. Another is that the superficial view that the war of a small state against a giant is hopeless should be countered by the observation that even a hopeless war is a war just the same. Besides, certain factors operating within the "giant" countries—the outbreak of revolution, for example—can turn a "hopeless" war into a very "hopeful" one.

We have dwelt in detail on the erroneous proposition that "national wars are no longer possible" not only because it is patently erroneous from the theoretical point of view—it would certainly be very lamentable if the "Left" were to reveal a light-hearted attitude to Marxist theory at a time when the establishment of the Third International is possible only on the basis of unvulgarized Marxism. But the mistake is very harmful also from the standpoint of practical politics, for it gives rise to the absurd propaganda of "disarmament," since it is alleged that there can be no wars except reactionary wars. It also gives rise to the even more ludicrous and downright reactionary attitude of indifference to national movements. And such an attitude becomes chauvinism when members of the "great" European nations, that is, the nations which oppress the mass of small and colonial peoples, declare with a pseudo-scientific air: "national wars are no longer possible!" National wars *against* the imperialist powers are not only possible and probable; they are inevitable, *progressive* and *revolutionary; though,* of course, to be *successful,* they require either the concerted effort of huge numbers of people in the oppressed countries (hundreds of millions in our example of India and China), or a *particularly* favorable conjuncture of international conditions (e.g., the fact that the imperialist powers cannot interfere, being paralyzed by exhaustion, by war, by their antagonism, etc.), or the *simultaneous* uprising of the proletariat against the bourgeoisie in one of the big powers (this latter eventuality holds first place as the most desirable and favorable for the victory of the proletariat).

—"The Junius Pamphlet," V. I. Lenin, *Collected Works,* Vol. 22, 1964, pp. 305–12; written in July 1916.

14

Marxism and Insurrection

V. I. LENIN

One of the most vicious and probably most widespread distortions of Marxism resorted to by the dominant "socialist" parties is the opportunist lie that preparation for insurrection, and generally the treatment of insurrection as an art, is "Blanquism."

Bernstein, the leader of opportunism, has already earned himself unfortunate fame by accusing Marxism of Blanquism, and when our present-day opportunists cry Blanquism they do not improve on or "enrich" the meager "ideas" of Bernstein one little bit.

Marxists are accused of Blanquism for treating insurrection as an art! Can there be a more flagrant perversion of the truth, when not a single Marxist will deny that it was Marx who expressed himself on this score in the most definite, precise and categorical manner, referring to insurrection specifically as an *art,* saying that it must be treated as an art, that you must *win* the first success and then proceed from success to success, never ceasing the *offensive* against the enemy, taking advantage of his confusion, etc., etc.?

To be successful, insurrection must rely not upon conspiracy and not upon a party, but upon the advanced class. That is the first point. Insurrection must rely upon a *revolutionary upsurge of the people.* That is the second point. Insurrection must rely upon that *turning-point* in the history of the growing revolution when the activity of the advanced ranks of the people is at its height, and when the *vacillations* in the ranks of the enemy and *in the ranks of the weak, half-hearted and irresolute friends of the revolution* are strongest. That is the third point. And these three conditions for raising the question of insurrection distinguish *Marxism from Blanquism.*

Once these conditions exist, however, to refuse to treat insurrection as an *art* is a betrayal of Marxism and a betrayal of the revolution.

To show that it is precisely the present moment that the party *must* recognize as the one in which the entire course of events has objectively placed *insurrection* on the order of the day and that insurrection must be treated as an art, it will perhaps be best to use the method of comparison, and to draw a parallel between July 3–4 and the September days.*

On July 3–4 it could have been argued, without violating the truth, that the correct thing to do was to take power, for our enemies would in any case have accused us of insurrection and ruthlessly treated us as rebels. However, to have decided on this account in favor of taking power at that time would have been wrong, because the objective conditions for the victory of the insurrection did not exist.

(1) We still lacked the support of the class which is the vanguard of the revolution.

---

* The strikes and demonstrations in July and the defeat of General Kornilov's counter-revolutionary revolt against the Provisional Government in September 1917.

We still did not have a majority among the workers and soldiers of Petrograd and Moscow. Now we have a majority in both Soviets. It was created *solely* by the history of July and August, by the experience of the "ruthless treatment" meted out to the Bolsheviks,* and by the experience of the Kornilov revolt.

(2) There was no country-wide revolutionary upsurge at that time. There is now, after the Kornilov revolt; the situation in the provinces and assumption of power by the Soviets in many localities prove this.

(3) At that time there was *no vacillation* on any serious political scale among our enemies and among the irresolute petty bourgeoisie. Now the vacillation is enormous. Our main enemy, Allied and world imperialism (for world imperialism is headed by the "Allies"), *has begun to waver* between a war to a victorious finish and a separate peace directed against Russia. Our petty-bourgeois democrats, having clearly lost their majority among the people, have begun to vacillate enormously, and have rejected a bloc, i.e., a coalition, with the Cadets.

(4) Therefore, an insurrection on July 3-4 would have been a mistake; we could not have retained power either physically or politically. We could not have retained it physically even though Petrograd was at times in our hands, because at that time our workers and soldiers would not have *fought and died* for Petrograd. There was not at the time that "savageness," or fierce hatred *both of* the Kerenskys *and of* the Tseretelis and Chernovs.† Our people had still not been tempered by the experience of the persecution of the Bolsheviks in which the Socialist-Revolutionaries and Mensheviks participated.

We could not have retained power politically on July 3-4 because, *before the Kornilov revolt,* the army and the provinces could and would have marched against Petrograd.

Now the picture is entirely different.

We have the following of the majority of a *class,* the vanguard

---

* In July 1917, the Provisional Government under Kerensky suppressed workers' demonstrations and started repressions against the Bolsheviks and their press.

† Alexander F. Kerensky, Socialist-Revolutionary and head of the Provisional Government since July 1917; Iraky G. Tsereteli, Menshevik leader who in July became Minister of the Interior in the Kerensky cabinet; Victor M. Chernov, Socialist-Revolutionary leader and Minister for Agriculture in the Provisional Government.

of the revolution, the vanguard of the people, which is capable of carrying the masses with it.

We have the following of the *majority* of the people, because Chernov's resignation, while by no means the only symptom, is the most striking and obvious symptom that the peasants *will not receive land* from the Socialist-Revolutionaries' bloc (or from the Socialist-Revolutionaries themselves). And that is the chief reason for the popular character of the revolution.

We are in the advantageous position of a party that knows for certain which way to go at a time when *imperialism as a whole* and the Menshevik and Socialist-Revolutionary bloc as a whole are vacillating in an incredible fashion.

Our victory is assured, for the people are close to desperation, and we are showing the entire people a sure way out; we demonstrated to the entire people during the "Kornilov days" the value of our leadership, and then *proposed* to the politicians of the bloc a compromise, *which they rejected,* although there is no let-up in their vacillations.

It would be a great mistake to think that our offer of a compromise had not *yet* been rejected, and that the Democratic Conference* may *still* accept it. The compromise was proposed *by a party to parties*; it could not have been proposed in any other way. It was rejected by *parties.* The Democratic Conference is a *conference,* and nothing more. One thing must not be forgotten, namely, that the *majority* of the revolutionary people, the poor, embittered peasants, are not represented in it. It is a conference of *a minority of the people*—this obvious truth must not be forgotten. It would be a big mistake, sheer parliamentary cretinism on our part, if we were to regard the Democratic Conference as a parliament; for even *if it were* to proclaim itself a permanent and sovereign parliament of the revolution, it would nevertheless *decide nothing.* The power of decision lies *outside it* in the working-class quarters of Petrograd and Moscow.

All the objective conditions exist for a successful insurrection. We have the exceptional advantage of a situation in which *only* our victory in the insurrection can put an end to that most painful thing on earth, vacillation, which has worn the people out; in which only our victory in the insurrection will give the peasants land immediately; a situation in which *only our* victory

---

* Called by the Kerensky government, following the Kornilov revolt, in the attempt to secure a broader base among the petty bourgeoisie.

in the insurrection can *foil* the game of a separate peace directed against the revolution—foil it by publicly proposing a fuller, juster and earlier peace, a peace that will *benefit* the revolution.

Finally, our party alone *can*, by a victorious insurrection, save Petrograd; for if our proposal for peace is rejected, if we do not secure even an armistice, then *we* shall become "defensists," we shall place ourselves *at the head of the war parties*, we shall be the *war party par excellence*, and we shall conduct the war in a truly revolutionary manner. We shall take away all the bread and boots from the capitalists. We shall leave them only crusts and dress them in bast shoes. We shall send all the bread and footwear to the front.

And then we shall save Petrograd.

The resources, both material and spiritual, for a truly revolutionary war in Russia are still immense; the chances are a hundred to one that the Germans will grant us at least an armistice. And to secure an armistice now would in itself mean to win the *whole world*.

Having recognized the absolute necessity for an insurrection of the workers of Petrograd and Moscow in order to save the revolution and to save Russia from a "separate" partition by the imperialists of both groups, we must first adapt our political tactics at the Conference to the conditions of the growing insurrection; secondly, we must show that it is not only in words that we accept Marx's idea that insurrection must be treated as an art.

At the Conference we must immediately cement the Bolshevik group, without striving after numbers, and without fearing to leave the waverers in the waverers' camp. They are more useful to the cause of the revolution *there* than in the camp of the resolute and devoted fighters.

We must draw up a brief declaration from the Bolsheviks, emphasizing in no uncertain manner the irrelevance of long speeches and of "speeches" in general, the necessity for immediate action to save the revolution, the absolute necessity for a complete break with the bourgeoisie, for the removal of the present government, in its entirety, for a complete rupture with the Anglo-French imperialists, who are preparing a "separate" partition of Russia, and for the immediate transfer of all power to *revolutionary democrats, headed by the revolutionary proletariat.*

Our declaration must give the briefest and most trenchant formulation of *this* conclusion in connection with the program proposals of peace for the peoples, land for the peasants, confiscation of scandalous profits, and a check on the scandalous sabotage of production by the capitalists.

The briefer and more trenchant the declaration, the better. Only two other highly important points must be clearly indicated in it, namely, that the people are worn out by the vacillations, that they are fed up with the irresolution of the Socialist-Revolutionaries and Mensheviks; and that we are definitely breaking with these *parties* because they have betrayed the revolution.

And another thing. By immediately proposing a peace without annexations, by immediately breaking with the Allied imperialists and with all imperialists, either we shall at once obtain an armistice, or the entire revolutionary proletariat will rally to the defense of the country, and a really just, really revolutionary war will then be waged by revolutionary democrats under the leadership of the proletariat.

Having read this declaration, and having appealed for *decisions* and not talk, for *action* and not resolution-writing, we must *dispatch* our entire group to the *factories and the barracks.* Their place is there, the pulse of life is there, there is the source of salvation for our revolution, and there is the motive force of the Democratic Conference.

There, in ardent and impassioned speeches, we must explain our program and put the alternative: either the Conference adopts it *in its entirety,* or else insurrection. There is no middle course. Delay is impossible. The revolution is dying.

By putting the question in this way, by concentrating our entire group in the factories and barracks, *we shall be able to determine the right moment to start the insurrection.*

In order to treat insurrection in a Marxist way, i.e., as an art, we must at the same time, without losing a single moment, organize a *headquarters* of the insurgent detachments, distribute our forces, move the reliable regiments to the most important points, surround the Alexandrinsky Theatre, occupy the Peter and Paul Fortress, arrest the General Staff and the government, and move against the officer cadets and the Savage Division [Caucasion mountaineer troops] those detachments which would rather die than allow the enemy to approach the strategic points of the city. We must mobilize the armed workers and call them to fight the last desperate fight, occupy the telegraph and the telephone exchange at once, move *our* insurrection headquarters to the central telephone exchange and connect it by telephone with all the factories, all the regiments, all the points of armed fighting, etc.

Of course, this is all by way of example, only to *illustrate* the fact that at the present moment it is impossible to remain loyal to Marxism, to remain loyal to the revolution *unless insurrection is treated as an art.*

—V. I. Lenin, *Selected Works*, Vol. 2, pp. 365–70; this letter to the Central Committee of the Russian Social-Democratic Labor Party (Bolshevik), was written September 13–14, 1917, and was first published in 1921 in *Proletarskaya Revolutsia*, No. 2.

15

Emancipation of the Peoples of the East

V. I. LENIN

... We have witnessed Soviet Russia's complete triumph over Kolchak.* Here we undoubtedly have practical proof that the united forces of workers and peasants who have been emancipated from the capitalist yoke can perform real miracles. Here we have practical proof that when a revolutionary war really does attract and interest the working and oppressed people, when it makes them conscious that they are fighting the exploiters—such a revolutionary war engenders the strength and ability to perform miracles.

I think that what the Red Army has accomplished, its struggle, and the history of its victory, will be of colossal, epochal significance for all the peoples of the East. It will show them that, weak as they may be, as invincible as may seem the power of the European oppressors, who in the struggle employ all the

---

* Admiral Kolchak, a White Guard officer, headed the imperialist-backed intervention in the Soviet Far East and Siberia in 1918–19.

marvels of technology and of the military art—nevertheless, a revolutionary war waged by oppressed peoples, if it really succeeds in arousing the millions of working and exploited people, harbors such potentialities, such miracles, that the emancipation of the peoples of the East is now quite practicable, from the standpoint not only of the prospects of the international revolution, but also of the direct military experience acquired in Asia, in Siberia, the experience of the Soviet Republic, which has suffered the armed invasion of all the powerful imperialist countries.

Furthermore, the experience of the Civil War in Russia has shown us and the Communists of all countries that, in the crucible of civil war, the development of revolutionary enthusiasm is accompanied by a powerful inner cohesion. War tests all the economic and organizational forces of a nation. In the final analysis, infinitely hard as the war has been for the workers and peasants, who are suffering famine and cold, it may be said on the basis of these two years' experience that we are winning and will continue to win, because we have a hinterland, and a strong one, because, despite famine and cold, the peasants and workers stand together, have grown strong, and answer every heavy blow with a greater cohesion of their forces and increased economic might. . . .

Permit me . . . to say something about the situation that is developing in respect to the nationalities of the East. You are representatives of the Communist organizations and Communist parties of various Eastern peoples. I must say that the Russian Bolsheviks have succeeded in forcing a breach in the old imperialism, in undertaking the exceedingly difficult, but also exceedingly noble task of blazing new paths of revolution, whereas you, the representatives of the working people of the East, have before you a task that is still greater and newer. It is becoming quite clear that the socialist revolution which is impending for the whole world will not be merely the victory of the proletariat of each country over its own bourgeoisie. That would be possible if revolutions came easily and swiftly. We know that the imperialists will not allow this, that all countries are armed against their domestic Bolshevism and that their one thought is how to defeat Bolshevism at home. That is why in every country a civil war is brewing in which the old Socialist compromisers are enlisted on the side of the bourgeoisie. Hence, the socialist revolution will not be solely, or chiefly, a struggle of the revolutionary proletarians in each country against their bourgeoisie—no, it will be a struggle of all the imperialism-oppressed colonies and countries, of all dependent countries, against international imperialism. Characterizing the approach of the world social revolution in the Party Program we adopted last March, we said that the civil war of the working people against the imperialists and exploiters in all the advanced countries is beginning to be combined with national wars against international imperialism. That is confirmed by the course of the revolution, and will be more and more confirmed as time goes on. It will be the same in the East.

We know that in the East the masses will rise as independent participants, as builders of a new life, because hundreds of millions of the people belong to dependent, underprivileged nations, which until now have been objects of international imperialist policy, and have only existed as material to fertilize capitalist culture and civilization. And when they talk of handing out mandates for colonies, we know very well that it means handing out mandates of spoliation and plunder—handing out to an insignificant section of the world's population the right to exploit the majority of the population of the globe. That majority, which up till then had been completely outside the orbit of historical progress, because it could not constitute an independent revolutionary force, ceased, as we know, to play such a passive role at the beginning of the 20th century. We know that 1905 was followed by revolutions in Turkey, Persia and China, and that a revolutionary movement developed in India. The imperialist war likewise contributed to the growth of the revolutionary movement, because the European imperialists had to enlist whole colonial regiments in their struggle. The imperialist war aroused the East also and drew its peoples into international politics. Britain and France armed colonial peoples and helped them to familiarize themselves with military technique and up-to-date machines. That knowledge they will use against the imperialist gentry. The period of awakening of the East in the contemporary revolution is being succeeded by a period in which all the Eastern peoples will participate in deciding the destiny of the whole world, so as not to be simply objects of the enrichment of others. The peoples of the East are becoming alive to the need for practical action, the need for every nation to take part in shaping the destiny of all mankind.

That is why I think that in the history of development of the world revolution—which, judging by its beginning, will continue for many years and will demand much effort—that in the revolutionary struggle, in the revolutionary movement you will be called upon to play a big part and to merge with our struggle against international imperialism. Your participation in the international revolution will confront you with a complicated and difficult task, the accomplishment of which will serve as the foundation for our common success, because here the majority of the people for the first time begin to act independently and will be an active factor in the fight to overthrow international imperialism.

Most of the Eastern peoples are in a worse position than the most backward country in Europe—Russia. But in our struggle against feudal survivals and capitalism, we succeeded in uniting the peasants and workers of Russia; and it was because the peasants and workers united against capitalism and feudalism that our victory was so easy. Here contact with the peoples of the East is particularly important, because the majority of the Eastern peoples are typical representatives of the working people—not workers who have passed through the school of capitalist factories, but typical representatives of the working and exploited peasant masses who are victims of medieval oppression. The Russian Revolution showed how the proletarians, after defeating capitalism and uniting with the vast diffuse mass of working peasants, rose up victoriously against medieval oppression. Our Soviet Republic must now muster all the awakening peoples of the East and, together with them, wage a struggle against international imperialism.

In this respect you are confronted with a task which has not previously confronted the Communists of the world: relying upon the general theory and practice of communism, you must adapt yourselves to specific conditions such as do not exist in European countries; you must be able to apply that theory and practice to conditions in which the bulk of the population are peasants, and in which the task is to wage a struggle against medieval survivals and not against capitalism. That is a difficult and unique task, but a very thankful one, because masses that have taken no part in the struggle up to now are being drawn into it, and also because the organization of Communist cells in the East gives you an opportunity to maintain the closest contact with the Third International.* You must find specific forms for this alli-

---

* The Communist International, 1919–43.

ance of the foremost proletarians of the world with the laboring and exploited masses of the East whose conditions are in many cases medieval. We have accomplished on a small scale in our country what you will do on a big scale and in big countries. And that latter task you will, I hope, perform with success. Thanks to the Communist organizations in the East, of which you here are the representatives, you have contact with the advanced revolutionary proletariat. Your task is to continue to ensure that Communist propaganda is carried on in every country in a language the people understand.

It is self-evident that final victory can be won only by the proletariat of all the advanced countries of the world, and we, the Russians, are beginning the work which the British, French or German proletariat will consolidate. But we see that they will not be victorious without the aid of the working people of all the oppressed colonial nations, first and foremost, of Eastern nations. We must realize that the transition to communism cannot be accomplished by the vanguard alone. The task is to arouse the working masses to revolutionary activity, independent action and to organization, regardless of the level they have reached; to translate the true communist doctrine, which was intended for the Communists of the more advanced countries, into the language of every people; to carry out those practical tasks which must be carried out immediately, and to join the proletarians of other countries in a common struggle.

Such are the problems whose solution you will not find in any Communist book, but will find in the common struggle begun by Russia. You will have to tackle that problem and solve it through your own independent experience. In that you will be assisted, on the one hand, by close alliance with the vanguard of the working people of other countries, and, on the other, by ability to find the right approach to the peoples of the East whom you here represent. You will have to base yourselves on the bourgeois nationalism which is awakening, and must awaken, among those peoples, and which has its historical justification. At the same time, you must find your way to the working and exploited masses of every country and tell them in a language they understand that their only hope of emancipation lies in the victory of the international revolution, and that the international proletariat is the only ally of all the hundreds of millions of working and exploited peoples of the East.

Such is the immense task which confronts you, and which, thanks to the era of revolution and the growth of the revolutionary movement—of that there can be no doubt—will, by the joint efforts of the Communist organizations of the East, be successfully accomplished and crowned by complete victory over international imperialism.

—"Address to the Second All-Russian Congress of Communist Organizations of the Peoples of the East," V. I. Lenin, *Selected Works,* Vol. 3, pp. 285, 289–93. The Address was given on November 22, 1919.

PART TWO

Contemporary Theory and Practice

I. THE SOVIET UNION

The practical application of Lenin's views on revolutionary armed struggle is, of course, most plainly seen in Soviet experience with guerrilla warfare, as illustrated in the following selections, as well as in Soviet overall military policies which Lenin personally had a hand in shaping. A vast Soviet literature on guerrilla experience, ranging from Alexander Fadayev's great novel, *The Nineteen,* to a host of personal accounts of guerrilla life in the war against the Nazis, has established a familiar background on the subject, sharing a common theoretical approach to guerrilla strategy and tactics.

In the case of the Soviet Union, it is not merely experience in armed struggle that is drawn upon by national liberation and revolutionary movements generally, but more significantly its role as external factor in providing both moral and material assistance for revolutionary struggles.

The Soviet position on this was stated by Sharaf R. Rashidov, Alternate Member of the Presidium of the CPSU Central Committee, at the First Solidarity Conference of Asia, Africa and Latin America (the Tricontinental Conference), held in Havana, Cuba, January 3–15, 1966. He asserted that "the Soviet people support people's wars and the armed struggle of oppressed peoples for freedom and independence." As an example, he described in detail the extensive aid being rendered by the Soviet Union to the Vietnamese people.

Rashidov stated that the Soviet view that "relations between sovereign states with different social systems must be built on the principle of peaceful coexistence" did not alter its international revolutionary duties, affirming that "it is clear that there is not and cannot be any peaceful coexistence between oppressed peoples and their oppressors, the colonialists and the imperialists, between the imperialist aggressors and their victims."

1

Guerrillas in the Civil War

I. MINZ

The Civil War [1917–21] was a great war of liberation, the first great patriotic war of the Soviet people. In the course of it were created and built up the Red Army and Navy, and the fine traditions of loyalty and devotion to country, of courage and heroism, to which the Red Army has always adhered, were laid down.

The Red Army was victorious because it was loyal to the Soviet people. The Soviet people knew that the Whiteguards wanted to restore the detestable old regime; they knew that the foreign invaders wanted to transform their country into a colony, as Germany had tried to do with the Ukraine. That is why they sent their best sons into the Red Army and supported it by every means in their power.

It was this devotion and determination of the workers and peasants that enabled the poorly-armed Red Army to defeat the well-armed and numerically superior forces of the Whiteguards and the invaders. Russians and Kazakhs, Ukrainians and Tajiks, Byelorussians and Uzbeks, Caucasian highlanders and the Northern peoples fought shoulder to shoulder in the Red Army and this served to tighten still further the bonds of fraternity that united the different peoples of the Soviet Republic. All the peoples of the Soviet Republic headed by the Great-Russian people jointly defended their motherland, jointly liberated the Ukraine and Byelorussia, Azerbaijan and Turkmenistan. The blood they shed for their motherland served to cement the friendship of the peoples of the Soviet Union.

Concerning the victory of the Red Army Lenin wrote: "We were victorious because we could be and were united."

Another important factor that contributed to the victory of the Red Army was that the government, guided by the Communist Party, succeeded in organizing the country to serve the forces fighting to defend it. The whole country was transformed into a united camp which devoted all its efforts to the service of the Red Army.

The Red Army's victory was ensured by the invaluable assistance it received from the guerrillas fighting in the enemy's rear. The experience and traditions of this heroic guerrilla warfare are indelibly inscribed in the annals of the Soviet people and inspire them in their struggle against the fascist hordes today [1942]. In every region and every republic occupied by foreign invaders or Russian Whiteguards, guerrilla warfare broke out. Each region had its own specific methods of fighting, adapted to their local conditions; but taken as a whole it was another "minor war" in the enemy's rear. . . . This "minor war" was most vigorously pursued in the Ukraine, Byelorussia and in the Baltic countries.

With an army of over 300,000 men the Germans invaded the Ukraine in quest of grain. Actually, this was a vast foraging expedition. German garrisons were stationed not only in towns, but also in the large villages. Large forces were continuously marching from village to village. These circumstances moulded the character of the guerrilla warfare of the Ukrainian people. It was almost impossible to form big guerrilla units, for these would soon have been discovered and crushed by the large concentrations of German troops. The character of the country—the vast steppes and scarcity of woods in which to take cover—also precluded the formation of large units.

A guerrilla unit usually consisted of 30 to 50 men. These were carefully chosen, and only those known for their devotion to the Soviet regime and for their courage and experience were enrolled. The guerrillas lived in their different villages, and engaged in their ordinary occupations. Their arms were carefully hidden in secret but easily accessible places. When the commander of the group intended to make a raid on a German garrison he informed all the members of his group through scouts, and on the appointed day they gathered at a given spot with their arms. If a very large operation was to be undertaken as many as several hundred men would be concentrated. After the raid had been carried out and the German garrison wiped out, the guerrillas would disperse to their villages again, carefully conceal their arms and go on with their work as before. These units were very mobile and after a raid could move quickly to places scores of miles from the scene of operations. On receiving information of a raid having taken place the German Command would send out a force of several hundred men, and sometimes a whole division, to attempt to capture the guerrillas. They surrounded whole *uyezds* [districts], combed the woods and scoured the plains, but all in vain.

The guerrilla warfare in Byelorussia had its own peculiar features. True, the large stretches of forest and marsh provided excellent cover; nevertheless, this did not permit the formation of large groups. The invaders kept to the main roads and railways, fearing to follow the cross-country tracks that wound deviously through the marshes and forests. This made their lines of communication very vulnerable and compelled them to guard the roads, and particularly the bridges, with the aid of armored trains, armored cars and special infantry units armed with machine guns. This strong protection compelled the guerrillas, who were poorly armed, closely to coordinate their activities with the operations of the regular Red Army.

This warfare was particularly effective when the guerrillas were able to establish direct contact with the headquarters of the Red Army units. In such cases they received instructions where to make raids, which bridges to destroy, etc., in conformity with the operations the Red Army Command had in view. As a consequence of this close cooperation the Red Army was able to inflict more effective blows on the enemy.

These guerrilla activities wore down the enemy and kept him in a state of constant tension. They gave him no rest and compelled him to fight on two fronts. Night and day the German invaders were made to feel that they were in enemy territory; danger lurked in every hut and in every bush.

Guerrilla warfare was conducted on an exceptionally wide scale in Kolchak's rear, in Siberia. Here, hundreds of guerrilla units were formed. In view of the vast area of the country, the Whiteguards could not maintain garrisons everywhere. They were stationed only in large towns, and along the railways from which they dared not venture more than 20 kilometers or so. This facilitated the formation of large guerrilla units and even whole armies, with divisions and regiments. The guerrilla army led by Shchetinkin and Kravchenko numbered tens of thousands of men. Whole regions behind Kolchak's lines remained in the control of the Soviets. Here the machinery of Soviet local government functioned in the ordinary way, and Soviet newspapers were published regularly. The guerrilla forces were organized in regiments and divisions, and had a well-organized supply service. All the secret operations were conducted by arrangement with the General Staff of the Eastern Front of the Red Army.

To counteract the operations of the guerrillas, Kolchak was compelled to divert a large part of his forces. A force of 200,000 men was employed to guard the railway, but even this proved to be inadequate and Kolchak was compelled to withdraw men from the front. Hard pressed by the Red Army, the Whiteguard forces retreated, but their line of retreat was constantly harassed by guerrillas. Under these double blows Kolchak's army dwindled. Whole divisions went over to the side of the Red Army. Eventually, by the combined efforts of the Red Army and the guerrillas, Kolchak was routed.

—I. Minz, *The Army of the Soviet Union*, Foreign Languages Publishing House, Moscow, 1942, pp. 90–93.

2

Soviet Partisans in World War II

A. FYODOROV

The Germans were developing their offensive. The western part of the Ukraine had become a war zone. And although enemy planes had made dozens of flights over Chernigov and repeatedly bombed the towns of the region, to us, the heads of the Chernigov region, it seemed incredible that the Germans could invade our area in the heart of the Ukraine.

At a meeting of the workers of the Chernigov Railway Depot on July 4, I said that the fascists would not break through to our town, that we could go on working calmly. And I sincerely believed it.

When I returned to the R. C. [Regional Committee] headquarters from that meeting I learned that Comrade Korotchenko, a secretary of the Ukrainian Central Committee, had come from Kiev. He did not stay long in Chernigov, no more than a day.

With his help the regional organizations planned which people, industrial equipment and valuables were to be evacuated first. Before leaving he advised us to register the people who had been partisans in the Civil War. "Their experience, Comrade, may come in handy!"

That evening I received a telegram from the Central Committee summoning me to Kiev. I left immediately by car.

Nikita Sergeyevich [Khrushchev]* received me that same night. He described the situation at the fronts and said that we had to face the facts. The German offensive should not be underestimated, he said, and the advance of the enemy army into the heart of the country must not find us unprepared.

Nikita Sergeyevich suggested that we begin immediate preparations for a Bolshevik underground movement and organize a partisan detachment in every district in good time. "On your return to Chernigov get down immediately to the selection of people, set up bases in the forests for the partisans and start on the military training of the people you have chosen. You'll get detailed instructions from Comrade Burmistrenko."

Mikhail Alexeyevich Burmistrenko told me how to choose people for underground work, what a partisan detachment ought to be like and how it should be formed and gave me the codes. What amazed me was that the Central Committee had already mapped out the entire organizational scheme of an underground movement...

On my arrival in Chernigov I called a meeting of the R. C. bureau. My announcement that an underground movement was to be organized came like a bolt from the blue to them. Organize an underground movement! The very words sounded bookish, unreal. "The Bolshevik underground"—why, that was something out of the history of the party. Yet there we were, men past the first flush of youth, true enough, but Soviet-bred, and we were to prepare to go underground....

All the members of the R. C. bureau decided to remain in Chernigov region. At the same meeting we nominated an underground R. C. of seven. We also named substitutes in case any of us were caught; that, too, was taken into account. Then we assigned the functions and discussed a preliminary plan of action.

Everybody soon became accustomed to the new situation. There were now two regional party committees: the legal and

---

* Then secretary of the party in the Ukraine.

the underground. The existence of the second was known only to its members. A few days later an underground R. C. of the Komsomol [Young Communist League] was organized in a similar way. Technically I remained secretary of both the legal and underground regional committees, but at the very outset I transferred almost all my legal work to other comrades while I got busy preparing for the new, unknown life.

The Central Committee of the party demanded that we members of the R. C. make thorough preparations. We had to provide for every detail, including the everyday needs of the partisans-to-be.

The future partisan commanders were already attending special courses where they were taught to blow up bridges, fire tanks, steal German staff documents. They had already taken leave of their families, while the underground party workers had taken leave of their real names as well; they trained themselves not to respond when hailed by their old names . . .

We divided up the work among ourselves. It was my task to organize the underground district party and Komsomol committees. I also handled the evacuation of the population and the wealth of the region. Nikolai Nikitich Popudrenko was put in charge of the training of sappers. Petrik, the secretary for propaganda and agitation, was given the job of selecting literature, setting up a printshop, collecting and packing newsprint; Novikov, Yaremenko and Rudko picked and checked on the fitness of people for the primary village and factory underground nuclei. Kapranov set up food dumps. In a month we picked and sent off more than 900 people to the districts for underground work.

Active preparations for underground work and partisan operations were underway in the districts. Alongside the telephone and telegraph reports on the evacuation of industrial equipment and the harvesting of the grain crop, the R. C. received daily reports on these preparations—in code, of course . . . .

There was an extermination battalion consisting of volunteers operating in the Kholmy district. Comrade Kurochka correctly decided that the men of this battalion, who had already acquired a certain amount of experience in fighting the enemy in the woods, under conditions approximating those the partisans would be in, might make up the core of a detachment. All the 240 men of the extermination battalion agreed to remain behind in the enemy rear and enlisted as partisans.

In Kholmy district all the party members of the district committee, the district executive committee and the People's Commissariat of Internal Affairs joined the detachment in a body. The detachment had begun target practice and grenade drill and was studying partisan warfare tactics. In the machine shop of the distillery the local Osoaviakhim* training machine gun was remodelled for combat use....

Fifteen days before Kholmy district was occupied, the extermination battalion and all the volunteers who had joined it took to the forest to allow the front to pass them by.

In Koryukhovka district, where Comrade Korotkov was first secretary of the party committee, the entire *active* left for the villages directly after Comrade Stalin's radio address to the people. Without waiting to be called by the R. C., they went to prepare the Communists and the leading collective farmers for the eventuality of German occupation and partisan warfare against the enemy. They organized 11 underground Communist nuclei in good time. Everybody who agreed to remain behind in the enemy rear received detailed instructions.

Comrade Stratilat, secretary of the Nosovka district committee, later one of the gifted partisan commanders, made a very interesting decision long before occupation of the area. All recent arrivals in the district and all the young Communists were called to the district committee. Those who agreed to remain in the underground and were suited for the work, were sent to the villages and small towns where no one knew them. On their arrival they took minor jobs in the village Soviets, the kolkhozes, hospitals, etc. They organized secret meeting places and built up resistance groups.

Oster district reported that a base for 100 partisans had already been outfitted. Enough food for approximately eight months, arms, ammunition and many other supplies were cached there. Two detachments had been organized in the district, one of 15 men and the other of 20, and a meeting had been held of all the Communists in the district who were to go underground. There was not a single district that did not send in similar reports.

Vasili Logvinovich Kapranov, former vice-chairman of the Chernigov Regional Executive Committee and now a member of the underground R. C., was in charge of outfitting the partisan bases. The work of this small, rotund man with the kindest of hearts was shrouded in the deepest secrecy.

---

* Society for Air and Chemical Defense, a civilian defense organization.

Tons of flour, cases of canned goods and barrels of alcohol were turned over to him at the warehouses. Trucks drew up, loaders piled heavy sacks on them, bookkeepers made out invoices. But Kapranov alone knew what these supplies were destined for. A truck would stop somewhere in a field, at the fringe of a wood, unload and turn back. When the empty truck had driven out of sight a cart would come out of the wood and men would load the supplies on it. The farm horse at first moved along the cart track and then would turn off into the wood. The men who accompanied the cart covered the wheel tracks with twigs and grass. But more frequently there was no cart. The men lugged the supplies on their backs. These were partisans-to-be at work. They received a great variety of goods: sugar, biscuits, cartridges, machine guns, felt boots, printer's type....

The typical dump was an excavation three meters deep and some 30 to 40 meters square. The walls were reinforced with heavy logs, in best sapper fashion. Of course, the trees for the logs were cut down at some distance from the dumps, at least 300 paces away. The floor was tamped down and then covered with branches as a protection against the dampness. The waste was carried off as far as possible and scattered or else thrown into a stream or a gully.

Such a dump—actually a sturdily built underground warehouse—was roofed with logs, covered with earth and leveled to the surrounding surface. The next step was to cover it with turf or moss and plant bushes or small trees on it. Kapranov often led me to such camouflaged dumps and not once was I able to detect them. He showed me notches of trees and other signs by which I was to find them.

Kapranov's men built nine of these dumps. And they did the job well. Subsequently the fascists uncovered only one of them, and that by accident. In the region as a whole there were about 200 dumps, built by the district detachments. If this work had not been done, the partisan detachments would have had a hard time of it, particularly in the initial organizational period. The dumps saved many detachments. The population could not always feed us and we only began to capture food stores from the enemy after we had armed ourselves at his expense....

And so the people had been picked, the bases outfitted. As far as we could see we were prepared to receive our uninvited "guests." But had our underground workers come to realize that the most important thing was the support of the people, that it was our sacred duty to be with the people, to stir them to resistance when the enemy would be lording it in our region? After all, we Communists, the organizers, were only the core. This we had to bear in mind always. And if we did, no hostile force could break us. . . .

One of the main tasks the R. C. set the Communists and Komsomol members at that time was to fight for the strictest partisan discipline and against laxity, slackness and irresponsibility.

To some we had to make it plain that the party could not let the partisan movement take its own course, drift along. The party demanded discipline, planned action and organization from the partisan just as from the soldier, it expected the various detachments and men to help each other out.

A Communist is everywhere a Communist. Whether in the forest, or in underground work, or among his friends, or in the bosom of his family, a Communist may not forget that he is a Communist, he may not take a vacation from his party responsibilities or violate the party rules.

In some detachments, mainly those organized after occupation had set in, there arose the practice of electing officers, a practice long since condemned by the party. The R. C. condemned this practice and required that all detachments operating on the territory of Chernigov region be connected with regional headquarters and coordinate their actions with it. Simultaneously the R. C. worked to strengthen one-man leadership and the authority of the commander. The commander's word was law. The R. C. promptly nipped any attempts to hold meetings to discuss decisions taken or the orders of a commander.

The partisans were free citizens in the occupied regions. But this was not freedom to wander through the woods at will. The partisans in this war had to look upon themselves as fighting men of the Red Army.

"You serve in the army because the fundamental law of the Soviet state obliges you to do so," we told each partisan. "And don't forget, dear comrade, that although the enemy has entered the Ukraine it remains a part of the great Soviet Union. You are a partisan because the conscience of a Soviet citizen obliges you to be one. And so observe discipline willingly and conscientiously. The fact that you volunteered does not mean you are free to be undisciplined." . . .

The following order, issued by Fyodorov under his guerrilla name, illustrates the activity of the Soviet guerrillas and what was demanded of them.

ORDER OF THE DAY OF THE REGIONAL HEADQUARTERS
OF THE CHERNIGOV PARTISAN MOVEMENT (OMBISHI FOREST)

November 9, 1941

The regional headquarters of the partisan movement notes that the leaders of the Ichnya detachment—Comrade P. P. Sychov, commander of the detachment, Comrade V. D. Gorbaty, commissar, and Comrade Popko, secretary of the underground district party committee—have carried through organizational work resulting in the establishment of a firm core of a partisan detachment capable of developing effective combat operations against the German fascist invaders. But the leadership of the partisan detachment has not yet exploited these opportunities: it has not launched extensive party and mass political work among the population; has not launched extensive recruiting of the finest men and women into the partisan detachment; has not organized good intelligence; is not waging an all-out ruthless struggle against the German fascist invaders; has not taken the initiative in fighting the German invaders; has not replied to the terror perpetrated by the fascists and their agents with Red Terror and powerful blows at the fascist invaders, who have already killed dozens of totally innocent people in Ichnya district: political instructor Comrade Yaroshenkov in the village of Buromka, a kolkhoz member in the village of Rozhnovka, a Red Army man in the village of Zaudaika.

The regional headquarters of the partisan movement *orders* the command of the Ichnya partisan detachment:

To cripple the Kiev-Bakhmach railway without delay; to blow up the railway bridge between Kruty and Plisky; to derail German trains without letup; to destroy motor vehicles, armories and ammunition depots; to exterminate the Germans and their agents; to wipe out the German detachments in Ichnya, Parafievka and Kruty.

To seize the registration list of Communists prepared by the Germans. To put to death the *starosta* [village elder] and the Ukrainian nationalists in the village of Zaudaika. To hold conferences of Communists in groups within the next ten days, to place before them the tasks of fighting the German invaders.

Immediately to launch extensive recruiting of the finest men and women into the partisan detachment.

To organize systematic distant reconnaissance and contact with every village in the district and with the adjacent districts; to have two women messengers and, if possible, a boy and an old man in the detachment for this purpose. To have two or three persons in every village for reconnaissance and contact, so as to know daily and hourly what is happening in the villages and in the district.

Every partisan is a champion of the directives of the party and the government; hence it is the task of every partisan to conduct mass political work among the population, to concern himself with the material welfare of the working people, to defend them and help them in questions pertaining to their material interests.

To ensure fulfillment of all these measures, the detachment is to march through the villages of the district in battle formation at regular intervals, and, if the necessity arises, through other districts as well, carrying out on the march all the tasks facing it: the wiping out of all hostile elements; the destruction of enemy bases, bridges, trains, motor vehicles, etc.; the conduct of mass political work among the population; the arrangement of tangible material assistance to the working people, etc.

The guiding principles of partisan activity must be fulfillment of combat assignments hand in hand with the conduct of political educational work among the population: the partisan must enhance his ideological and political level, maintain close contact with the population and help them in every way, and everywhere and always wage a ruthless struggle against the German invaders.

Fulfillment of this order is to be reported to the Regional Headquarters of the Chernigov Partisan Movement.

Chief of Staff, Regional Headquarters,

Fyodor Orlov

—A. Fyodorov, *The Underground Committee Carries On,* Foreign Languages Publishing House, Moscow, 1952, pp. 15–27, 262–63, 198–200. Fyodorov was secretary of the Chernigov Regional Committee of the Communist Party of the Ukraine in 1941 and became commander of one of the largest partisan units in the Ukraine during the war.

II. EUROPE

Since World War I, Europe has been the scene of many revolutionary armed struggles. Besides those in Ireland, Spain and Austria cited in the Introduction, there should be mentioned the mutinies in the French army in 1917 on the western front and in the French navy on the Black Sea in 1919 during the imperialist intervention against the new Soviet Republic.

The civil war in Spain (1936–1939) produced one of the outstanding examples of readiness for armed struggle when necessary on the part of Communists in Europe (and in the United States): the International Brigades. Communists from many countries who enrolled in the Brigades also participated in the guerrilla units operating behind Franco's lines and later put their experience to good use as members of or in allied liaison teams working with guerrilla resistance movements in World War II.

Space has not permitted inclusion of selections from all guerrilla resistance movements that arose during and after World War II: the following selections have been made for relevance to contemporary questions. Resistance movements existed in every Nazi-occupied country and in the fascist countries themselves. The Yugoslav movement led by Yugoslav Communists developed in classical style from partisan beginnings to regular warfare. In Greece, the ELAS forces were so strong at war's end that only intervention by British troops prevented their establishment of a postwar government. Albanian guerrillas, like those in Yugoslavia, were the foundation of the Albanian socialist state that emerged after the war. In Italy, the partisan forces carried out important operations in Rome and in other cities as well as in the countryside. Czechoslovak guerrillas fought throughout the war and liberated part of their territory before the Soviet Red Army arrived. Guerrilla forces rose to strike at retreating Nazi armies in Poland, Hungary, Bulgaria and Rumania, while Norway, Denmark, the Netherlands and Belgium, as well as France, produced guerrillas that had long and proud fighting records against the fascists. In every case, Communists played a major leading role in their organization.

It will be noted that the article on street fighting by James Connolly, which forecast the tactics in the insurrection in Dublin in 1916, might have been written about the fighting in Saigon, Hué and other cities in South Vietnam conducted by the National Liberation Front.

1

Street Fighting

JAMES CONNOLLY

> *This is one of a series of articles written by the Irish Marxist, James Connolly, in the newspaper* Workers' Republic *during May–July 1915. The articles analyzed insurrections in cities from 1830 to 1905, concluding that the Russian experience in 1905 "succeeded in establishing the fact that even under modern conditions the professional soldier is, in a city, badly handicapped in a fight against really determined civilian revolutionists." Connolly prefaced his articles with the expressed hope that they would "enlighten and instruct our members in the work they are banded together to perform" and urged that they be read "from the standpoint of their value to those who desire to see perfected a Citizen Army able to perform whatever duty may be thrust upon it." The duty was performed in the Easter Rising in 1916.*

In the military sense of the term what after all is a *street?* A street is a defile in a city. A defile is a narrow pass through which troops can only move by narrowing their front, and therefore making themselves a good target for the enemy. A defile is also a difficult place for soldiers to maneuver in, especially if the flanks of the defile are held by the enemy.

A mountain pass is a defile the sides of which are constituted by the natural slopes of the mountain sides, as at the Scalp. A bridge over a river is a defile the sides of which are constituted by the river. A street is a defile the sides of which are constituted by the houses in the street.

To traverse a mountain pass with any degree of safety the sides of the mountain must be cleared by flanking parties ahead of the main body; to pass over a bridge the banks of the river on each side must be raked with gun or rifle fire while the bridge is being rushed; to take a street properly barricaded and held on both sides by forces in the houses, these houses must be broken into and taken by hand-to-hand fighting. A street barricade placed in a position where artillery cannot operate from a distance is impregnable to frontal attack. To bring artillery within a couple of hundred yards—the length of the average street—would mean the loss of the artillery if confronted by even imperfectly drilled troops armed with rifles.

The Moscow revolution, where only 80 rifles were in the possession of the insurgents, would have ended in the annihilation of the artillery had the number of insurgent rifles been 800.

The insurrection of Paris in June 1848 reveals how districts of towns, or villages, should be held. The streets were barricaded at tactical points, *not on the main streets* but commanding them. The houses were broken through so that passages were made inside the houses along the whole length of the streets. The side walls were loopholed, as were also the front walls, the windows were blocked by sandbags, boxes filled with stones and dirt, bricks, chests and other pieces of furniture with all sorts of odds and ends piled up against them.

Behind such defenses the insurgents poured their fire upon the troops through loopholes left for the purpose.

In the attack upon Paris by the allies fighting against Napoleon a village held in this manner repulsed several assaults by the Prussian allies of England. When these Prussians were relieved by the English these latter did not dare attempt a frontal attack, but instead broke into an end house on one side of the village street, and commenced to take the houses one by one. Thus all the fighting was inside the houses, and musket fire played but a small part. On one side of the street they captured all the houses, on the other they failed, and when a truce was declared the English were in possession of one side of the village, and their French enemies of the other.

The truce led to a peace. When peace was finally proclaimed the two sides of the village street were still held by opposing forces.

The defense of a building in a city, town, or village is governed by the same rules. Such a building left unconquered is a serious danger even if its supports are all defeated. If it had been flanked by barricades, and these barricades were destroyed, no troops could afford to push on and leave the building in the hands of the enemy. If they did so they would be running the danger of perhaps meeting a check further on, which check would be disastrous if they had left a hostile building manned by an unconquered force in their rear. Therefore, the fortifying of a strong building, as a pivot upon which the defense of a town or village should hinge, forms a principal object of the preparations of any defending force, whether regular army or insurrectionary.

In the Franco-Prussian War of 1870 the chateau, or castle, of Geissberg formed such a position in the French lines on August 4. The Germans drove in all the supports of the French party occupying this country house, and stormed the outer courts, but were driven back by the fire from the windows and loopholed walls. Four batteries of artillery were brought up to within 900 yards of the house and battered away at its walls, and battalion after battalion was hurled against it. The advance of the whole German army was delayed until this one house was taken. To take it caused a loss of 23 officers and 329 men, yet it had only a garrison of 200.

In the same campaign the village of Bazeilles offered a similar lesson of the tactical strength of a well-defended line of houses. The German army drove the French off the field and entered the village without a struggle. But it took a whole army corps seven hours to fight its way through to the other end of the village.

A mountainous country has always been held to be difficult for military operations owing to its passes or glens. A city is a huge maze of passes or glens formed by streets and lanes. Every difficulty that exists for the operation of regular troops in mountains is multiplied a hundredfold in a city. And the difficulty of the commissariat which is likely to be insuperable to an irregular or popular force taking to the mountains, is solved for them by the sympathies of the populace when they take to the streets.

The general principle to be deducted from a study of the example we have been dealing with is that the defense is of almost overwhelming importance in such warfare as a popular force like the Citizen Army might be called upon to participate in. Not a mere passive defense of a position valueless in itself, but the active defense of a position whose location threatens the supremacy or existence of the enemy. The genius of the commander must find such a position, the skill of his subordinates must prepare and fortify it, the courage of all must defend it. Out of this combination of genius, skill and courage alone can grow the flower of military success.

The Citizen Army and the Irish Volunteers are open for all who wish to qualify for the exercise of these qualities.

—James Connolly, *Revolutionary Warfare* (pamphlet), New Books Publications, Dublin and Belfast, 1968, pp. 32–34.

2

Guerrilla Warfare in Spain, 1939–1951

ENRIQUE LISTER

The people of Spain and the Communist Party have no little experience in both peaceful and non-peaceful revolutionary action. I need not refer to the distant past, rich in fighting experience, to make my point. I shall confine myself to the nine years from December 1930 to April 1939. That brief span witnessed such events as the abortive rising of democratic army officers in December 1930; the victory—won without recourse to armed struggle—which in April 1931 led to the abolition of the military dictatorship, the overthrow of the monarchy, and the establishment of the Republic; the abortive mutiny of reactionary officers in August 1932; the popular revolt in October 1934, and the victory of the Popular Front in February 1936. Then there was the July 1936 revolt of fascists, both military and civilian, which, after nearly three years of civil war and a toll of a million lives, ended in victory for them in 1939, thanks to armed intervention by Mussolini and Hitler.

What I want to write about, however, is not the civil war and its lessons, but the guerrilla war which the people waged against the Franco dictatorship for many years after the civil war.

A powerful guerrilla movement behind Franco's lines became a possibility even before the civil war had ended. It could have been based on the thousands of patriots operating in the mountains in the territory held by Franco's fascists. But the successive Republican governments and their war ministers failed to seize the opportunity.

Guerrilla units came into being spontaneously, and fought in Galicia, Leon, Zamora, Andalusia, Estremadura, Asturias and elsewhere. Their operations, and those of the 14th Guerrilla Corps, formed in the Republican zone, compelled Franco to use tens of thousands of troops to safeguard his communication lines and munition plants.

The period immediately following the defeat of the Republic in 1939 was a period of great hardship for the thousands of antifascists who sought refuge in the mountains. There was no guerrilla warfare proper for some time after the Republican defeat. The guerrillas confined themselves to defense against the Franco bloodhounds and to procuring provisions and clothing.

The Communists strove to guide the struggle of the thousands who had escaped into the mountains. As a result, the guerrilla movement soon regained its combative character. This renewed the people's faith in the return of freedom and greatly helped them to prevent Franco from embroiling Spain in Hitler's war.

Throughout the Second World War, and for a number of years after, the guerrilla units in Asturias-Santander, Galicia-Leon, Andalusia, Catalonia, Levante and Aragon, Estremadura and Castille, fought the government troops and the so-called forces of public order. They raided barracks, supply and communication centers, and military trains. A mere 500 men of the Levante and Aragon formation tied down 40,000 Franco troops in the Valencia, Cuenca, Castellon de la Plana and Teruel provinces.

We Spanish Communists believed that the defeat of Hitler in the war would be followed by the downfall of Franco. This conviction, however, did not mean that our forces became complacent. After the defeat of Hitler, when the United States began to aid and comfort Franco, we continued the fight against his regime. In point of fact we stepped up our effort, hoping to impel the people to revolt.

Between 1945 and 1948 the guerrilla movement reached its peak organizationally, politically and militarily.

During those years our party did everything to support the movement. Besides sending its members, material and funds, the party as a whole was virtually placed at the disposal of the movement inside the country. It called on the workers and peasants to back the guerrillas. It worked hard to coordinate the struggle of the workers, peasants and guerrillas against Franco and to compel him to disperse his forces.

In some areas the guerrillas won the full support of the peasants. But such areas were few and small, which enabled the fascists to blockade them and terrorize the population by killing some and removing others. In this way the guerrillas were deprived of support in those areas.

The party also formed guerrilla groups in the towns, and in some towns they carried out daring operations. However, this form of struggle did not become widespread because of the savage terror which prevailed at the time....

Some day we will be able to tell about the many tons of supplies which over a number of years were delivered to Spain by land and sea, about the courage of the many party members who made their way into Spain over mountain trails often at 20° C below zero, carrying 30 to 35 kilos of arms and equipment on their backs. In some cases the men managed to elude the Franco outposts at the frontier and along their route. At times they had to fight, and many of them fell in the unequal battle. Those gallant men set up hundreds of dumps for guerrilla use. The party made extensive use of radio to propagandize our struggle, transmit coded instructions to guerrilla formations, expose informers and reveal enemy plans to the guerrillas.

To help the guerrillas, the party carried on propaganda work among the Civil Guard and in the Army, particularly among young officers and men. This activity bore good fruit....

Guerrilla units were a vital necessity at the time and they played a tremendous role. But the guerrillas alone could not deliver Spain from Franco. The overthrow of the dictatorship necessitated the participation of the people on a mass scale.

As we fought, it became clear to us that guerrilla units and the party could not by themselves hold their own against the regime. Besides, it was becoming increasingly difficult to supply the guerrillas with arms and other necessities. Surveillance had been tightened and the persecution had become fiercer. From 1944 to 1950 the regime steadily reinforced the troops stationed along the frontier. These troops, holding a zone 60 kilometers deep, were made up of 450,000 regulars plus Civil Guard and police units.

These circumstances impelled us to try and form Resistance Councils with a view, among other things, of broadening the struggle.

But the attempts failed as a result of the defeat sustained by the people in 1939 and because of the terror, which was now intensified. Another factor was the lack of unity among the forces opposing Franco, and the noncommittal attitude taken by most of the leaders of these forces whenever the question of using arms was raised.

In October 1948 the Political Bureau of the Communist Party of Spain and the Executive of the United Socialist Party of Catalonia held a joint meeting with a number of political and guerrilla leaders. The meeting assessed the experience of recent years and the outlook for the future, and decided on a change of tactics. The new tactics provided, in particular, for dissolving the underground trade unions and switching to work in the official trade unions, membership of which was compulsory, abandoning the guerrilla warfare and instructing the more efficiently organized and reliable units to safeguard the party committees in the mountains, whence they guided the activities of the party. The other units were to be disbanded.

It was painful to have to discontinue the guerrilla movement in which so many men and women had fought with supreme courage. The dissolution of the guerrilla movement was necessary also for political reasons. Looking back I would say that perhaps the only thing for which we could be blamed is that we should have done it a couple of years earlier....

I would like now to touch on some principles of guerrilla warfare, which are well known but are not always applied.

A guerrilla war can be waged only under certain conditions and for specific reasons. Let us recall some of these conditions and reasons.

A guerrilla war may break out against an invading army which has overrun part of the national territory. In that case it will supplement the nation's regular army in the just war continued by the army in the battlefield. The peoples of the Soviet Union furnished a splendid example of this during the Second World War.

A guerrilla war may break out against a foreign army which is waging an unjust war, a war of aggression, and which has just defeated the armed forces of the invaded country. In that case remnants of the defeated army, helped by civilians, may resort to guerrilla warfare to prevent the invader from consolidating his positions and to pave the way for the use of higher forms of struggle. This was the case in Spain in 1808, and in France and elsewhere during the last war.

A guerrilla war may continue the struggle of the people defeated by the reactionaries of their own country in a civil war or national revolutionary war, as was the case in Spain in 1939.

A guerrilla war may rouse the people to an armed struggle against the reactionary regime in their country.

To be sure, there are other forms of guerrilla warfare, and new forms will appear as time goes on.

In organizing a guerrilla movement one should never confuse popular sympathy with popular support; these are two different things. In Spain the guerrillas enjoyed the sympathy of the people who regarded them as heroes. But the sympathy did not go beyond that. It never became the active and massive support for the guerrilla operations which was essential and on which the guerrillas had counted.

It may be argued that that was because the people had just emerged from three years of a civil war in which they were defeated, and that when guerrilla warfare develops in more favorable conditions it can meet with much greater support. That, of course, may or may not be the case. Everything depends on the timing. Popular sentiment has changed rapidly in Spain since the time of the guerrilla war, and a new generation has grown up. But in my view, if we were to renew guerrilla war, to call on the people to take up arms, we would not be any more successful than we were in the past.

I cannot say for certain how, ultimately, the Spanish question will be settled. But I feel that a call for armed struggle, for a solution based on the use of force, would be foolhardy, to say the least. Only the vanguard would respond to the call. As to the mass of the people, the main force, they might admire us, and I am sure they would be cast down by our defeat, but as things are today they would not join with us in an armed fight. Furthermore, in the present situation, the self-sacrifice of the vanguard would hardly make a dent in the dictatorship, just as the many years of guerrilla warfare failed to do. On the contrary, it may well be that it would strengthen the dictatorship, since it would unite around Franco all the reactionary and bourgeois elements, some of whom would like to see Franco ousted. True, things may change, and change quickly, and we must be prepared for such a contingency. . . .

Our experience has taught us that a party which is thinking in terms of initiating a guerrilla war should know that guerrilla operations, which are a form of political struggle, cannot be isolated from other forms used by the people. A guerrilla movement cannot exist unless supported by the people. It can grow into a mass movement provided the people take part in it, using the forms suggested by the actual situation and objective conditions in the country, including armed insurrection.

It is important to remember that the guerrilla operations should be in harmony with the sentiment and aspirations of the people. The moment this harmony ceases, we get instead of a guerrilla war, terrorism and acts of vengeance, and these bring little benefit to the revolution.

The guerrilla units have the character of an insurrectionary mass movement against a foreign invader, against internal oppressors in the event of civil war, or of a popular struggle to abolish a tyrannical regime. But in each case, and particularly the latter, the political factor is decisive.

That is as it should be. A guerrilla movement cannot exist and spread unless it is understood and supported by the people, and forms part of the people's fight against a common enemy. We, at any rate, realized that it was not guerrilla units but the people as a whole that could end the Franco regime by rising against it, and we did all in our power to organize such a rising.

One conclusion we drew was that in a country with an average standard of development—to say nothing of a highly developed country—it is hard to wage a protracted guerrilla war without carrying on a mass revolutionary struggle, as well as armed operations, in the towns. In other words, to be successful the armed struggle must be a nation-wide struggle.

The experience of Spain shows that it is difficult simultaneously to carry on an armed fight in the countryside and an extensive struggle in the towns, combining legal and illegal forms, unless there is an acute revolutionary crisis. In a country where the state commands a strong coercive machinery and lines of communication enabling it to deploy and maneuver its forces, it is difficult to fight a guerrilla war for long if a general revolutionary situation is lacking.

There is much talk nowadays to the effect that a revolutionary situation can be developed from a particular "center." In some cases attempts are made to prove this in practice. This claim is refuted by the Marxist-Leninist doctrine of this form of struggle, and is disproved by revolutionary experience. A revolutionary situation cannot be created at will. No "center" or "centers" in themselves create a revolutionary situation.

Guerrilla warfare may serve as a catalyst in creating a revolutionary situation. But it can do so only in definitely favorable conditions, if it is part of other forms of struggle involving the mass of the people.

Lenin always spoke of guerrilla units associated with the struggle of the people as a product of the high intensity of this struggle and not an exclusive means. "The party of the proletariat," he wrote, "can never regard guerrilla warfare as the only, or even the chief, method of struggle . . . this method must be subordinated to other methods . . . must be commensurate with the chief methods of warfare."*

We Spanish Communists have some experience in this matter as well. I have said that guerrilla operations in Spain in the years immediately after the civil war were aimed at defending the people against the fascist marauders, raising the morale of the people and convincing them that the Franco regime would not last forever. This struggle helped to prevent Spain from being embroiled in the war as an ally of Hitler and Mussolini. Afterward we tried to use the guerrilla movement as a means of creating a revolutionary situation. But because the conditions were lacking, things did not turn out as we thought they would, despite dozens of guerrilla "centers" in the country.

Another lesson we have learned—and Spain is no exception—is that one must be able to call off the guerrilla warfare in good time, must "trim one's sails" and tack before it is too late, when it becomes evident that the method chosen is not the best one and may exhaust the revolutionary vanguard. . . .

—"Lessons of the Spanish Guerrilla War (1939–51)," *World Marxist Review*, February 1965, pp. 35–39. Lister was a general in the Spanish Republican Army during the Civil War.

---

* See V. I. Lenin, "Guerilla Warfare," in Part One, above.

3

Specific Features of the Yugoslav Liberation Struggle

JOSIP BROZ TITO

Many people abroad, even certain left-wingers who are friendly to our country, have explained (and still persist in doing so) that not only the heroic people's liberation struggle but also the revolutionary transformation, the exceptional achievements in the creation of the new Yugoslavia, of a new social system, and the attainments in the country's development, are the result of certain fortuitous circumstances, certain coincidences, and so on. The nation-wide people's uprising and the victorious outcome of the people's liberation struggle are senselessly attributed to such factors as the high mountains, the forests, or the national inequalities that existed in pre-war Yugoslavia, and even a certain fatalistic attitude toward life and death, typical of primitive peoples, which our people are supposed to have.

All of these reasons are, of course, inaccurate, senseless and humiliating. Such arguments are an offense to our people, for they aim to portray the uprising in Yugoslavia as an act of unconscious spontaneity, as a desperate step bordering on adventure and suicide, and not as the result of the profound social consciousness and complete awareness of the people of Yugoslavia of the full difficulty of that struggle and the sacrifices they would have to make in it.

Furthermore, such arguments either forget or deliberately overlook the boundless hatred felt by the peoples of Yugoslavia toward the fascist occupiers who invaded the country and enslaved it; they ignore the traditional love of our peoples for liberty and independence for which our ancestors have shed blood and made sacrifices for centuries, giving up what they held dearest when the need arose. They forget, or underestimate, the most important factor which not only made the uprising possible but assured its success, that is, the organized character and proper guidance of the insurrection for which the Communist Party of Yugoslavia deserves the credit. Its members selflessly remained with the people in the most agonizing days in their history, they were the first to take arms in hand and go into combat, to offer heroic examples of loyalty to the people. It is also true that from the very first days of their grueling struggle our peoples were profoundly convinced that the great land of socialism—the Soviet Union—was invincible; they therefore took their place by its side and contributed their share to the fight against the common enemies.

Yugoslavia does not consist of mountains and forests alone. The uprising flared up throughout the whole country, in the plains of Srem as well as in hilly Bosnia, and elsewhere. Our people went into battle because they loved life, loved freedom. Our young people did not go to war and die because they hated life but because they loved life, because they believed in a better and happier life, in a better future. The national inequality, the hatred and intolerance warping prewar Yugoslavia through the fault of its rulers could not be the motive force behind the uprising; on the contrary, these factors were exploited by the invaders the more easily to enslave the peoples of Yugoslavia....

A great deal of perseverance was necessary to convince all nationalities that only a people's liberation struggle, only a struggle against the invaders and domestic, treacherous reactionaries could win national rights and thus create a new Yugoslavia, rid of its former rulers, on entirely new foundations. When all the peoples of Yugoslavia became convinced this policy was correct, as outlined to the masses by the Communist Party of Yugoslavia, the national question, too, became a powerful lever in the liberation struggle....

What were the specific features of the liberation struggle of the peoples of Yugoslavia?

First, owing to the cowardice, incompetence and betrayal of the senior officers, the Yugoslav Army capitulated after a few days of weak resistance; most of the men were herded into prisoner-of-war camps while all the weapons and military equipment fell into the hands of the invaders. Betrayed by the military and government leaders, the people were left without an army, without arms, face to face with the greatest enemy our peoples have ever known, an enemy who came not only to enslave but to exterminate.

Second, the government apparatus disintegrated while the government, headed by the king, fled abroad, leaving the subjugated country to its fate.

Third, left to their own resources, without an army, without weapons, without supply depots, without generals and officers (with a few exceptions)—the peoples of Yugoslavia rose, under the leadership of the Communist Party of Yugoslavia, to do battle against the invaders, wresting weapons from the enemy with their bare hands, and fighting a life and death struggle for freedom and independence.

Fourth, as the armed struggle by the people against the invaders dawned, no coalition with other parties existed, as many of the leaders of these parties had placed themselves at the disposal of the invaders while others had become passive and were waiting to see what would happen. This was the case in all parts of Yugoslavia (except in Slovenia where the Liberation Front had been formed). At the call of the Communist Party, the people went to war regardless of party, national or religious affiliation.

Fifth, as the war proceeded we saw the steeling and development of a new people's army, the nucleus of which consisted of the first partisan detachments, headed by new officers who had sprung up from the people and won their training on the battlefield in ceaseless and bloody fighting to the death.

Sixth, neither the partisan detachments nor the new people's army (the first brigade of which had been formed by December 1941 along the lines of a regular army unit, followed in rapid succession by new brigades, then divisions and then the powerful People's Liberation Army which came into existence by 1942) were engaged in episodic fighting. They fought a permanent war, a grueling war with all the consequences, a war of extermination against the invaders and domestic traitors. It was a nation-wide war, well organized, guided from a center—the Supreme HQ, which combined partisan warfare with frontal combat, depending upon the existence of free territories and the formation of large military units, divisions and corps.

Seventh, regardless of the enemy's immense numerical and technical superiority, and although the liberation war was being fought in all parts of Yugoslavia and the Julian Marsh with much poorer equipment than the enemy's, he nevertheless did not succeed in destroying the people's forces anywhere at any time during the war. On the contrary, these forces usually emerged stronger after heavy fighting.

Eighth, regardless of the extremely arduous and uncompromising struggle which demanded tremendous sacrifices in men and property, the people never wavered, nor did they turn back from the struggle. On the contrary, these great sacrifices in men and material (frequently entire regions, with all the property in them, were laid waste) aroused in the people an even greater determination to endure to the end.

Ninth, the people of Yugoslavia were fighting not only against the invaders but also their allies, the local traitors—the gangs of Pavelic, Nedic, Rupnik and Draza Mihailovic. Despite the fact that the invaders and domestic traitors linked forces, the people prevailed in their great struggle.

Therein lie the specific features of the liberation struggle of the peoples of Yugoslavia, therein lies its greatness. No other occupied country in Europe can boast of such a struggle and our people have the right to be proud of it.

A new type of state emerged in the course of the liberation war. It was a state with an entirely different social system from that of pre-war Yugoslavia, a better and more just system for the broad masses. The Federal People's Republic of Yugoslavia was created, a republic replacing the former incompetent monarchy. It was a state which had solved the national question correctly, a state based on new democratic foundations, with a new social and economic pattern. How was this possible when it is generally known that such a major transformation can usually be achieved only by a revolution, an open struggle against those who hold power against the will of the people?

Therein lies the specific feature of the creation and development of the new Yugoslavia.

The new Yugoslavia was created in the process of the liberation struggle, on the ruins of pre-war Yugoslavia, the state apparatus of which disintegrated as soon as the country was occupied. The frightful tragedy that befell our peoples through occupation and betrayal by the reactionary ruling clique opened the eyes of all patriots. Owing to the treason and cowardice of the former ruling clique, the anti-national policy of the pre-war regimes, the peoples of Yugoslavia came to hate the past and determined never to allow it to return. . . . Simply calling upon the people to struggle against the invaders without giving them to understand that their struggle would lead to something new, something better, that the old would not return, would not have sufficed to impel them into struggle nor would the broad masses have been so directly concerned in it, nor could they endure it to the end, finally to emerge victorious.

Consequently, at the very beginning of the struggle, as early as 1941, we had to shed the previous form of government both in the villages and in the towns, and start creating new organs of power which we called people's liberation committees, the name deriving from their character. The features of these committees make them the most democratic government of a new type. That we had judged the mood of the people correctly was evident when they immediately started creating such committees not only everywhere on liberated territory but also on nonliberated, both in the towns and in the villages.

These were the nuclei of the new state which emerged gradually during the process of the liberation struggle against the invaders and local traitors. There was nothing casual and spontaneous about it; it was thoroughly prepared, deliberated and organized and carried through, not without difficulty, struggle and bloodshed, but rather with much hardship and bloody combat against the local traitors who waged an uncompromising war against the people on the side of the invaders, hoping to frustrate the creation of a new people's state and maintain the old system.

It is this twofold character of the armed struggle—the struggle against the invaders and the struggle against the traitorous domestic reactionaries—that gives the birth of the new state its specific character. . . .

It is evident from the foregoing facts that mobilization of all patriotic forces, persevering expansion and consolidation of the resistance front, is precisely what made it possible to surmount even the greatest difficulties in this war. This holds true of the war and just as much, if not more so, of the peaceful development of our country. . . .

—Josip Broz Tito, *Selected Military Works,* Belgrade, 1966, pp. 204–12. This excerpt is from an article first published in the Yugoslav journal, *Komunist,* No. 1, October 1946. Marshall Tito, now President of Yugoslavia, was Commander-in-Chief of Yugoslavia's People's Liberation Army.

4

The Party and the Liberation Army

JOSIP BROZ TITO

The party in your area [Macedonia] has taken an incorrect attitude toward military formations and the composition of military commands.

The party organization in the army has been so established that all party members in one company form a single cell. That is the party unit in the army: one company—one cell. If there are a large number of party members, the cell may be divided up into groups, by platoons. The cell secretary is simultaneously the deputy political commissar of the company. The secretaries of all company cells in a battalion or detachment comprise the party committee of a battalion or detachment. The secretary of the party committee is also the deputy political commissar of the battalion, or the detachment. He is the head of the party organization and maintains ties with party forums in the field, with the municipal committee and the district committee, both for purposes of party work in the army and party work in the field.

The HQs are military operational leaderships and as such are independent in making decisions on military and tactical assignments, on initiating and directing actions and commanding partisan units. The HQ of a company comprises: the commander, deputy commander, political commissar and deputy political commissar. The HQ is a collective leadership, but the responsibility is borne on behalf of the HQ, as regards commanding and leading troops and actions, by the commander. The HQ of the battalion or detachment comprises: the commander, the deputy commander, the political commissar, and the deputy political commissar. If possible, all members of the HQ should be party members, although the junior commander or commander may be non-members. The competent party forums implement party directives, instructions, suggestions and so on, through the HQ party cell. All members of the HQ who are party members comprise the party unit in the HQ (HQ cell). The deputy political commissar of the battalion, or the detachment, is the secretary of this cell. The company does not have a HQ cell, but rather the party members of the HQ become members of the company cell. The political commissar may not be the secretary of the HQ cell. As army men, HQ members are responsible to their military superiors. But as party members, they are also responsible for their performance to the party which can replace them if they are not suitable. The replacement is carried out through regular channels, through the army command. At cell meetings, party members, in addition to engaging in other kinds of party work, are to take a critical and self-critical attitude toward their activities. The party thus has insight into the work of the army and can keep a check on it; through party members in responsible posts, the party can influence and lead. Through political work and instruction, by explaining the aims and character of the people's liberation struggle and the role of the party, party members wield an educational influence over non-party partisans and prepare them for joining the party.

The political commissar is the party delegate in the Army. Political work and activities among all the partisans in the unit are his responsibility (this includes political, as well as cultural-educational and allied activities), as are concern for the well-being of the men (health and nutrition via the medical and supply services), general supervision of HQ work in the fulfilment of assignments and duties; finally, he is responsible for the fighting efficiency, the morale, the political level and the cohesion of his unit. The party organization helps him carry out large-scale duties, which include conferences (company, battalion), lectures, reports, study groups (theoretical and general education), courses for illiterates, choir practice, amateur theatrical groups, etc. He has political delegates in the platoons (party members); it is also his responsibility, aided by party organizations and all partisans, to develop educational and instructional activities among the population in the area where the detachment in question is located.

The deputy political commissar is the head of the party organization. As members of the HQ, both the political commissar and his deputy must take an interest in and show understanding of military matters and help the HQ along these lines.

You must see to it that the party organization in the detachment, and also party forums in the field, are not transformed into tutors of the HQ. The relationship must be placed on such a basis that the party actually does the leading while at the same time doing nothing to obstruct the independence and initiative of the military command and assuring implementation of party directives; on the other hand, in all matters the military command can count on the firm support and assistance of the party organization as the leading factor in the people's liberation struggle.

Care must be taken to prevent the "army line" (this term has come into general use) from overriding the party line, that is, party members in positions of military or political leadership must not attend exclusively to their official duties to the neglect of their party responsibilities, thereby reducing their relationship with their party organization to the execution of their military duties alone. This would detract from the political significance of the goal we are fighting for and the party would lose its leading role and its influence in the units. It has happened that certain military units, otherwise praiseworthy as such, neglected the political aspect of their activities with the result that the men simply became "militarized," a circumstance which can lead to negative results in certain situations (failure in combat, exhaustion, lack of food, etc., harmful political propaganda by the enemy or the discouraged elements, and so on). The party organization and party members must remain alert and party work must proceed without a break.

By consolidating the party organization, implementing the political line properly, educating and keeping vigil over our cadres, you will, comrades, unquestionably achieve success in short order.

Death to Fascism—Liberty to the People!

—*Ibid.*, pp. 268–71. From a letter written by Marshall Tito on January 16, 1943, to the Macedonia Provincial Committee of the Yugoslav Communist Party.

5

French Partisans in World War II

FERNAND GRENIER

> Many resistance movements against German fascist occupation in World War II operated for the most part in cities and towns, as in the case of the Communist-led French resistance movement. Its organization and activities are illustrated in the following selections from a contemporary pamphlet.

The FTP* are composed of squads, of detachments, and of companies. Their composition into battalions is in progress.

Each squad of the FTP is composed of seven members. At its head is a chief who has two responsible aides: (1) an aide responsible for equipment, in charge of procuring arms, ammunition, explosives and special equipment intended for sabotaging railroad lines, locomotives, freight cars, telegraph lines and electric power generators; and (2) an aide responsible for intelligence work, in charge of compiling the greatest amount of information on certain persons, on their habits and their domiciles, of collecting diagrams of railroad lines, power plants, police headquarters and barracks of police and of special troops. For security, each squad is divided into two groups of three men each. This is an application of the well-known principle of three: no group of three knows the members of any other group, and the one in charge of them does not know who is in charge of the higher echelon.

Three or four squads comprise a detachment. At the head of a detachment is a chief with two aides. In addition, the chief of a detachment is assisted by a staff member who carries out the functions of political instructor and supervisor of propaganda.

* *Francs-Tireurs et Partisans Français* (French Guerrillas and Partisans).

The detachments in a region come under a regional military committee. Whenever three detachments operate in a region and other squads are being formed, the regional military committee proceeds to organize a company. The staff of a company is composed of a captain in command, a political instructor, and a "technician" in charge of information and communication systems, supply dumps and mobilization.

Always the principle of three!

Not until several companies have been organized in a region does the regional military committee set up a battalion staff.

Such is the organization of the FTP. The regional military committees coordinate their activities through interregional military committees. These are responsible, in their turn, to a national military committee.

Attacks and liquidations are carried out by the squads. Seven men are enough to prepare a swiftly executed blow: one or two do the ambushing and the others cover the retreat. Attacks against trains or power stations are usually organized by detachments, for these operations require a large number of persons.

COMMUNIQUE NO. 20 (FTP), JANUARY 8–20, 1943

From the eighth to the 20th of January, the FTP have courageously carried out their struggle against the Hitler bandits and the traitors, also against the communications of the enemy. At Vimy, a train of equipment was derailed: the damage was great. Twenty freight cars and one locomotive of another train were destroyed. A freight car of fish, on its way to Germany, was destroyed, the people in the area seizing the fish.

In Lille, a German recreation center was attacked with a grenade: six killed. In another German establishment, in Bethune Street, there were 15 killed, 20 wounded; a Gestapo agent was killed in Bassée, five *boche* [Germans] in Sailly, three in Avion; a high tension pylon was demolished in Maubeuge. A brothel was grenaded in Caruin: two officers killed. High tension cables supplying the Heudemont factories in Louvroil have been cut: the factory was put out of commission for three days with 600 workers idle (armor plate is made there). A pylon knocked down at Valenciennes has halted work for the time being in several factories. The telephone exchange in Maubeuge-Aunoye has been destroyed.

In Falaise, the underground telephone cables have been cut. Two anti-aircraft guns here have been destroyed. Two warehouses containing the harvest of collaborators, reserved for the *boches,* have been burned. Arms and explosives have been seized. Several freight cars of straw have been burned, four German employment bureaus and two fascist headquarters have been burned in Seine-Inferieure. Three *boche* officers have been laid low. The transformer of the SNAM factory in Melante was burned. In Corbeil, 1,500 cwt. of corn and oats have been destroyed, 1,000 cwt. in Fitz Jeanne, 700 in Frame. Near Creil, a mine was exploded under a locomotive and under a trainload of *boche* equipment, and traffic was interrupted for 12 hours. A road has been damaged between Abbeville and Amiens (out of use for eight hours), a train was derailed, with two cars of German soldiers wiped out.

In Toul, an enemy detachment has been attacked with a grenade; in Homicourt, a mine was exploded under a trainload of equipment; 500 tons of requisitioned corn were dumped in the Meuse River. In Pompey, a pylon was burned, five freight cars and a locomotive were blown into the river: we counted 78 dead, the majority officers.

In Genlis (Côte D'or), a train of merchandise with 17 cars was derailed. A derailment was caused on the line between Châtellerault and Poitiers.

In Châtellerault, a detachment of Germans was attacked, leaving five dead and several wounded on the ground. In Angers, grenades thrown in a bar caused 15 dead and wounded. Wrecked signals halted railroad traffic for six hours. In Saŭmŭr, a distillery working for the *boche* was set on fire: 80,000 liters of alcohol were lost. In Cholet, a forage depot was burned. In Orléans, a bomb was thrown at a detachment of troops. Two Gestapo agents were slain in Bourges; three locomotives were sabotaged in Vierzon. In Bordeaux, the traitor Piquet has been executed. The telephone line of the local headquarters was cut.

In Nantes, two informers have been killed. Arms and ammunition were seized. In Lorient, a special restaurant for the Germans was burned: eight were killed. In Morlaix, the headquarters of the Legion, a hotel and a main building have been attacked. In Brest, in a raid on a German cinema, six *boches* were eliminated. The water tower of the St. Brieuc railroad station was burned. In the same town, a German restaurant was fired: five killed and wounded. Two *boche* restaurants have been grenaded in Lezardrieux. A railroad line has been hit. A steam shovel was destroyed; in the course of patriotic actions in Finistère, Morbihan and Côtes-du-Nord a curfew has had to be declared at 8:00 P.M. In Mans, a bomb was exploded in a German amusement center; six ambulances were needed to evacuate the dead and wounded. Two locomotives were sabotaged and a transformer destroyed.

In Paris, in the Rue Boissy d'Anglas, a *Speisslokal* has been attacked with a grenade; similar establishments have been grenaded in the Avenue de la Bourdonnais, the Rue Lafayette, and the Avenue Pierre 1er de Serbie. On the Rue de Laborde a German garage has been completely burned. Molotov cocktails were thrown into the German quarters on the Rue Coustou (18ème), the Avenue Daumsenil, and the Rue de Maubeuge. The Nazi studios in Billancourt have been burned; also a sawmill working for the Nazis. In Stains, near Versailles-Chantier, a German troop train was attacked.

In Lyon, the traitor Métral has been slain by the patriots. In Roanne, the power station was burned. In Grenoble, a bar frequented by Italians was destroyed by a bomb.

In Marseilles, a grenade was thrown at a group of Nazi officers at the entrance of the Grand Hotel, Boulevard Garibaldi: a captain was killed, a lieutenant-colonel and several other officers were wounded. Two carloads of gasoline were burned, 250 tons of coal tar and 85 freight cars were destroyed. In Nîmes, a gasoline truck was burned. In Saint Girons, a Nazi employment bureau was burned. A German train traveling from Clermont was derailed at St. Germain des Fosses. A locomotive was derailed at Pontmort wrecking 200 meters of track, and a train was derailed in Clermont-Ferrand. In Limoges, the power station and an aviation factory were burned.

In the course of all these operations in which a number of FTP distinguished themselves by their courage and discipline, all of the men got away without losses; we have four patriots wounded, of which one was serious.

—Fernand Grenier, *Francs-Tireurs et Partisans Français* (pamphlet), Cobbett, London, 1943, pp. 14–15, 21–25. Grenier acted for the resistance forces as liaison with the Allied forces.

6

The Greek Resistance Against Nazi Occupation

E. JOANNIDES

... Five days after the entry of the Germans into Salonika,* the district committee of the Communist Party met in secret and decided on armed struggle against the invader. Arms were found and within a few weeks small guerrilla groups began to form in the mountains of Langadas. In September 1941 the guerrillas gave the first blow to the occupationist forces in Kerdyllia in Macedonia.

The struggle against German power was not easy. It was an uphill fight. The Metaxas dictatorship† and the German conquest left a trail of havoc behind them in communications, in men and organizations. But gradually and painfully the different sections of the resistance movement were coming together; arming themselves with weapons taken from the dead enemy, or hidden away by the people, they began to form the nucleus of armed units operating both in the towns and the mountains.

EAM *(Ethniko Apeleftherotiko Metopo)*, National Liberation Front, came into being a few short months after the occupation. At first it comprised members of the Communist, the Agrarian and Socialist parties. All these parties had clean political records. None of them had been associated with any of the pre-war coups or dictatorships. All of them fought against Metaxas. Gradually, by persistent effort and sacrificial work, EAM extended its influence, broadened its organization and undertook the leadership of the struggle. Many other parties and organiza-

---

* The German invasion of Greece began on April 6, 1941, and they entered Salonika on April 9.

† General Metaxas became dictator in 1936, continuing until his death in January 1941, prior to which he prepared the way for Nazi attack.

tions joined its ranks, including a section of Progressive Liberals, the Liberal Youth, the General Unionist Confederation of Labor, the Civil Servants and Railwaymen's Unions, various women's organizations, etc. Every political and economic organization of the people that survived Metaxas and the Germans joined in this noble crusade for freedom. The former great Liberal Party, which incidentally has never been an organized political party, was completely broken up under the blows of the dictatorship. Its leaders, mostly aged persons, did not join with EAM, and at best remained neutral. Many Liberals, however, individually and in groups, joined with EAM. None of the traditional parties took part in the Resistance.

By the beginning of 1942, EAM was a force to be reckoned with. It unified the different guerrilla groups and brought them under one central authority, i.e., ELAS (Greek People's Liberation Army). The country was honeycombed with EAM committees; sabotage in the towns became organized and systematic, and in the mountains the guerrillas carried out planned military operations.

EAM drew up a plan of action calling upon all Greeks to sink their differences and unite against the common enemy. It declared its program:

(a) To liberate Greece from the fascist invaders and to restore full national sovereignty.

(b) To form, after the liberation, a provisional government consisting of truly anti-fascist elements. This government to be pledged to reinstate the people's democratic liberties, to ensure work and food for all, to secure the independence and integrity of Greece, to grant an amnesty to political prisoners, and to organize free elections.

(c) To punish the quislings and war criminals.

(d) The king should not return to Greece until the people could decide upon the question of the monarchy in free plebiscite....

EAM blossomed into full activity during the first hard winter of occupation. A hundred corpses were collected each morning from the streets and households of Athens, victims of the starvation policy of the Germans. The poor suffered most. As far as its power permitted, EAM arranged for the distribution of food and brought supplies secretly from the country for distribution among the peoples of the towns. Occasionally harsh measures had to be taken to make rich peasants and hoarders part with some of their stocks. It also organized the people of Athens and the Piraeus against the black marketeers and compelled the hoarders of food to open up their stores. In its military operations EAM was hampered by the knowledge of the cruel German reprisals taken against the people. Therefore, each attack had to be planned separately and carefully; it had to conform to a general pattern in order to be helpful to the Greek people and the allies, and its risks calculated. It was no longer an individualist war by a dozen scattered groups, but a planned national war. Planned as such, most encounters with the enemy proved successful. From these a welcome supply of arms flowed into EAM's military organization, ELAS.

Violent means of struggle were augmented by passive means of resistance. Every other Greek approached by a German was either deaf, dumb or illiterate. Nobody could understand orders! The methodical Germans were bewildered. On top of these were the strikes. Two strikes, general in character, organized by EAM in Athens and the Piraeus in April and September 1942, compelled the occupation authorities to increase wages and salaries, to pay the workers partly in kind, to set up soup kitchens for the working people and their families, and to declare that in future no foodstuffs would be exported from Greece. When, a few months later, the Germans tried to secure Greek labor for Germany, passive and active resistance was carried to such an extent that the Germans were compelled to modify their tactics. Instead of force they tried persuasion, but with an equal lack of success. Although many thousands were dragged to slavery in Germany, Greece has the honor of having contributed proportionately far less to the German Minotaur than any other conquered country.

—E. Joannides, *Bloody But Unbowed: The Story of the Greek People's Struggle for Freedom*, Hermes Press, London, 1949, pp. 20-23.

7
Lessons of the Greek Civil War

ZIZIS ZOGRAFOS

It has been conclusively proved that the British imperialists and the Greek reactionaries did their utmost to unleash civil war. It is they who have been responsible not only for the bloodshed (according to the official figures published in *Eleftheria* on March 18, 1952, the number of civil war victims was 154,561) but also for turning down the repeated offers of the Provisional Revolutionary Government to terminate the war, as well as the proposals made by the Soviet Union for a durable peace in Greece.

It should be pointed out that while the Right opportunist mistakes committed by the leadership of the Communist Party during the occupation* caused the popular movement to be ideologically, politically and organizationally unprepared to repulse the British armed intervention in December 1944, the Left opportunist mistakes made after December enabled the reactionaries and imperialists to start the civil war, which they saw as the only way to complete what they had started in December, to crush the democratic movement and to consolidate their power.

The Eighth Congress of our party (August 1961) held that the basic mistakes made by the party leadership of that time were the following: first, it incorrectly appraised the postwar situation (1945–46), underestimated the peaceful forms of struggle which could have helped to unite the majority of the people around the working class, and turned to armed struggle when the conditions did not warrant this; second, having decided on armed action, the party leadership prepared for it belatedly, and the enemy took advantage of this. These basic mistakes, as well as a number of others stemming from them and the generally Left

---

* The Nazi German occupation during World War II.

sectarian policy of the party leadership at the time, had disastrous consequences for the democratic movement.

Of the utmost importance in the revolutionary struggle is a correct assessment of the popular sentiment, which, though shaped by the objective conditions and pressures, must be channeled in the desired direction by advancing slogans giving concrete expression to a sound party policy.

Precise assessment of the mood of the masses and their readiness to take revolutionary action is all the more important when it comes to armed struggle, especially protracted partisan warfare.

The leadership of the Communist Party ignored these considerations when the struggle against the offensive of the Greek reactionaries and the imperialists reached the critical stage with the announcement of a general election to be held on March 31, 1946.

What was the situation in the country at that time and what was the mood of the masses?

A revolutionary crisis was maturing, but it had not yet come to a head. The Communist Party had the support of the majority of the working class (witness the trade union elections), around which the peasantry and the urban middle sections were rallying. Our party won these masses by waging the fight for independence, democracy and the peace so deeply desired by the people.

The only correct policy in these circumstances would have been participation in the elections with a view to rallying all the democratic forces around the slogan of "Out with the British fomentors of civil war!" and "For normal democratic life!" and action to avert the civil war. The whole situation called for this policy. If pursued it would have added to the prestige of the Communist Party and the EAM, strengthened their links with the masses, won them stronger positions (this is clear from the response to the party's call to boycott the elections), and opened new opportunities for winning democratic gains by peaceful means. Success for this line was a tangible *possibility* (inasmuch as it was supported by the overwhelming majority of the people, and the balance of forces in the world arena and in the Balkans was favorable). And if the home reactionaries and the British imperialists had persisted in fomenting civil war, the masses themselves would have realized that the only way out was to take to arms.

But at this critical juncture the leadership of the Communist Party, assuming without any justification that the masses who had followed our lead in the struggle for peace would automatically without proper preparation follow us also in armed struggle, decided to boycott the election, opted for armed struggle and, regardless of the fact that the situation was unfavorable, actually embarked upon civil war and thus played into the hands of the British imperialists and the home reactionaries.

Moreover, capitalizing on the inconsistency in the policy of the party leadership at the time, it should be noted that it aimed at carrying the revolution to its socialist stage without going through the anti-imperialist democratic stage. N. Zachariades* wrote subsequently that the Greek Democratic Army "fought *from the very beginning* for the socialist revolution" and that "wherever it was victorious it established the dictatorship of the proletariat."

This erroneous line gave rise to other mistakes, such as, for instance, the new attitude adopted on the Macedonian question, underestimation of our allies in the EAM, and a subjectivist approach to the armed struggle.

The Eighth Party Congress also pointed out that one of the basic mistakes of the party leadership at the time was that, having turned the party toward an armed struggle, it allowed 18 months to go by before any efforts were made to prepare for the struggle.

To begin with, the policy of the party leadership at this time was clearly contradictory and vacillating. Indicative in this respect were the decisions of the national conference held on April 16–17, 1946, which posed before the membership tasks that had nothing to do with the armed struggle, for which the Communist Party had opted two months earlier. The decision of the Seventh Congress (October 1945) dissolving the rural organizations of the party and instructing their members to join the Agrarian Party was now being implemented. This disorganized the party in the rural areas at a time when all its branches should have been strengthened in every way, and when, according to the instructions issued by the leadership, the armed struggle was to be started—and indeed had started—in the countryside.

* At the time, general secretary of the Greek Communist Party.

Secondly, the problem of reserves, which is one of the most important elements of revolutionary strategy, was not correctly solved. As we know, ensuring adequate forces and reserves for any armed struggle requires (1) a correct policy, (2) timely political, ideological and organizational preparation of forces, primarily the forces of the party, and (3) timely and determined action to forestall any attempt by the enemy to deprive the popular movement of its reserves. It is imperative to be ahead of the enemy in mastering reserves and in moving them into action.

The first condition, as can be seen from what has been said, was not met. The decision on armed struggle ran counter to the sentiment of the masses. Even many party functionaries and members did not agree with it. This made it much more difficult to ensure the second condition—the ideological, political and organizational preparation of forces for the armed struggle. For the party decision had to be implemented primarily by its functionaries and members.

"The masses," Lenin said, "must know that they are entering upon an armed, bloody and desperate struggle. Contempt for death must be widespread among them and will insure victory."*

Armed struggle, if only in the form of guerrilla action in the countryside, is sooner or later bound to lead to the banning of the party and all other democratic organizations. Consequently, it is essential to take steps in advance to insure underground party activities. This applies primarily to the urban centers which are under the direct control of the enemy and where practically the entire vanguard force of the revolution—the working class—is to be found.

But these things were not done, with the result that the steps taken by the enemy to isolate the party and the Democratic Army did not meet with resolute resistance.

With the party isolated, only part of its forces, and a small part at that, engaged in the struggle, cut off, moreover, from the other revolutionary forces and from the people generally. This was the result not only of the wrong policy of the party leadership but of the lack of proper preparation.

Third, a wrong approach was taken to the army. Lenin said, "the wavering of the troops, which is inevitable in every truly popular movement, leads to a real *fight for the troops* whenever

---

* V. I. Lenin, "Lessons of the Moscow Uprising," in Part One above.

the revolutionary struggle becomes acute. The Moscow uprising was precisely an example of the desperate, frantic struggle for the troops that takes place between the reaction and the revolution."*

An examination of the situation in the army at the time when the decision on armed struggle was taken and the party leaders' subsequent attitude toward it leaves no doubt that the Leninist principle of struggle to win over the troops in preparing for and waging an armed struggle was ignored.

In 1946, when the Central Committee decided to steer a course toward armed struggle, the situation in the army was favorable for the popular movement. Its numerical strength was no more than 60,000 and democratic sentiment was widespread among the men. Describing the situation in July 1946, General Tsakalotos mentioned that half the men of a brigade of the Second Army Corps in Larissa were under arrest. And this was not an isolated instance; it was characteristic of the entire army. Yet the party turned its attention to preparing for armed struggle 15 months after the Central Committee decision. By this time the army was far from what it had been in 1946 from the standpoint of both organization and personnel, officers as well as men. The reactionaries, using every device from intimidation, torture and the firing squad to "brainwashing," corruption and bribery, had succeeded in changing the situation.

It should also be borne in mind that the party leadership paid little attention to preserving the military cadres of ELAS, in particular the former regular army officers, whose training and skills were essential for building up the Democratic Army and especially for staff work.

Apart from the fact that for a long time there was no military center to direct the armed struggle, the *absence of a strategic plan* should be noted. For some time the local organizations of the party were left to their own devices and, lacking instruction, took haphazard action at their own discretion. The armed detachments which began to be formed in the spring of 1946 were left to decide for themselves whom to take in. In 1947, for instance, many detachments would not accept volunteers who offered to join, but sent them back to the villages where arrest awaited them.

The absence of a strategic plan, combined with all the other negative features, laid its imprint on the organization and direc-

* *Ibid.*

tion of operations, and ruled out a proper study of the enemy, of his possibilities, and the prospects of the struggle.

In the situation that developed in 1946 and 1947 the reactionaries were able to launch an offensive against the popular forces.

With the help of the British imperialists they reorganized their armed forces, set up a state administration and intensified the terror. The Communist Party was outlawed, the EAM disbanded, democratic organizations and 62 democratic newspapers were banned and restrictions were placed on the movements of the urban population.

By the end of 1947 the number of people in prison camps on the islands exceeded 30,000; 20,000 officers and men were held in a concentration camp in Makronisos, and 15,000 people were in jail.

The isolation of the towns, and of the working population, from the Democratic Army, the closing down of the party organizations and the consequent absence of mass actions in the towns, had a strongly negative effect on the armed struggle of the people during the civil war.

The fact that, after the formation of the first armed groups, the leadership of the party remained virtually inactive gave the enemy time to isolate the Democratic Army from the population of the countryside as well. Big tracts of land lay deserted because half a million peasants had been herded into camps set up in the vicinity of the towns. The Democratic Army was thus deprived of its last source of supply and information, its last means of contact with the urban population. The partisans were practically the sole inhabitants of the villages in the deserted mountain areas.

Thus before it had time to build up its strength the Democratic Army was isolated throughout the duration of the struggle. Because of the erroneous policy of the party leadership in boycotting the election, in launching a premature and ill-prepared uprising, and also owing to maneuvers taken by the enemy, the party, too, found itself cut off from the masses.

—"Some Lessons of the Civil War in Greece," *World Marxist Review,* November 1967, pp. 42–45. Zografos was a member of the political bureau of the Communist Party of Greece when this was written. In March 1968 he was expelled from the CPG for rightist factional reasons. This analysis, however, represented the view of the CPG's political bureau when written.

III. CHINA

Selections from the extensive literature on the vast range of Chinese guerrilla experience have been made with the intention of illustrating two features: (1) the stages in its development and in the elaboration of its theory, and (2) the strong emphasis placed on political education in the revolutionary armed forces.

Chinese strategy and tactics in guerrilla warfare evolved slowly out of experience and out of the changing problems that confronted the revolutionary movement at different stages: the Second Revolutionary Civil War or the War of Agrarian Revolution, 1927–37; the Anti-Japanese War, 1937–45, and the Third Revolutionary Civil War, 1945–49, which culminated in the establishment of the present Chinese People's Republic. (The First Revolutionary Civil War, 1924–27, was conducted by traditional means under the Kuomintang-Communist United Front.) The selections in this section, with the exception of the last, are from the years 1928 to 1938, during which a concrete analysis of China's peculiar conditions took place, a full-fledged theory of guerrilla warfare was evolved, and a transition occurred from civil war to a national war against an invader.

In the protracted Chinese Revolution, guerrilla warfare was generally characteristic, although its forms changed. During the long Second Revolutionary Civil War armed struggles took the form of guerrilla warfare, but as the strength of the Red Army grew it was developed to a higher level—mobile warfare with large bodies of troops, waged in guerrilla fashion. But with the beginning of the Anti-Japanese War there was a shift back to the older forms of guerrilla warfare. Again, in the last stage of this war and then especially in the period of the Third Civil War, the main form of armed struggle became regular warfare, finally emerging as large-scale operations with huge field armies able to storm the enemy's strongly-fortified positions.

It is important to compare the precise references to China's conditions on which these earlier stages of theory were based with the very generalized approach and conclusions contained in the selection by Marshal Lin Piao. This is the latest stage of officially defined theory emanating from Mao Tse-tung, seeking to claim for the Chinese experience and the conclusions derived from it a "universality" and an international validity. This selection has been included to illustrate the theory; the editor's view of it is contained in the Introduction.

1

The Military Problem

MAO TSE-TUNG

Since the struggle in the border area* is exclusively military, both the party and the masses have to be placed on a war footing. How to deal with the enemy and how to fight have become the central problems in our daily life. An independent regime must be an armed one. Wherever there are no armed forces, or the armed forces are inadequate, or the tactics for dealing with the enemy are wrong, the enemy will immediately come into occupation. As the struggle is getting fiercer every day, our problems have also become extremely complicated and serious. . . .

As to the composition of the Red Army, one part consists of workers and peasants and the other of *lumpen*-proletarians. It is of course inadvisable to have too large a proportion of *lumpen*-proletarians. But as fighting is going on every day and casualties mounting, it is already no easy matter to get for replacements the *lumpen*-proletarians, who are good fighters. In these circumstances the only thing to do is to intensify political training.

The majority of the Red Army soldiers came from mercenary armies; but once in the Red Army, they change their character. First of all the Red Army has abolished the mercenary system, making the soldiers feel that they are not fighting for somebody else but for themselves and the people. The Red Army has not

* The reference is to the adjoining areas of Hunan and Kiangsi provinces, where an independent Red regime had been established in April 1928.

to this day instituted a system of regular pay, but issues only rice, an allowance for oil, salt, firewood and vegetables, and a little pocket money. Land has been allotted to all Red Army officers and men who are natives of the border area, but it is rather hard to allot land to those from distant areas.

After receiving some political education, the Red Army soldiers have all become class-conscious and aquired a general knowledge about redistributing land, establishing political power, arming the workers and peasants, etc.; and they all know that they are fighting for themselves and for the working class and the peasantry. Hence they can endure the bitter struggle without complaint. Each company, battalion or regiment has its soldiers' council which represents the interests of the soldiers and carries out political and mass work.

Experience has proved that the system of party representatives must not be abolished. As the party branch is organized on the company basis, the party representative at the company level is particularly important. He has to supervise the soldiers' committee in carrying out political training, to direct the work of the mass movement, and to act at the same time as the secretary of the party branch. Facts have proved that the better the company party representative is, the better is the company, while the company commander can hardly play such an effective political role. As the casualties among the lower cadres are heavy, soldiers captured from the enemy a short time ago have often been made platoon or company commanders and some of these captured only last February or March are now [November] battalion commanders....

The average soldier needs six months' or a year's training before he can fight, but our soldiers, though recruited only yesterday, have to fight today with practically no training to speak of. Exceedingly poor in military technique, they fight by courage alone. As a long period for rest and training is impossible, we shall see whether we can find ways to avoid certain battles in order to gain time for training. For the training of lower officers we have formed a training corps of 150 men and intend to make it a permanent institution. We hope that the party center and the two provincial committees will send us more officers from the rank of platoon and company commanders upward.

The Hunan Provincial Committee has asked us to attend to the material life of the soldiers and to make it at least a little better than that of the average worker or peasant. At present the very reverse is the case, for, besides rice, each man gets only five cents a day for cooking oil, salt, firewood and vegetables, and it is hard even to keep this up. The monthly cost of these items alone amounts to more than 10,000 silver dollars, which are obtained exclusively through expropriating the local bullies.* We have now obtained cotton for the winter clothing of the whole army of 5,000 men but are still short of cloth. Cold as the weather is, many of our men are still wearing two suits of clothes of single thickness. Fortunately we are inured to hardships. Furthermore, all alike share the same hardships: everybody from the army commander down to the cook lives on a daily fare worth five cents, apart from grain. In the matter of pocket money, if two dimes are allotted, it is two dimes for everybody; if four dimes are allotted, it is four dimes for everybody.† Thus the soldiers harbor no resentment against anyone.

After each engagement there are a number of wounded soldiers. And a great many officers and men have fallen ill from malnutrition, exposure to cold and other causes. The hospital up in the mountains gives both Chinese and Western treatments, but is short of doctors as well as medicine. At present there are over 800 patients in the hospital. The Hunan Provincial Committee promised to procure medicine for us but so far we have not received any. We still have to ask the party center and the two provincial committees to send us some iodine and a few doctors with Western training.

Apart from the role played by the party, the reason the Red Army can sustain itself without collapse in spite of such a poor standard of material life and incessant engagements, is its practice of democracy. The officers do not beat the men; officers and men receive equal treatment; soldiers enjoy freedom of assembly and speech; cumbersome formalities and ceremonies are done away with; and the account books are open to the inspection of all. The soldiers handle the messing arrangements and, out of the daily five cents for oil, salt, firewood and vegetables, can even save a little sum for pocket money (called "mess savings") of approximately 60 or 70 cash‡ for each person every day. All

---

* This was only a temporary measure; with the growth of the army and the expansion of the territory, taxation became necessary and possible.

† This practice continued for a long time in the Red Army. Later, officers and men received slightly different treatment according to their ranks.

‡ A cash is nominally worth one-thousandth of a silver dollar.

these measures are very satisfactory to the soldiers. The newly captured soldiers in particular feel that our army and the Kuomintang's army are worlds apart. They feel that, though in material life they are worse off in the Red Army than in the White army, spiritually they are liberated. The fact that the same soldier who was not brave in the enemy army yesterday becomes very brave in the Red Army today shows precisely the impact of democracy. The Red Army is like a furnace in which all captured soldiers are melted down and transformed the moment they come over. In China not only the people need democracy but the army needs it, too. The democratic system in an army is an important weapon for destroying the feudal mercenary army.

The party organizations are now divided into four levels: the company branch, the battalion committee, the regimental committee and the army committee. In a company there is the branch, and in a squad, the group. An important reason why the Red Army has been able to undertake such severe struggle without falling apart is that the *party branch is organized on the company basis.* Two years ago our organizations in the Kuomintang army did not have any hold on the soldiers, and even among Yeh T'ing's troops* there was only one party branch in a regiment; this is why they could not stand up to any crucial test. In the Red Army today the ratio of party members to non-party men is approximately one to three, i.e. on the average there is one party member among every four men. Recently we have decided to recruit more party members among the combat soldiers, so as to attain a 50-50 ratio between party members and non-party men. At present the company branches are short of good secretaries and we ask the party center to send us for this purpose a large number of the activists from among those who can no longer stay where they are. . . .

The local armed forces are the Red guards and the workers' and peasants' insurrection corps. The insurrection corps is armed with spears and fowling pieces and organized on a township basis with a contingent in every township, the strength of which is proportional to the township population. Its job is to suppress counter-revolution, to protect the township government and, when the enemy comes, to assist the Red Army and the Red

* Troops which had participated in the Nanchang Uprising, August 1, 1927, against the Kuomintang; the origin of the Red Army is dated from that event.

guards in war. The insurrection corps was started in Yungsin as an underground force; it has come out in the open since we captured the entire county. The organization has now been expanded in other counties of the border area and the name remains unchanged. The arms of the Red guards are mainly five-round rifles but also include some nine-round and single-round ones. There are 140 rifles in Ningkang, 220 in Yungsin, 43 in Lienhwa, 50 in Chaling, 90 in Ling, 130 in Suichwan and 10 in Wanan, making a total of 683. While most of the rifles were supplied by the Red Army, a small number were captured from the enemy by the Red guards themselves. Fighting regularly against the peace preservation corps and the house-to-house militia of the landed gentry, most of the Red guards in the counties are daily increasing their fighting capacity.

Before the Incident of May 21,* there were peasant self-defense corps in all counties. They had 300 rifles in Yu, 300 in Chaling, 60 in Ling, 50 in Suichwan, 80 in Yungsin, 60 in Lienhwa, 60 in Ningyang (Yuan Wen-ts'ai's men) and 60 in the Chingkang mountains (Wang Tso's men), totalling 970. After the Incident, apart from the rifles of Yuan's and Wang's men in which no losses were incurred, only six in Suichwan and one in Lienhwa were saved while all the rest were seized by the landed gentry. Such inability on the part of the peasant self-defense corps to hold on to their rifles is the result of the opportunist line. At present the rifles of the Red guards in the counties are still far from being sufficient and are fewer than those of the landed gentry; the Red Army should continue to help the Red guards with arms. In so far as its own fighting capacity is not reduced the Red Army should do its best to help the people to arm themselves.

We have laid it down that each battalion of the Red Army is to be made up of four companies, with 75 rifles to each company; when these are added to the rifles of the special task company, the machine gun company, the trench mortar company and the headquarters detachments of the three battalions and of the regiment itself, each regiment will have 1,075 rifles. Rifles captured in action should be used as far as possible for arming the local forces. The commanders of the Red guards should be people who have been sent from the counties to the training corps instituted

---

* Beginning of the Chiang Kai-shek counter-revolutionary terror in Changsha, May 21, 1927.

by the Red Army and have finished the course. The Red Army should send fewer and fewer people from distant areas to be captains of local forces. Chu P'ei-teh is also arming his peace preservation corps and house-to-house militia and the landed gentry's armed forces in the counties in the border area are considerable in size and fighting capacity. All the more reason why there must not be a moment's delay in expanding our Red local forces.

The principle for the Red Army is concentration and that for the Red guards, dispersion. In the present period of the temporary stability of the reactionary regime the enemy can mass huge forces to attack the Red Army, and it is disadvantageous for the Red Army to disperse itself. In our experience, the dispersion of forces has almost always led to defeat, while the concentration of forces to fight an enemy whose strength was inferior, equal or slightly superior to ours often led to victory. The area in which the Party Central Committee has instructed us to develop guerrilla warfare is too extensive, covering several thousands of *li** in length and breadth; this is probably due to an over-estimation of our strength. For the Red guards, dispersion is advantageous and at present the Red guards in the counties have all resorted to dispersed operations.

In the propaganda directed to the enemy forces, the most effective means are releasing the captured soldiers and giving medical treatment to their wounded. Whenever soldiers or platoon, company or battalion commanders of the enemy forces are captured, propaganda is immediately carried on among them; they are divided into those who wish to stay and those who wish to leave, and the latter are given traveling expenses and set free. This immediately shatters the enemy's calumny that "the Communist bandits kill everyone on sight." Concerning this measure, Yang Ch'ih-sheng's *Ten Day Review of the Ninth Division* once exclaimed in astonishment: "Deadly indeed." The comfort given by Red Army soldiers to the captured soldiers and the farewell made to them are extremely warm-hearted, and at every "Farewell Party to New Brothers" the captured soldiers make speeches to express in return their heartfelt gratitude. Medical treatment for the enemy wounded is also a very effective means. Recently, in imitation of us, clever persons on the enemy side, *e.g.* Li Wen-pin, kill no prisoners and give medical attention to the wounded ones. Despite this, it has twice happened that at the next engage-

*A *li* is about one third of a mile.

ment some of our men have rejoined us with their arms. In addition, we have done as much written propaganda, *e.g.* slogan painting, as possible. Wherever we go, we write slogans all over the walls. But we are short of people skilled in drawing pictures, and hope that the party center and the two provincial committees will send us a few.

—"The Struggle in the Chingkang Mountains," Mao Tse-tung, *Selected Works*, Vol. 1, International Publishers, 1954, pp. 79–86. Excerpted from a report submitted to the Central Committee of the Chinese Communist Party, November 25, 1928.

2

On the Purely Military Viewpoint

MAO TSE-TUNG

The purely military viewpoint is unusually widespread among a number of comrades in the Red Army. It manifests itself as follows:

1. To regard military work and political work as opposed to each other; to fail to recognize military work as only one of the means for accomplishing political tasks. Even to declare, "When military work is well done, political work will naturally be well done; when military work is not well done, political work cannot be well done either"—this is to go a step farther and to regard military work as leading political work.

2. To regard the task of the Red Army as similar to that of the White army—merely fighting. To ignore the fact that the Chinese Red Army is an armed force for carrying out the political tasks of the revolution. Especially at the present time, certainly the Red Army exists not merely to fight; besides fighting to destroy the enemy's military strength, it should also shoulder such important tasks as agitating the masses, organizing them, arming them, and helping them to set up revolutionary political power, and even establishing organizations of the Communist Party. When the Red Army fights, it fights not merely for the sake of fighting but to agitate the masses, to organize them, to arm them,

and to help them to establish revolutionary political power; apart from such objectives, fighting loses its meaning and the Red Army the reason for its existence.

3. Organizationally, therefore, to subordinate the organs of the Red Army's political work to those of its military work, and to put forward the slogan, "Army HQ deals with the public." If such an idea continues to develop, it may lead to estrangement from the masses, to domination of the government by the army, and to a departure from proletarian leadership—in a word, to the same path of warlordism as that followed by the Kuomintang army.

4. At the same time, in agitational work, to overlook the importance of the agitation teams. In organizing the masses, to overlook the organization of the soldiers' councils in the army and the organization of the local masses of workers and peasants. As a result, both agitational and organizational work are abandoned.

5. To be conceited when a battle is won and to be dejected when it is lost.

6. Group egoism, i.e., to approach everything only in the interests of the Fourth Army without understanding that to arm the local masses is one of the Red Army's important tasks. This is an enlarged form of cliquism.

7. Limited by the immediate environment of the Fourth Army, a small number of comrades think that no other revolutionary forces exist. Hence the extremely deep-rooted idea of conserving its strength by avoiding action. This is a remnant of opportunism.

8. To disregard the subjective and objective conditions, to be seized with revolutionary impetuosity, to hate to take pains over any minor, detailed work among the masses, but to wish only to do big things and to be chock-full of illusions. This is a remnant of adventurism.*

---

* For a brief period after the defeat of the revolution in 1927, following the betrayal by Chiang Kai-shek, a "Left adventurist" tendency arose in the Communist Party. Regarding the Chinese revolution as a "permanent revolution" and the revolutionary situation in China as one of a "permanent upsurge," the adventurists refused to organize an orderly retreat and, adopting the methods of authoritarianism and relying on a small number of party members and a small section of the masses, erroneously attempted to stage throughout the country a series of local uprisings which had no prospects of success. This had subsided by 1928 but some adventurist sentiments remained.

The source of the purely military viewpoint:

1. The low political level. Hence the failure to recognize the role of political leadership in the army or to recognize the fact that the Red Army and the White army are basically different.

2. The ideology of the mercenary troops. As soldiers captured from the enemy in battles are very numerous, such elements, when taken into the Red Army, have brought with them their deep-rooted ideology of the mercenary troops, thereby providing a rank-and-file basis for the purely military viewpoint.

3. From the two preceding causes arises a third, namely, overconfidence in military strength and lack of confidence in the strength of the masses of the people.

4. The party's failure actively to attend to and discuss military work is also a cause for the emergence of the purely military viewpoint among a number of the comrades.

The methods of rectification:

1. To raise the political level in the party by means of education, to eradicate the theoretical roots of the purely military viewpoint, to recognize clearly the basic differences between the Red Army and the White army. At the same time, to eliminate also the remnants of opportunism and adventurism and to break down the group egoism of the Fourth Army.

2. To intensify the political education of both officers and men, especially the education of soldiers captured from the enemy. At the same time, let the local governments select, by all possible means, workers and peasants experienced in struggle to join the Red Army, thus organizationally weakening and even eradicating the root of the purely military viewpoint.

3. To arouse the local party organizations to make criticism of the party organizations in the Red Army, and the organs of mass political power to make criticisms of the Red Army in order to influence the party organizations in the Red Army and officers and men of the Red Army.

4. The party must actively pay attention to military work and hold discussions on it. After being discussed and decided upon by the party, all work is to be carried out through the masses.

5. To draw up rules and regulations which clearly define the tasks of the Red Army, the relationship between the organs for military work and those for political work, the relationship between the Red Army and the masses of the people, and the powers and functions of the soldiers' council and its relationship with the military and political organs.

—"On the Rectification of Incorrect Ideas in the Party," Mao Tse-tung, *Selected Works,* Vol. 1, pp. 106–08. Excerpts from a report written for the Ninth Conference of the party organization of the Fourth Army of the Red Army, December 1929.

3

Characteristics of China's Revolutionary War

MAO TSE-TUNG

1. The Importance of the Subject

People who will not admit, who do not know, or who do not care to know that China's revolutionary war has its own characteristics have treated the war waged by the Red Army against the Kuomintang forces as similar in nature to wars in general or the civil war in the Soviet Union. The experience of the civil war in the Soviet Union directed by Lenin and Stalin has indeed a world-wide significance. All Communist parties, including the Chinese Communist Party, regard this experience and its theoretical summing-up by Lenin and Stalin as their guiding compass. Yet this does not mean that we are to make use of this experience mechanically under our own conditions. China's revolutionary war is distinguished by many characteristics from the civil war in the Soviet Union. Failure to reckon with these characteristics or denial of them is of course erroneous. This point has been fully proved in the ten years of our war.

Our enemy also made similar mistakes. He refused to admit that fighting the Red Army requires strategy and tactics different from those for fighting other forces. Relying on his superiority in various respects, he underestimated us and stuck to his old methods of warfare. This was the case both before and during his fourth campaign of "encirclement and annihilation" in 1933; as a result, he courted a series of defeats. The reactionary Kuomintang general Liu Wei-yuan first—and after him Tai Yo—

suggested a new approach to the Kuomintang army. Their recommendations were eventually accepted by Chiang Kai-shek. This was how Chiang Kai-shek established his Officers Training Corps at Kuling* and acquired the new reactionary military principles† he applied in his fifth campaign of "encirclement and annihilation."‡

But when the enemy modified his military principles to suit the conditions of warfare against the Red Army, there appeared in our own ranks a group of people who returned to the "old way." Advocating a return to conditions of a general nature and refusing to reckon with any special circumstances, they rejected the experience in the history of the Red Army's bloody fights, under-estimated the strength of imperialism and the Kuomintang as well as that of the Kuomintang army, and deliberately ignored the new reactionary principles the enemy had adopted. As a result, all the revolutionary bases were lost except the Shensi-Kansu border area, the Red Army was reduced from 300,000 to a few tens of thousands, the membership of the Chinese Communist Party was reduced from 300,000 to a few tens of thousands, and the party organizations in Kuomintang areas were almost entirely wiped out. In short, we received an extremely great historical punishment. This group of people called themselves Marxist-Leninists, but had actually not learned even an iota of Marxism-Leninism. Lenin said that "the most essential thing in Marxism, the living soul of Marxism," is "the concrete analysis of concrete conditions." These comrades had forgotten exactly this point.

It can thus be seen that failure to understand the characteristics of China's revolutionary war means inability to direct it or lead it to victory.

---

* Set up in July 1933 in Kuling, mountain summer resort in Kiukang, Kiangsi province, to train anti-Communist military cadres, who received fascist political and military training from German, Italian and American instructors.
† The strategy of building blockhouses and making slow but steady advance.
‡ From 1930 to 1934, Chiang Kai-shek launched five large-scale offensives against the Red area centered in Kiangsi; the fifth began in October 1933. A year later the Red Army began its Long March of 8,000 miles, arriving in northern Shensi in October 1935.

2. What Are The Characteristics Of China's Revolutionary War?

What then are the characteristics of China's revolutionary war?

I think there are four.

The first is that China is a vast semi-colonial country which is unevenly developed both politically and economically, and which has gone through the revolution of 1924–27.

This characteristic indicates that it is possible for China's revolutionary war to develop and attain victory. We pointed this out (at the First Party Conference of the Hunan-Kiangsi Border Area, May 20, 1928) when, in late 1927 and early 1928 soon after guerrilla warfare was started in China, some comrades in the Hunan-Kiangsi border area—the Chingkang mountains—raised the question: "How long can the red flag be kept flying?" For this was a most fundamental question; without answering the question whether in China's revolutionary base areas the Chinese Red Army could exist and develop, we would not advance a single step. The Sixth National Congress of the Chinese Communist Party in 1928 again answered the question. Henceforth the Chinese revolutionary movement has been provided with a correct theoretical basis.

Let us now analyse this characteristic.

The unevenness of political and economic development in China—the coexistence of a frail capitalist economy and a preponderant semi-feudal economy; the coexistence of a few modern industrial and commercial cities and the boundless expanses of stagnant rural districts; the coexistence of several millions of industrial workers on the one hand and, on the other, hundreds of millions of peasants and handicraftsmen under the old regime; the coexistence of big warlords controlling the central government and small warlords controlling the provinces; the coexistence of two kinds of reactionary armies, i.e. the so-called Central army under Chiang Kai-shek and the troops of miscellaneous brands under the warlords in the provinces; and the coexistence of a few railway and steamship lines and motor roads on the one hand and, on the other, the vast number of wheelbarrow paths and trails for pedestrians only, many of which are even difficult for them to negotiate.

China is a semi-colonial country—the disunity among the imperialist countries has caused the disunity among the various ruling blocs in China. A semi-colonial state controlled by several countries is different from a colony controlled by a single country.

China is a vast country—"When the east is still dark, the west is lit up; when night falls in the south, the day breaks in the north"; hence one need not worry about whether there is room enough to move around.

China has gone through a great revolution which has provided us with the seeds of the Red Army, the Chinese Communist Party which leads the Red Army, and the masses who have participated in a revolution.

We have said, therefore, that the first characteristic of China's revolutionary war is that China is a vast semi-colonial country which has gone through a revolution and is unevenly developed politically and economically. This characteristic basically determines not only our political strategy and tactics, but also our military strategy and tactics.

The second characteristic is the great strength of the enemy.

What is the situation of the Kuomintang, the enemy of the Red Army? It is a party that has seized political power and has relatively stabilized it. It has gained the support of the principal counter-revolutionary countries in the world. It has remodeled its army, which has thus become different from any other army in Chinese history and on the whole similar to the armies of the modern states in the world; its army is supplied much more abundantly with arms and other equipment than the Red Army, and is greater in numerical strength than any army in Chinese history, even than the standing army of any country in the world. There is a world of difference between the Kuomintang army and the Red Army. The Kuomintang controls the key positions or lifelines in the politics, economy, communications and cultures of China; its political power is nationwide in character.

The Chinese Red Army is confronted with such a powerful enemy. This is the second characteristic of China's revolutionary war. This characteristic inevitably makes the war waged by the Red Army different in many ways from wars in general, from the civil war in the Soviet Union and from the Northern Expedition.*

* Launched from Canton in July 1926, under the Kuomintang-Communist United Front, against the Northern warlords, by mid-1927 the greater part of China proper was in Nationalist hands.

The third characteristic is that the Red Army is weak and small.

The Chinese Red Army was born after the failure of the first great revolution, starting as guerrilla units. It finds itself existing not only in a period of reaction in China but in a period of relative political and economic stability in the reactionary capitalist countries of the world.

Our political power is dispersed and isolated in mountainous or remote regions, and is deprived of any outside help. In economic and cultural conditions the revolutionary base areas are more backward than the Kuomintang areas. The revolutionary bases embrace only rural districts and small towns. They were extremely small in the beginning and have not grown much larger since. Moreover, they are often shifted and the Red Army possesses no really consolidated bases.

The Red Army is small in numbers, its arms are poor, and its access to food, bedding, clothing and other supplies is extremely difficult.

This characteristic presents a sharp contrast to the preceding one. The strategy and tactics of the Red Army are based on this sharp contrast.

The fourth characteristic is the Communist Party's leadership and the agrarian revolution.

This characteristic is the inevitable result of the first one. It gives rise to the following two features. On the one hand, China's revolutionary war, though taking place in a period of reaction in China and throughout the capitalist world, can yet be victorious because it is led by the Communist Party and supported by the peasantry. Because we have secured the support of the peasantry, our base areas, though small, possess great political power and stand firmly opposed to the political power of the Kuomintang which encompasses a vast area; in a military sense this creates colossal difficulties for the attacking Kuomintang troops. The Red Army, though small, has great fighting capacity, because its men under the leadership of the Communist Party have sprung from the agrarian revolution and are fighting for their own interests, and because officers and men are politically united.

On the other hand, our situation contrasts sharply with that of the Kuomintang. Opposed to the agrarian revolution, the Kuomintang is deprived of the support of the peasantry. Despite the great size of its army it cannot arouse the bulk of the soldiers or many of the lower-rank officers, who used to be small producers, to risk their lives voluntarily for its sake. Officers and men are politically disunited and this reduces its fighting capacity.

3. *Our Strategy And Tactics Ensuing From These Characteristics*

A vast semi-colonial country that is unevenly developed politically and economically and that has gone through a great revolution; a powerful enemy; a weak and small Red Army; and the agrarian revolution—these are the four principal characteristics of China's revolutionary war. They determine the guiding line for China's revolutionary war and its strategic and tactical principles. The first and fourth characteristics determine the possibility of the Chinese Red Army growing and defeating its enemy. The second and third characteristics determine the impossibility of the Chinese Red Army growing speedily and defeating its enemy quickly, or in other words, they determine the protracted nature of the war and, if things go wrong, the possibility of the war ending in failure.

These are the two aspects of China's revolutionary war. They exist simultaneously, that is, there are favorable as well as difficult conditions. This is the fundamental law of China's revolutionary war, from which many other laws are derived. The history of ten years of our war has proved the validity of this law. He who has eyes but does not see these laws of a fundamental nature cannot direct China's revolutionary war, cannot lead the Red Army to win victories.

It is quite clear that, in order to determine correctly our strategic direction, it is necessary to solve correctly all problems of principle, as for instance: *against* adventurism during offensive operations, *against* conservatism while on the defensive, and *against* flightism when shifting our forces; *against* guerrillaism in the Red Army, yet *for* its guerrilla character; *against* protracted campaigns and a strategy of quick decision, and *for* a strategy of protracted war and campaigns of quick decision; *against* fixed operational fronts and positional warfare, and *for* fluid operational fronts and mobile warfare; *against* the mere routing of the enemy, and *for* a war of annihilation; *against* the principle of striking with both fists, and *for* the principle of striking with one fist; *against* a large rear area and *for* a small rear area; *against* absolute centralized command and *for* a relatively centralized command; *against* the purely military viewpoint and the idea of roving insurgents, but *for* the view that the Red Army is a propagandist and organizer of the Chinese revolution; *against* banditry and *for* strict political discipline; *against* warlordism and *for* a democratic way of life within limits and authoritative military discipline; *against* an incorrect sectarian cadres policy and *for* a correct cadres policy; *against* isolationism and *for* the winning over of all possible allies; and finally, *against* keeping the Red Army at its old stage and *for* striving to bring it to a new stage.

—"Strategic Problems of China's Revolutionary War," Chapter III, Mao Tse-tung, *Selected Works*, Vol. 1, pp. 192–98. Originally given as lectures at the Red Army College in northern Shensi, December 1936.

4

Base Areas in the Anti-Japanese Guerrilla War

MAO TSE-TUNG

The third strategic problem of anti-Japanese guerrilla war* is the establishment of base areas. It is necessary and important to raise this problem because the war is protracted and ruthless. Since our lost territories cannot be recovered until a nation-wide strategic counter-offensive is launched, the enemy's front will,

---

* The six strategic problems of the anti-Japanese guerrilla war as defined by Mao Tse-tung were these: "(1) on our own initiative, with flexibility and according to plan carry out offensives in a defensive war, battles of quick decision in a protracted war, and exterior line operations within interior line operations; (2) coordinate with regular warfare; (3) establish base areas; (4) undertake strategic defensive and strategic offensive; (5) develop into mobile warfare, and (6) establish correct relationship of command." (*Selected Works*, Vol. II, pp. 122–23.)

prior to that, extend far into the central part of China and cut it lengthwise, and a part or even a greater part of our territories will fall into the hands of the enemy and become his rear. We must spread a guerrilla war all over this vast enemy-occupied area, converting the enemy's rear into his front and forcing him to fight ceaselessly throughout his occupied areas. As long as our strategic counter-offensive is not launched and our lost territories are not recovered, the guerrilla war in the enemy's rear must, beyond any doubt, be firmly kept up—though we cannot yet tell for how long: this is what we mean by the protracted nature of the war. At the same time, in order to safeguard his interests in his occupied areas, the enemy will certainly intensify every day his activities against the guerrillas, and he will certainly begin his relentless suppression of the guerrillas, especially after his strategic offensive has come to a halt. Thus, as the war is at once protracted and ruthless, it is impossible to sustain guerrilla war in the enemy's rear without base areas.

What, then, are the base areas for a guerrilla war? They are the strategic bases on which a guerrilla war relies for carrying out its strategic tasks as well as for achieving the goals of preserving and expanding oneself and annihilating or expelling the enemy. Without such strategic bases there will be nothing to depend on for carrying out all the strategic tasks and fulfilling all the war objectives. Operating without a rear is a characteristic of guerrilla warfare behind the enemy line, for it is detached from the nation's general rear. But guerrilla war could not be maintained and developed for long without base areas, which are indeed its rear.

There have been in history many peasant wars of the roving insurgent type, but they all failed. In the present age of advanced communications and technology, it is more than ever an entirely groundless illusion to attempt to win victory after the fashion of the roving insurgents. However, the idea of roving insurgents still exists among the impoverished peasants, and this idea, when reflected in the minds of leaders of guerrilla warfare, becomes the view that base areas are neither necessary nor important. Therefore, to rid the minds of leaders in the guerrilla war of such an idea is a prerequisite for formulating a definite policy of establishing base areas. The question whether to have or not to have base areas, to value or not to value them, or, in other words, the conflict between the idea of holding base areas and the idea of behaving like roving insurgents, arises in every guerrilla war and, to a certain extent, it has arisen in the anti-Japanese guerrilla war, which is no exception to this general rule. Therefore, it is necessary to wage a struggle against the idea of roving insurgents. Only when the idea of roving insurgents is thoroughly eradicated and the policy of establishing base areas put forward and carried out can a long sustained guerrilla war be facilitated.

The necessity and importance of base areas having now been made clear, the following problems must be understood and solved in the course of actually establishing them: types of base areas, guerrilla areas and base areas, conditions for the establishment of base areas, consolidation and expansion of base areas, and types of encirclement by enemy forces and by our own forces.

1. *Types of Base Areas*

The base areas of the anti-Japanese guerrilla war are mainly of three types: those in the mountains, on the plains, and in the river-lake-estuary regions.

The advantage of setting up base areas in mountain regions is known to all, and the base areas which have been, are being, or will be established in the Changpai, Wutai, Taihang, Tai, Yen and Mao mountains, are all of this kind. All these base areas are places where the anti-Japanese guerrilla war can hold out for the longest time, and are important strongholds in the anti-Japanese war. We must develop guerrilla warfare and set up base areas in all mountain regions behind the enemy lines.

Plains are of course inferior to mountains, but one must not rule out the possibility of developing guerrilla warfare or establishing some sort of base areas on the plains. That guerrilla war can be developed on the plains is proved by the extensive guerrilla war developing on the plains of Hopeh and northern and northwestern Shantung. As to the possibility of establishing on plains base areas that can hold out for a long time, it is not yet confirmed; but the establishment of temporary base areas has been proved possible, and that of base areas for small units or for seasonal use ought to be possible. As on the one hand the enemy has not sufficient troops at his disposal and is pursuing a barbarous policy unprecedented in human history, while on the other hand China possesses a vast territory and a vast population fighting Japan, objective conditions are present for developing guerrilla warfare as well as setting up temporary base areas on the plains; with the addition of a correct command, the establishment of unfixed but long-term base areas for small guerrilla units should naturally be possible.*

Generally speaking, when the enemy has concluded his strategic offensive and entered the stage of holding fast his occupied areas, he will no doubt launch ruthless attacks on all base areas of guerrilla war, and the guerrilla base areas on the plains will naturally bear the brunt. When that happens, the large guerrilla corps operating on the plains will be unable to keep fighting for long in the same places, and must gradually shift to the mountain regions in a way suitable to the circumstances—witness the shift of the guerrillas from the Hopeh plains to the Wutai and Taihang mountains, or from the Shantung plains to the Tai mountains and to the Kiaotung peninsula. But under conditions of a national war, it is not impossible for numerous small guerrilla units to scatter themselves in various counties over the broad plains and adopt a fluid mode of fighting, i.e. to shift their base areas from one place to another. It is definitely possible to conduct a seasonal guerrilla war by taking advantage of the "green curtain" in summer (*kaoliang* fields) and of the frozen rivers in winter. As the enemy has at present no energy to spare on us and will have not much energy to spare on us in the future, it is absolutely necessary, for the present, to decide on a policy of expanding guerrilla warfare on the plains and of establishing temporary base areas; and for the future, a policy of preparing small units for keeping up a guerrilla war, or at least one of a seasonal nature, and of establishing unfixed base areas.

Regarding the objective conditions, the possibility of developing guerrilla warfare and establishing base areas in the river-lake-estuary regions is greater than on the plains, only less so than in the mountain regions. In our history countless battles have been dramatically fought by "pirates" and "water-bandits," and in the Red Army days the guerrilla warfare round the Hung Lake went on for several years; all these prove that it is possible to develop guerrilla warfare and establish base areas in river-lake-estuary regions. However, the anti-Japanese parties and groups and the anti-Japanese masses of people have so far paid

---

* Experience in the Anti-Japanese War proved that it was possible to establish on the plains base areas which can be held for a long time or even permanently.

little attention to this. Although the subjective conditions are not yet present, we should undoubtedly attend to it and proceed with it. As one aspect in the development of a nation-wide guerrilla war, such a war should be properly organized in the Hungtze lake region, north of the Yangtze river, in the Tai lake region south of the Yangtze river, and in all river-lake-estuary regions in the enemy-occupied areas along the Yangtze river and the sea coast, and permanent base areas should be created right in them or close by them. To overlook this aspect is tantamount to facilitating the enemy's transport by water, and constitutes a defect in the strategic planning of the anti-Japanese war, a defect to be remedied in time.

2. *Guerrilla Areas and Base Areas*

In a guerrilla war conducted in the enemy's rear, guerrilla areas are distinguished from guerrilla base areas. Areas which are surrounded by the enemy but whose central parts are not occupied by him or have been recovered from his occupation, like certain counties in the Wutai mountain region (i.e. the Shansi-Chahar-Hopeh border area) and in the Taihang and Tai mountain regions, are ready-made base areas where the guerrilla units can conveniently develop guerrilla warfare. But the situation is different in other sections than in these base areas, like the eastern and northern parts of the Wutai mountain region— certain sections in western Hopeh and southern Chahar and many places east of Paoting and west of Tsangchow—which at the beginning of the guerrilla war the guerrillas could not completely occupy but could only constantly harass and attack, which were recovered by the guerrillas only when they arrived and lost to the puppet regime as soon as they left, and which consequently are not yet guerrilla base areas but only guerrilla areas. Such guerrilla areas will be transformed into base areas when they have gone through the necessary processes in a guerrilla war, that is, when a large number of enemy troops have been annihilated or defeated, the puppet regime destroyed, the activity of the people called forth, popular anti-Japanese organizations formed, the people's armed forces developed, and an anti-Japanese political power established. By the expansion of base areas is meant the addition of these base areas to the original one.

In the guerrilla war in some places, eastern Hopeh for instance, the whole field of operation formed from the beginning a guerrilla area. In eastern Hopeh, where there already existed a long-established puppet regime, people's armed forces that had grown out of local uprisings and guerrillas that had been dispatched from the Wutai mountains, the whole field of operation was a guerrilla area from the beginning. At the outset of their operations, the guerrillas could only select in this area comparatively suitable localities as their temporary rear or temporary base areas. Only when the enemy forces are annihilated and the masses aroused can these guerrilla areas be transformed into relatively stabilized base areas.

To convert a guerrilla area into a base area is therefore a painstaking process of creation, for whether a guerrilla base has been transformed into a base area depends on how far the enemy is annihilated and the masses of the people are aroused.

Many regions will remain guerrilla areas for a long time. In these regions the enemy, though exerting his utmost to maintain his control, cannot set up a stabilized puppet regime, and though we have developed a guerrilla war by every possible means, we cannot succeed in establishing an anti-Japanese political power, as witness the regions along the enemy-controlled railway lines, the environs of big cities and certain districts on the plains.

As the big cities, the railway stations and certain districts on the plains, which the enemy controls with strong forces, are under a relatively stabilized puppet regime and hence in a different situation, guerrilla war can be extended only to their vicinities but not right into them.

As a result of our erroneous leadership or the enemy's strong pressure, the above-mentioned state of affairs may change into its opposite, i.e., a guerrilla base area may change into a guerrilla area, and a guerrilla area may become an area under the relatively stabilized occupation of the enemy. This may occur sometimes and deserves the vigilant attention of the leaders of guerrilla war.

As a result of guerrilla warfare and the struggle between the enemy and ourselves, any of the enemy-occupied territories falls into one of the following three categories: first, anti-Japanese base areas controlled by our guerrilla units and our organs of political power; secondly, areas in the grip of Japanese imperialism and the puppet regime; and thirdly, intermediate zones contested by both sides, i.e., guerrilla areas. The duty of the leaders of guerrilla war is to exert their utmost to expand the territories of the first and third kinds and to reduce the territories of the second kind. This is the strategic task of guerrilla warfare.

3. Conditions For the Establishment of Base Areas

The basic condition for the establishment of base areas is that there should be an anti-Japanese armed force employed to defeat the enemy and to arouse the people into action. So the first problem in establishing base areas is the problem of an armed force. Leaders in guerrilla war must exert their utmost to build up one or several guerrilla units and, in the course of the struggle, develop them gradually into guerrilla corps and eventually into regular units and regular corps. The build-up of an armed force is the most fundamental link in establishing a base area; without an armed force or with one that is not strong enough, nothing can be done. This is the first condition.

The second condition inseparable from the establishment of base areas is that the armed forces should be employed in coordination with the masses of the people to defeat the enemy. All places under enemy control are enemy base areas but not guerrilla base areas, and it is evident that the former cannot be transformed into the latter unless the enemy is defeated. Even in guerrilla-controlled regions, if we do not repulse the enemy's attacks and defeat him, these regions under our control will become enemy-controlled ones, and then the establishment of base areas will also be impossible.

The third condition inseparable from the establishment of base areas is that all power, including the armed forces, should be employed to arouse the people to struggle against Japan. In the course of such struggles we must arm the people, i.e., organize self-defense corps and guerrilla units. In the course of such struggles we must form mass organizations; workers, peasants, youth, women, children, merchants and members of the free professions, according to the degree of their political consciousness and fighting enthusiasm should all be organized into the various indispensable anti-Japanese public bodies which are to expand gradually. If they are unorganized, the masses of the people will not be able to demonstrate their strength in fighting the Japanese. In the course of such struggles we must proceed with the elimination of the forces of collaborators in the open or under cover, a task which we can accomplish only by relying on the strength of the people. It is particularly important to arouse, through such struggles, the masses of the people to establish or consolidate the local organs of anti-Japanese political power. Where the original Chinese organs of political power have not been destroyed by the enemy we must, on the basis of the support of the broad masses, proceed to reform and consolidate them; where the original Chinese organs of political power have been destroyed by the enemy we must, on the basis of the effort of the broad masses, proceed to rebuild them. Such organs of political power must carry out the policy of the Anti-Japanese National United Front and must unite all the forces of the people to fight against our sole enemy, Japanese imperialism with its jackals—the collaborators and reactionaries.

A base area for guerrilla war can be actually established only when the three afore-mentioned basic conditions have been gradually secured, i.e., the build-up of the anti-Japanese armed forces, the defeat of the enemy and the mobilization of the masses of the people.

Furthermore, the geographical and economic conditions should be pointed out. In an earlier section on the types of base areas I have already touched on the question of geographical conditions and pointed out the three different cases; and I shall only mention here the major requirements, i.e., the extensiveness of the area. In places encircled by the enemy on four or three sides, mountain regions naturally offer the best conditions for establishing base areas where we can hold out for a long time; but the main thing is that there must be enough room for the guerrillas to maneuver, namely, an extensive area. With this condition—an extensive area—guerrilla warfare can be developed and sustained even on plains, not to say in river-lake-estuary regions. Owing to the vastness of China's territory and the enemy's insufficiency in armed forces, guerrilla warfare in China is generally provided with this condition. As far as the possibility of guerrilla warfare is concerned, this is an important or even the primary condition; in small countries like Belgium, the possibility is very little or nil, because this condition is lacking. In China, however, this condition is not an objective to be fought for, or a difficulty to be solved but is something provided by nature for us to exploit.

The economic condition, viewed from its natural aspect, presents the same picture as the geographical condition. For now we are not discussing the establishment of base areas in a desert, where no enemy is to be found, but the establishment of base areas in the enemy's rear; wherever the enemy can go, there must have long been Chinese inhabitants as well as an economic basis for making a living, hence in establishing base areas the question of choosing them according to economic conditions simply does not arise. We should exert our utmost to develop guerrilla warfare and establish permanent or temporary base areas in all places where there are both Chinese inhabitants and the enemy, irrespective of the economic condition. But in a political sense the economic condition presents a quite different picture; in this respect there is a problem, namely, the problem of economic policy, which is of vital importance to the establishment of base areas. The economic policy for the guerrilla base areas must be based on the principles of the Anti-Japanese National United Front, i.e., reasonable distribution of the financial burden and protection of commerce; neither the local political power nor the guerrilla units must violate these principles, for otherwise the establishment of base areas and the effort to keep up the guerrilla war will be adversely affected. To distribute the financial burden reasonably means to implement the principle of "those who have money give money"; the peasants, however, are required also to supply, within a certain limit, foodstuffs to the guerrilla units. Protection of commerce will be realized by the guerrilla observance of a strict discipline; the confiscation of any stores, except those owned by confirmed collaborators, is to be strictly prohibited. This is a difficult matter, but it is also a determined policy that must be put into effect.

4. *The Consolidation and Expansion of Base Areas*

In order to confine the enemy invading China to a few strongholds, namely, to big cities and main communication lines, it is absolutely necessary for the guerrillas in various base areas to endeavor to extend the war to all their environs, closing in on all enemy strongholds, threatening the enemy's existence and shaking his morale while expanding the base areas. Conservatism in guerrilla warfare must be opposed. Conservatism, which is either due to love of comfort or to an overestimation of the enemy's strength, can only bring losses to the anti-Japanese war as well as harm to the guerrilla war and its base areas themselves. Furthermore, we should not overlook the consolidation of the base areas, in which the chief task is to arouse and organize the people as well as to train guerrilla units and local armed forces.

Such consolidation is necessary for keeping up the war as well as for expanding it, for without consolidation no vigorous expansion is possible. If we only attend to expansion and forget about consolidation in guerrilla warfare, we cannot withstand the enemy's attacks, and the result is that not only is the territory gained in the course of expansion lost, but the very existence of the base areas is endangered. The correct principle is expansion through consolidation—a good method to attain a position where we can be on the offensive or the defensive as we choose. So long as it is prolonged war, the question of consolidating and expanding the base areas is one that constantly arises for every guerrilla unit. The specific solution of this problem depends, of course, on circumstances. In one period, emphasis may be placed on expansion, i.e., on expanding guerrilla areas and enlarging guerrilla units. In another period, emphasis may be placed on consolidation, i.e., on organizing the people and training the troops. As the tasks of expansion and consolidation are different in nature, military dispositions and the execution of our tasks will differ accordingly; to shift the emphasis from one to the other according to the time and circumstances is the only way to solve the problem properly.

5. *Types of Encirclement By Enemy Forces And By Our Own Forces*

Taking the anti-Japanese war as a whole, we are no doubt in the midst of strategic encirclement by the enemy, because of his strategic offensive and exterior-line operations and our strategic defensive and interior-line operations. This is the first kind of encirclement the enemy imposes on us. Because we have, with numerically preponderant forces, adopted a policy for offensive campaigns and battles and exterior-line operations against the enemy forces which advance on us in several columns from the exterior-line, each of the separately advancing enemy columns will find itself within our encirclement. This is the first kind of encirclement we impose on the enemy. Furthermore, considering the guerrilla base areas in the enemy's rear, each isolated base area is surrounded by the enemy on four sides, like the Wutai mountain regions, or on three sides, like the northwestern region of Shansi. This is the second kind of encirclement the enemy imposes on us. But if we look at the interconnections of the various base areas as well as the interconnections of these guerrilla base areas with the fronts of the regular forces, we shall see that we have in turn surrounded a great number of the enemy units; in Shansi, for instance, we have encircled the Tatung-Puchow railway area on three sides (the east and west flanks and the southern terminus of the railway) and the city of Taiyuan on four sides; similar encirclements can also be found in provinces like Hopeh and Shantung. This is the second kind of encirclement we impose on the enemy. Thus the enemy and ourselves have each imposed two kinds of encirclement on the other, and this is roughly similar to a game of *weich'i*;* campaigns and battles between us and the enemy are comparable to the capture of the other's pieces, and the enemy strongholds and our guerrilla base areas are comparable to the blank spaces secured to forestall encirclement. It is in the matter of securing the blank spaces that the strategic role of the guerrilla base areas behind the enemy lines reveals its great significance. To bring up this problem in the anti-Japanese war is to demand that the nation's military authorities as well as the guerrilla leaders in various areas all put on their agenda the development of guerrilla warfare behind the enemy lines and the establishment of base areas wherever possible, and carry these out as their strategic tasks. If on the international plane we could succeed in forming an anti-Japanese front in the Pacific region, with China as one strategic unit, and with the Soviet Union and perhaps some other countries which may participate in it each also as a strategic unit, we would impose one more kind of encirclement on the enemy than he has imposed on us and, operating on an exterior line in the Pacific region, would be able to encircle and annihilate fascist Japan. To be sure, this is of little practical significance at present, but it does point to a possible future development.

—"Strategic Problems in the Anti-Japanese Guerrilla War," Chapter VI, Mao Tse-tung, *Selected Works*, Vol. II, International Publishers, 1954, pp. 134–45. Written in May 1938.

* An old Chinese game of chess.

5

International Significance of Comrade Mao Tse-tung's Theory of People's War

LIN PIAO

The Chinese revolution is a continuation of the great October Revolution. The road of the October Revolution is the common road for all people's revolutions. The Chinese revolution and the October Revolution have in common the following basic characteristics: (1) Both were led by the working class with a Marxist-Leninist party as its nucleus. (2) Both were based on the worker-peasant alliance. (3) In both cases state power was seized through violent revolution and the dictatorship of the proletariat was established. (4) In both cases the socialist system was built after victory in the revolution. (5) Both were component parts of the proletarian world revolution.

Naturally, the Chinese revolution had its own peculiar characteristics. The October Revolution took place in imperialist Russia, but the Chinese revolution broke out in a semi-colonial and semi-feudal country. The former was a proletarian socialist revolution, while the latter developed into a socialist revolution after the complete victory of the new-democratic revolution. The October Revolution began with armed uprisings in the cities and then spread to the countryside, while the Chinese revolution won nation-wide victory through the encirclement of the cities from the rural area and the final capture of the cities.

Comrade Mao Tse-tung's great merit lies in the fact that he has succeeded in integrating the universal truth of Marxism-Leninism with the concrete practice of the Chinese revolution and has enriched and developed Marxism-Leninism by his masterly generalization and summation of the experience gained during the Chinese people's protracted revolutionary struggle.

Comrade Mao Tse-tung's theory of people's war has been proved by the long practice of the Chinese revolution to be in accord with the objective laws of such wars and to be invincible. It has not only been valid for China, it is a great contribution to the revolutionary struggles of the oppressed nations and peoples throughout the world.

The people's war led by the Chinese Communist Party, comprising the War of Resistance and the Revolutionary Civil Wars, lasted for 22 years. It constitutes the most drawn-out and most complex people's war led by the proletariat in modern history, and it has been the richest in experience.

In the last analysis, the Marxist-Leninist theory of proletarian revolution is the seizure of state power by revolutionary violence, the theory of countering war against the people by people's war. As Marx so aptly put it, "Force is the midwife of every old society pregnant with a new one."

It was on the basis of the lessons derived from the people's wars in China that Comrade Mao Tse-tung, using the simplest and the most vivid language, advanced the famous thesis that "political power grows out of the barrel of a gun."*

He clearly pointed out: "The seizure of power by armed force, the settlement of the issue by war, is the central task and the highest form of revolution. This Marxist-Leninist principle of revolution holds good universally, for China and for all other countries."

War is the product of imperialism and the system of exploitation of man by man. Lenin said that "war is always and everywhere begun by the exploiters themselves, by the ruling and oppressing classes." † So long as imperialism and the system of exploitation of man by man exist, the imperialists and reactionaries will invariably rely on armed force to maintain their reactionary rule and impose war on the oppressed nations and peoples. This is an objective law independent of man's will.

In the world today, all the imperialists headed by the United States and their lackeys, without exception, are strengthening their state machinery, and especially their armed forces. U.S. imperialism, in particular, is carrying out armed aggression and suppression everywhere.

---

* "Problems of War and Strategy," Mao Tse-tung, *Selected Works,* Vol. 2, p. 272.

† "The Revolutionary Army and the Revolutionary Government," V. I. Lenin, *Collected Works,* Vol. 8, Moscow, 1962, p. 565.

What should the oppressed nations and the oppressed peoples do in the face of wars of aggression and armed suppression by the imperialists and their lackeys? Should they submit and remain slaves in perpetuity? Or should they rise in resistance and fight for their liberation?

Comrade Mao Tse-tung answered this question in vivid terms; he said that after long investigation and study the Chinese people discovered that all the imperialists and their lackeys "have swords in their hands and are out to kill. The people have come to understand this and so act after the same fashion."* This is called doing unto them as they do unto us.

In the last analysis, whether one dares to wage a tit-for-tat struggle against armed aggression and suppression by the imperialists and their lackeys, whether one dares to fight a people's war against them, means whether one dares to embark on revolution. This is the most effective touchstone for distinguishing genuine from fake revolutionaries and Marxist-Leninists.

In view of the fact that some people were afflicted with the fear of the imperialists and reactionaries, Comrade Mao Tse-tung put forward his famous thesis that "the imperialists and the reactionaries are paper tigers." He said, "All reactionaries are paper tigers. In appearance, the reactionaries are terrifying, but in reality they are not so powerful. From a long-term point of view, it is not the reactionaries but the people who are really powerful."†

The history of people's war in China and other countries provides conclusive evidence that the growth of the people's revolutionary forces from weak and small beginnings into strong and large forces is a universal law of development of class struggle, a universal law of development of people's war. A people's war inevitably meets with many difficulties, with ups and downs and setbacks in the course of its development, but no force can alter its general trend toward inevitable triumph.

Comrade Mao Tse-tung points out that we must despise the enemy strategically and take full account of him tactically.

To despise the enemy strategically is an elementary requirement for a revolutionary. Without the courage to despise the

---

* "The Situation and Our Policy after the Victory in the War of Resistance against Japan," Mao Tse-tung, *Selected Works,* Vol. 5, New York, 1961, pp. 14–15.

† "Talk with the American Correspondent Anna Louise Strong," Mao Tse-tung, *Selected Works,* Vol. IV, New York, 1961, p. 100.

enemy and without daring to win, it will be simply impossible to make revolution and wage a people's war, let alone to achieve victory.

It is also very important for revolutionaries to take full account of the enemy tactically. It is likewise impossible to win victory in a people's war without taking full account of the enemy tactically, and without examining the concrete conditions, without being prudent and giving great attention to the study of the art of struggle, and without adopting appropriate forms of struggle in the concrete practice of the revolution in each country and with regard to each concrete problem of struggle.

Dialectical and historical materialism teaches us that what is important primarily is not that which at the moment seems to be durable and yet is already beginning to die away, but that which is arising and developing, even though at the given moment it may not appear to be durable, for only that which is arising and developing is invincible.

Why can the apparently weak new-born forces always triumph over the decadent forces which appear so powerful? The reason is that truth is on their side and that the masses are on their side, while the reactionary classes are always divorced from the masses and set themselves against the masses.

This has been borne out by the victory of the Chinese revolution, by the history of all revolutions, the whole history of class struggle and the entire history of mankind.

The imperialists are extremely afraid of Comrade Mao Tsetung's thesis that "imperialism and all reactionaries are paper tigers," and the revisionists are extremely hostile to it. They all oppose and attack this thesis and the philistines follow suit by ridiculing it. But this cannot in the least diminish its importance. The light of truth cannot be dimmed by anybody.

Comrade Mao Tse-tung's theory of people's war solves not only the problem of daring to fight a people's war, but also that of how to wage it.

Comrade Mao Tse-tung is a great statesman and military scientist, proficient at directing war in accordance with its laws. By the line and policies, the strategy and tactics he formulated for the people's war, he led the Chinese people in steering the ship of the people's war past all hidden reefs to the shores of victory in most complicated and difficult conditions.

It must be emphasized that Comrade Mao Tse-tung's theory of the establishment of rural revolutionary base areas and the encirclement of the cities from the countryside is of outstanding and universal practical importance for the present revolutionary struggles of all the oppressed nations and peoples, and particularly for the revolutionary struggles of the oppressed nations and peoples in Asia, Africa and Latin America against imperialism and its lackeys.

Many countries and peoples in Asia, Africa and Latin America are now being subjected to aggression and enslavement on a serious scale by the imperialists headed by the United States and their lackeys. The basic political and economic conditions in many of these countries have many similarities to those that prevailed in old China. As in China, the peasant question is extremely important in these regions. The peasants constitute the main force of the national-democratic revolution against the imperialists and their lackeys. In committing aggression against these countries, the imperialists usually begin by seizing the big cities and the main lines of communication, but they are unable to bring the vast countryside completely under their control. The countryside, and the countryside alone, can provide the broad areas in which the revolutionaries can maneuver freely. The countryside, and the countryside alone, can provide the revolutionary bases from which the revolutionaries can go forward to final victory. Precisely for this reason, Comrade Mao Tsetung's theory of establishing revolutionary base areas in the rural districts and encircling the cities from the countryside is attracting more and more attention among the people in these regions.

Taking the entire globe, if North America and Western Europe can be called "the cities of the world," then Asia, Africa and Latin America constitute "the rural areas of the world." Since World War II, the proletarian revolutionary movement has for various reasons been temporarily held back in the North American and West European capitalist countries, while the people's revolutionary movement in Asia, Africa and Latin America has been growing vigorously. In a sense, the contemporary world revolution also presents a picture of the encirclement of the cities by the rural areas. In the final analysis, the whole cause of world revolution hinges on the revolutionary struggles of the Asian, African and Latin American peoples who make up the overwhelming majority of the world's population. The socialist countries should regard it as their international duty to support the people's revolutionary struggles in Asia, Africa and Latin America.

The October Revolution opened up a new era in the revolution of the oppressed nations. The victory of the October Revolution built a bridge between the socialist revolution of the proletariat of the West and the national-democratic revolution of the colonial and semi-colonial countries of the East. The Chinese revolution has successfully solved the problem of how to link up the national-democratic with the socialist revolution in the colonial and semi-colonial countries.

Comrade Mao Tse-tung has pointed out that, in the epoch since the October Revolution, anti-imperialist revolution in any colonial or semi-colonial country is no longer part of the old bourgeois, or capitalist world revolution, but is part of the new world revolution, the proletarian socialist revolution.

Comrade Mao Tse-tung has formulated a complete theory of the new-democratic revolution. He indicated that this revolution, which is different from all others, can only be, nay, must be, a revolution against imperialism, feudalism and bureaucrat-capitalism waged by the broad masses of the people under the leadership of the proletariat.

This means that the revolution can only be, nay, must be, led by the proletariat and the genuinely revolutionary party armed with Marxism-Leninism, and by no other class or party.

This means that the revolution embraces in its ranks not only the workers, peasants and the urban petty bourgeoisie, but also the national bourgeoisie and other patriotic and anti-imperialist elements.

This means, finally, that the revolution is directed against imperialism, feudalism and bureaucrat-capitalism.

The new-democratic revolution leads to socialism, and not to capitalism.

>—"Long Live the Victory of People's War," *People's Daily*, Peking, August 1966. Marshal Lin Piao is now commander of China's armed forces.

IV. SOUTHEAST ASIA

Guerrilla liberation movements in Southeast Asia have had a long history. From the 16th century every colonial power that seized territory in the region met with resistance that took a guerrilla form—the Dutch in the East Indies, the British in the Malay states and in Burma, the French in Indochina, the Spaniards and the Americans in the Philippines.

The theory that there is an "Asian model" of contemporary guerrilla liberation struggles (it is assumed to be patterned on the Chinese experience) breaks down with a close examination of each struggle. This has been pointed out in the Introduction, but it needs to be stressed further that liberation movements in the region have been variegated, each with its own historical roots, deriving from the peculiar nature of the colonial system in each colony, and each pursuing its own course of development.

In Malaya, racial and social divisions, traceable to British policies of decentralized feudal sultanate rule that stifled nationalism and of imported Chinese and Indian labor and commercial strata, created difficulties for the Communist-led Malayan People's Liberation Army that did not occur elsewhere in Southeast Asia.

In the East Indies, a greater degree of centralized colonial administration by the Dutch, in which a minimum of representative government was allowed and in which sufficient Indonesian technical and professional personnel was trained and employed to inspire a bourgeois nationalist force, influenced the development of an Indonesian liberation movement that was largely (including its armed forces) under bourgeois nationalist control, with the Communists in a subordinate role, a situation quite different from that in neighboring countries.

Extremely restrictive French colonial policy in Indochina of prohibiting any representative government or nationalist political activity of either a bourgeois or a proletarian character led to the very broad Vietnamese national liberation movement in which Communist leadership soon came to the fore, with developed bourgeois political elements lacking.

In contrast, American colonial policy in the Philippines, coming after a very restrictive Spanish rule, had permitted extensive bourgeois political activity and representative government by Filipinos that established strong colonial ruling class influences, which made it difficult for the Huk national liberation movement to advance beyond its essentially proletarian character. (Filipino contemporary guerrilla movements, incidentally, have drawn their inspiration far more from their own historical background, such as the revolutionary Katipunan movement at the end of the 19th century and the guerrilla-style large-scale Filipino war of resistance to American conquest that went on for nearly a decade from 1899, than from other Asian sources.)

From the time of World War II three successive stages of liberation struggles have had their impact on these varied national situations. The first of these was resistance to Japanese wartime occupation, which dislocated established colonial rules and imposed its harsher form. Each wartime guerrilla movement that arose in the region in reaction to this followed the pattern of its own national conditions.

A second stage occurred in the immediate postwar period when the displaced colonial powers returned to reoccupy their colonies and to suppress nationalist aspirations for independence that had been augmented by the struggle against Japanese fascism. In Vietnam (Indochina) and in Indonesia independent republics had been proclaimed in 1945, and the French and Dutch imperialists, despite years of suppressive warfare, were unable to regain control, the Indonesians winning independence under bourgeois nationalist leadership in 1949, the Vietnamese partially freeing their country under Communist leadership in 1954. In the Philippines and Malaya, on the other hand, the narrower scope of the liberation struggles, combined with the imperialist use of colonial class allies, enabled American and British imperialism to restore their control.

A third stage of liberation struggles followed 1954, when American imperialism began efforts to dominate Southeast Asia and to reverse postwar liberation victories in Vietnam and in Indonesia. The third stage of the Vietnamese guerrilla war for liberation has been the main feature of this period, but American military policies, military presence and expansion in the region have also been the direct cause of the spread of guerrilla movements in Laos and Thailand, and of a revival of guerrilla action in the Philippines.

The inadvisability of referring to an "Asian model" of guerrilla warfare to fit any of these stages is perhaps best indicated by the nature of the guerrilla forces in Indonesia during the two independence wars against the Dutch, in 1946–47 and in 1948–49. During these struggles groups with Communist leadership fought in Java, but the other guerrilla forces were under the direction of the bourgeois republic's chief of staff, General Abdul Haris Nasution, a Dutch-trained army officer who prevented the influence of any political party or of political ideas (except "patriotism") among guerrillas, who were kept under the control of his regular army. In his book *Fundamentals of Guerrilla Warfare* [Praeger, 1965], (which imperialists have made use of more for its anti-guerrilla principles), Nasution places in charge of recruitment and guidance of guerrillas at village level the traditional landlord headman, the *lurah,* who had been utilized by the Dutch in their local control apparatus. After independence, Nasution converted these forces, still under the *lurah,* into anti-guerrilla internal security elements. This has undoubtedly been one of the factors that Indonesian Communists have confronted in developing armed resistance to the counter-revolution that began in October 1965.

The following selections illustrate stages of the guerrilla struggles in Vietnam and in the Philippines, and aspects of the Indonesian liberation struggle. Original material assessing the complicated guerrilla warfare in Burma was not available. A number of other guerrilla movements of an anti-imperialist or anti-feudal character also sprang up in southern or southeast Asia in the post-World War II period, among them the extensive guerrilla struggle in the Telengana district in Bengal, India, in 1948–1952, the revolt in Brunei (northern Borneo or Kalimantan) in 1962, and the guerrilla resistance in Sarawak against the creation of Malaysia in 1963.

1

Instruction to Establish the Vietnam Propaganda Unit for National Liberation

HO CHI MINH

1. The Vietnam Propaganda Unit for National Liberation* shows by its name that greater importance should be attached to the political side than to the military side. It is a propaganda unit. To act successfully in the military field, the main principle is concentration of forces; therefore, in accordance with the new instructions of the Organization [Communist Party of Indochina], the most resolute and energetic officers and men will be picked out of the ranks of the guerrilla units in the provinces of Cao Bang, Bac Can and Lang Son and a great amount of weapons will be concentrated to establish our main force.

Because ours is national resistance by the whole people, we must mobilize and arm the whole people; therefore, when concentrating our forces to set up the first unit, we must maintain the local armed forces, coordinating their operations and assist each other in all aspects. On its part, the main unit has the duty to guide the cadres of the local armed units, assist them in drilling, and supply them with weapons if possible, thus helping these units to grow unceasingly.

2. With regard to the local armed units, we will gather their cadres for training, send trained cadres to various localities to exchange experience, maintain liaison, and coordinate military operations.

---

* This unit was set up on December 27, 1944, comprising 34 men and officers with but a few rudimentary weapons, under the command of Vo Nguyen Giap. It is considered the origin of the present Vietnam People's Army. For background see the following excerpt from Vo Nguyen Giap.

3. Concerning tactics, we will apply guerrilla warfare, which consists in being secret, rapid, active, now in the East, now in the West, arriving unexpectedly and leaving unnoticed.

The Vietnam Propaganda Unit for National Liberation is the first-born unit. It is hoped that other units will soon come into being.

At first its size is small; however, its prospect is brilliant. It is the embryo of the Liberation Army and can move from North to South, throughout Vietnam.

—Ho Chi Minh, *Selected Works*, Foreign Languages Publishing House, Hanoi, 1961, Vol. II, pp. 155–56.

2

The General Insurrection of August 1945

VO NGUYEN GIAP

As early as 1941, the eighth session of the Central Committee [Communist Party of Indochina] took care to set out clearly what the conditions should be when people could be led to carry out the insurrection:

"The revolution in Indochina must be ended with an armed uprising; in order to wage an armed insurrection, conditions must be as follows:

"The National Salvation Front is already unified all over the country;

"The masses can no longer live under the French-Japanese yoke, and are ready to sacrifice themselves in launching the insurrection;

"The ruling circles in Indochina are driven to an economic, political and military crisis;

"The objective conditions are favorable to the uprising such as the Chinese army's great triumph over the Japanese army, the outbreak of the French or Japanese revolution, the total victory of the democratic camp in the Pacific and in the Soviet Union, the revolutionary fermentation in the French and Japanese colonies, and particularly the landing of Chinese or British-American armies in Indochina."

The instructions on *Preparation for the Insurrection,* issued by the Viet Minh* Central Committee in May 1944, also pointed out clearly the moment the people should rise up:

"1. The enemy's ranks at that moment are divided and dismayed in the extreme.

"2. The organizations for national salvation and the revolutionaries are resolved to rise up and kill the enemy.

"3. Broad masses whole-heartedly support the uprising and determinedly help the vanguard.

"If we launch the insurrection at the right time, our revolution for national liberation will certainly triumph. We must always be on the alert to feel the pulse of the movement and know the mood of the masses, estimate clearly the world situation and the situation in each period in order to seize the right opportunity and lead the masses of people to rise up in time."

The shifting from political struggle to armed struggle was a very great change that required a long period of preparation. If insurrection is said to be an art, the main content of this art is to know how to give to the struggle forms appropriate to the political situation at each stage, how to maintain the correct relation between the forms of political struggle and those of armed struggle in each period. At the beginning, the political struggle was the main task, the armed struggle a secondary one. Gradually, both the political struggle and armed struggle became equally important. Later, we went forward to the stage when the armed struggle occupied the key role. But even in this period, we had to define clearly when it occupied the key role within only a certain region and when throughout the nation. We had to base ourselves on the guiding principle with regard to forms of struggle to clearly lay down the guiding principles for our work and for the forms of organization. In the then situation, the struggle between the enemy and us was extremely hard and fierce. If guidance in struggle and organization was not precise, that is to say, did not correctly follow the guiding principle of both determination and carefulness, and of knowing how to estimate the subjective conditions and compare the revolutionary forces with the counter-revolutionary forces, we would certainly have met with difficulty and failure. The correct leadership in

---

* Revolutionary Front for the Independence of Vietnam.

the preparation for armed insurrection had to secure steady and timely development of the revolutionary forces until the time for launching the insurrection was ripe.

It was clearly pointed out at the eighth session of the Central Committee:

"To prepare forces for an insurrection our party has to:

"1. Develop and consolidate the organizations for national salvation.

"2. Expand the organizations to the cities, enterprises, mines and plantations.

"3. Expand the organizations to the provinces where the revolutionary movement is still weak and to minority areas.

"4. Steel the party members' spirit of determination and sacrifice.

"5. Steel the party members so that they may have capacity and experience to enable them to lead and cope with the situation.

"6. Form small guerrilla groups and soldiers' organizations. . . ."

When speaking of insurrection, V.I. Lenin stressed that "uprising must rely upon the high tide of the revolutionary movement of the masses," and "not upon a conspiracy." To speak of preparations for armed insurrection and of insurrection does not mean that we will pay no more attention to the political movement of the masses; on the contrary, insurrection could not be victorious without a deep and wide political movement waged by the revolutionary masses. Therefore, to make good preparations for armed insurrection, the most essential and important task was to make propaganda among the masses and organize them, to "develop and consolidate the organizations for national salvation." Only on the basis of strong political organizations could semi-armed organizations be set up firmly, guerrilla groups and guerrilla units organized which have close connection with the revolutionary masses, eventually to further their activities and development.

In the early years, as the political movement of the masses was not strong enough and the enemy's forces still stable, the political mobilization among the masses had all the more to be considered as the main task for the preparation of armed insurrection. The propaganda and organization of the masses carried out everywhere in the country, particularly at the key points, was of decisive importance. Viet Bac mountain regions were soon chosen by the Party Central Committee as the armed bases, the two central areas being Bac Son-Vu Nhai and Cao Bang. In the then prevailing conditions, the armed bases had to be held secret, had to be localities where the revolutionary movement was firm and the mass organizations strong; on the basis of the political organizations of the masses, self-defense groups and fighting self-defense groups* were set up which swelled afterwards to local armed groups, or armed platoons freed or partially freed from production, and eventually to bigger guerrilla units. Underground operating cadres' teams, underground militarized teams, armed shock teams and local armed groups and platoons gradually appeared. The most appropriate guiding principle for activities was *armed propaganda;† political activities were more important than military activities, and fighting less important than propaganda.* Armed activity was used to safeguard, consolidate and develop the political bases.

Once the political bases were consolidated and developed, we proceeded one step further to the consolidation and development of the semi-armed and armed forces. These had to be in strict secrecy with central points for propaganda activity or for dealing with traitors. Their military attacks were strictly secret and carried out with rapidity. Their movements had to be phantom-like. A position of legal struggle was maintained for the broad masses. The setting up of revolutionary power was not then opportune. There were regions in which the masses as a whole took part in organizations of national salvation, and the village Viet Minh Committees, as a matter of course, had full prestige among the masses as an underground organization of the revolutionary power. But even in these localities, we had not to attempt to overthrow the enemy, but try to win over and make use of him. It was in keeping with that direction that the Party Central Committee gave instructions to the armed units for national salvation at Bac Son-Vu Nhai. It was in line with that direction that President Ho Chi Minh pointed out the guiding principle of armed propaganda for the armed organizations at Cao Bang-Bac Can, chiefly when giving orders for the setting up of the Vietnam Liberation Armed Propaganda Unit. Experience has proved that in the first period of the preparation for armed insurrection, if

---

* Self-defense forces ensure public security and order in the villages and take part in the fighting in the last extremity only. Fighting self-defense forces have the task of fighting the enemy as soon as he arrives at the village.

† Propaganda carried out by armed units.

the above-mentioned guiding principles were not thoroughly understood, the revolutionary movement would often meet with temporary difficulties and losses, thus affecting the preparations for armed insurrection. . . .

The August General Insurrection was a great victory* for our people and our party. This was a successful uprising of a colonial and semi-feudal country, under the leadership of the Communist Party. Through a long political struggle, it developed into a regional armed struggle in the pre-insurrectionary period. In the end, seizing the right opportunity, when the enemy was in utter crisis, and making use mainly of the masses' political forces with the support of the armed and semi-armed forces, we heroically rose in the cities and the countryside, smashed the rule of the imperialists and feudalists and set up people's democratic power. The success of the August General Insurrection proves that the liberation movement of the oppressed nations, in given historical conditions, can be victorious through insurrection.

—Vo Nguyen Giap, *People's War, People's Army*, Foreign Languages Publishing House, Hanoi, pp. 76–87. The text of this section of General Giap's work has been rearranged somewhat for condensation.

3

The Resistance War Against French Imperialism

VO NGUYEN GIAP

As at the beginning of World War II, the policy advanced by the party was to prepare for armed uprising to liberate our country. In the years 1945–46, immediately after the establishment of the democratic republican regime, the party put forward the policy of uniting the entire people resolutely to wage

* The August Revolution liquidated colonial rule and established the Democratic Republic of Vietnam, with Ho Chi Minh as President.

the Resistance War to safeguard the achievements of the August Revolution and newly-recovered independence.

Following the success of the Revolution, the party clearly realized the danger of aggression from the French colonialists. Even in the Declaration of Independence and in the Oath of Independence, the party called for a heightening of vigilance, and mobilized the people to be prepared to defend the fatherland.

The French colonialists' aggressive war broke out in Saigon when people's power had not yet been consolidated and great difficulties in all fields lay ahead of us. Never had our country borne the yoke of so many foreign armies. The Japanese had capitulated but were still in possession of their arms. The Chiang Kai-shek army which landed in the North, did its best to assist the Vietnam Quoc Dan Dang [Vietnamese Kuomintang] to overthrow the people's power. In the South, British forces occupied the country up to the 16th parallel and tried to help the French colonialists expand their aggressive war.

Our party led the people in Nam Bo* to wage a resistance war against the French colonialists. To spearhead all the forces at the principal enemy, the party carried out the line of winning more friends and creating less enemies, endeavored to widen the national united front, founded the Vietnam National United Front (called Lien Viet, for short), united all forces which could be united, neutralized all those which could be neutralized, and differentiated between forces which could be differentiated. At the same time, it consolidated power, developed and consolidated the armed forces, elected the National Assembly and formed the government of coalition for the Resistance.

In its foreign policy, our party tried by every means to realize a cordial policy with the Chiang Kai-shek army and avoid all conflicts. Dealing with the main enemy, the French aggressive colonialists, on the one hand, our party led the people and army in Nam Bo resolutely to resist their aggressive army, mobilized the entire people throughout the country to do their best in supporting the South, sent troops there and at the same time actively prepared for resistance in case the war spread. On the

---

* The lower part of South Vietnam, formerly known as Cochin-China. The other two zones of Vietnam are Trung Bo, formerly Annam (now divided by the demarcation line at the 17th parallel), and Bac Bo, the former Tonkin in the upper part of North Vietnam.

other hand, it did not miss any opportunity to take advantage of the contradictions between the French and Chiang Kai-shek forces and to negotiate with the French government to secure a detente and preserve peace.

The signing of the Preliminary Convention on March 6, 1946, between the French and our forces was the result of this correct policy and strategy. Due to the concession granted by us, part of the French army could land at certain localities in north Vietnam to relieve the Chiang troops. On the French government's side, it recognized that the Democratic Republic of Vietnam was a free country within the framework of the French Union, having its own government, army, parliament, finance, etc. Thus, we succeeded in driving 200,000 Chiang Kai-shek troops out of our country. Following this, the counter-revolutionary army of the Vietnam Quoc Dan Dang, which still occupied five provinces along the frontier and the midland of north Vietnam, was also annihilated. The democratic republican regime grew stronger.

With the Preliminary Convention, we had carried out the policy of "making peace to go forward." Immediately after the signing of the Convention, there was a time when illusions of peace partly influenced our vigilance toward the colonialists' reactionary schemes. But in general, the party kept on making efforts to consolidate peace, while increasing our forces, ready to cope with all the enemy's plots. On the one hand, it adhered to the Convention which had been signed, on the other hand, it resolutely carried out a self-defense struggle against all enemy acts sabotaging this Convention. The French colonialists' schemes were revealed with every passing day. The more concessions we made, the further they trespassed. They openly tore up the Convention they had signed, carried on mopping-up operations in the provisionally occupied areas in the South, indulged in provocative acts, step by step encroached upon our rights in numerous localities, including Haiphong and Hanoi Capital. They did their utmost to occupy our country. Therefore, realizing that possibilities for maintaining peace no longer existed, the party called on the entire people to wage the Resistance War.

Realities clearly showed the people that our party and government had done their utmost to maintain the policy of peace, but the French colonialists were determined to invade our country once more. It was obvious that there was no other way for our nation but to take up arms resolutely to safeguard the fatherland. Practical deeds had clearly shown to the French people and peace-loving peoples all over the world that we wished to live in peace, but the French colonialists determinedly provoked war. That is why our People's War of Resistance won even greater sympathy and support from the broad masses in France and the world over.

Our party's policy of resistance was a precise one, in conformity with the masses' requirements, whose wrath toward the aggressors had reached a climax. For this very reason, in response to President Ho's appeal for carrying out a resistance war, our army and people did not shun hardships and sacrifices. Like one man, they were determined to wage the War of Resistance to final victory and annihilate the aggressors.

The Resistance War waged by our people was the continuation of the national democratic revolution by armed struggle. Therefore, to hold firm the line of national democratic revolution in leading the Resistance War was a nodal, decisive question.

Vietnam was originally a colonial and semi-feudal country. Our society underwent great changes as a result of the August Revolution. Imperialist rule had been overthrown. The power of the king and mandarins, the imperialists' stooges representing the most reactionary section of the feudal landlord class, had been overthrown. However, this class still existed in our society and the land question was only partly solved.

French colonial troops rekindled the aggressive war. The basic contradiction between our people and imperialism reappeared in the most acute form. Who was the aggressive enemy? Obviously the French imperialists. At the beginning, owing to the fact that there were progressive elements in the French government and due to tactical necessity, we named as our enemy French reactionary colonialists. But later, especially from 1947 on, the French government definitely became reactionary, the aggressors were unmistakeably the French imperialists who were the enemy of our entire people and were invading our country. In this situation, the national factor was of utmost importance. To fight French imperialism, it was necessary to unite the whole nation, all revolutionary classes and patriotic elements, to strengthen the National United Front. Our party obtained great success in its policy of uniting the people. The slogan, "Unity, unity and broad unity—success, success and great success," put forth by President Ho Chi Minh, became a great reality. The anti-imperialist National United Front in our country was a model of the broadest national front in a colonial country.

The revolution for national liberation under the leadership of the Communist Party never deviated from the democratic revolution. The anti-imperialistic task always went side by side with the anti-feudal task, although the former was the more urgent; Vietnam was a backward agricultural country and the great majority of the population were peasants. While the working class is the class leading the revolution, the peasantry is the main force of the revolution, full of anti-imperialist and anti-feudal spirit. Moreover, in waging the Resistance War, we relied on the countryside to build our bases from which to launch guerrilla warfare in order to encircle the enemy in the towns and eventually arrive at liberating the towns. Therefore, it was of particular importance to pay due attention to the peasant question and to the anti-feudal question to step up the long Resistance War to victory.

How did our party solve the anti-feudal question with a view to mobilizing the peasant force during the Resistance War? In the August Revolution, after we had overthrown the power of the king and mandarins, a number of traitors were punished, their land allotted to the peasants. Colonialists' land was also temporarily given to the peasants. After the French imperialists re-invaded our country, the collusion between the imperialists and the most reactionary section of the feudal landlord class took shape. The essential contradiction in our society at that time was the contradiction, on the one side, between our nation, our people, and on the other, the French imperialists and their henchmen, the reactionary feudalists. We accordingly put forth the slogan "To exterminate the reactionary colonialists and the traitors." As a result, as early as the first years of the Resistance War, a number of the most reactionary of the landlord class were repressed in the course of the operations against local puppet administrations and traitors. Their land and that belonging to the absent landlords were allotted outright or given to the trusteeship of the peasants. Thus, in practice, the anti-feudal task was carried on.

However, due to a vague conception as early as 1941 of the content of the revolution for national liberation, in the first years of the Resistance War, in our minds as well as in our policies, the anti-feudal task was somewhat neglected and the peasant question underestimated in importance. Only by 1949–1950 was this question put in a more definite way. In 1952–1953, our party decided to mobilize the masses for a drastic reduction of land rent and to carry out land reform, implementing the slogan "land to the tiller." Hence, the resistance spirit of millions of peasants was strongly roused, the peasant-worker alliance strengthened, the National United Front made firmer, the administration and army consolidated and resistance activities intensified. There were errors in land reform but they were, in the main, committed after the restoration of peace and thus did not have any effect on the Resistance War. It should be added that not only was land reform carried out in the North, but in south Vietnam land was also distributed to the peasants after 1951. The carrying out of land reform during the Resistance War was an accurate policy of a creative character of our party.

Looking back, on the whole our party stuck to the line of national democratic revolution throughout the Resistance War. Thanks to this, we succeeded in mobilizing our people *to launch the people's war,* using the enormous strength of the people to vanquish the aggressors.

Launching the Resistance War, our party accurately assessed the strong and weak points of the enemy as well as our own, and clearly saw the balance of forces and the strategic schemes of the enemy in order to define our strategic principle.

The *enemy,* an imperialist power much weakened after World War II, was still strong as compared with us. Moreover, he possessed a seasoned professional army equipped with up-to-date arms, well supplied and experienced in aggressive wars. His weak point lay in the unjust character of his war. As a result, he was internally divided, not supported by the people of his own country, and did not enjoy the sympathy of world opinion. His army was strong at the beginning but its fighting spirit was deteriorating. French imperialism had other weak points and difficulties, namely: limited manpower and wealth, their dirty war was strongly condemned by their countrymen, etc.

On *our side,* our country was originally a colonial and semi-feudal country whose independence was newly won back. Thus, our forces in all fields were not yet consolidated, our economy was a backward agrarian one, our army untried guerrilla troops with few and obsolete arms, our supplies insufficient and our cadres lacking experience. Our strong point lay in the just nature of our Resistance War. Hence, we succeeded in uniting our entire people. Our people and troops were always imbued with the spirit of sacrificing themselves in fighting the enemy, and enjoyed the deep sympathy and support of people throughout the world.

These were the main features of the two sides in the last Resistance War. They clearly pointed out that the enemy's strong points were our weak ones and our strong points were his weak ones, but the enemy's strong points were temporary while ours were basic.

Owing to the above-mentioned characteristics, *the enemy's strategic principle was to attack swiftly and win swiftly.* The more the war was protracted the lesser would be his strong points, and his weak points would grow weaker. This strategic principle was in contradiction with the French imperialists' limited forces, which had grown much weaker after World War II. Consequently, in schemes for invading our country, he was compelled to combine the plan of attacking swiftly and winning swiftly with that of invading step by step, and even of negotiating with us in a time-serving policy to muster additional forces. Despite the difficulties and obstacles caused by his weak points, whenever the enemy had the possibility, he would immediately carry out the plan of attacking swiftly and winning swiftly, hoping to end the war by a quick victory. From the very beginning of the war, French colonialists had the ambition to complete the occupation and "pacification" of south Vietnam within a few weeks. The nation-wide Resistance War broke out. On the failure of their attempt to wipe out our main forces in the cities, they did their utmost to regroup their forces and launched a big offensive in Viet Bac, expecting to annihilate our leading organs and main forces in order to score a decisive success. The offensive in Viet Bac was brought to failure, the enemy was forced to protract the war and switch over to "pacifying" the areas in his rear, but he had not as yet given up his strategic plan of attacking swiftly and winning swiftly. The reshuffling of generals time and again, especially the sending of General Navarre to Indochina, were all aimed at striking decisive blows in order to quickly end the aggressive war.

Realizing clearly the enemy's strong and weak points and ours, to cope with the enemy's strategic scheme *our party set forth the guiding principle of a long-term Resistance War.* Facing an enemy who temporarily had the upper hand, our people were not able to strike swiftly and win swiftly but needed time to overcome their shortcomings and increase the enemy's weak points. Time was needed to mobilize, organize and foster the forces of the Resistance, to wear out the enemy's forces, gradually reverse the balance of forces, turning our weakness into strength and concurrently availing ourselves of the changes in the international situation which was growing more and more advantageous to our Resistance, eventually to triumph over the enemy.

The general law of a long revolutionary war is usually to go through three stages: defensive, equilibrium and offensive. Fundamentally, in the main directions, our Resistance War also followed this general law. Of course, the reality on the battlefields unfolded in a more lively and more complicated manner. Implementing the guiding principle of a long war, after a period of fighting to wear out and check the enemy troops, we carried out a strategic withdrawal from the cities to the countryside in order to preserve our forces and defend our rural bases. Following the failure of the enemy offensive in Viet Bac, equilibrium gradually came into being. We decided to launch an extensive guerrilla war. From 1950 onward, campaigns of local counter-offensives were successively opened and we won the initiative on the northern battlefront. The Dien Bien Phu campaign in early 1954 was a big counter-offensive which ended the Resistance War with a great victory.

To make everyone understand thoroughly the strategic guiding principle of long-term war was not only a big work of organization, militarily and economically, but also a process of ideological education and struggle within the party and among the people against erroneous tendencies which appeared many a time in the years of the Resistance War. One was pessimistic defeatism which presumed that our country being small, our population thin, our economy backward and our armed forces young and weak, we would be unable to face the enemy, let alone perseveringly wage a long Resistance War. Other erroneous tendencies were subjectivism, loss of patience, eagerness to win swiftly, that came out at the start of the Resistance War in the operational plans of a number of localities which were unwilling to withdraw their force to preserve our main force, and also in their plan of general counter-offensive put forth in 1950, when this was not yet permitted by objective and subjective conditions.

Utmost efforts were made by the party to correct these erroneous tendencies, to educate the people, enabling them to see clearly our difficulties and advantages, stimulating the entire people to keep firm their determination to fight. The booklet *The Resistance War Will Win,* written by Comrade Trung Chinh, was an important contribution to the thorough understanding of the line of Resistance War and the policies of the party. Here, emphasis should be laid upon the great effect of the resolutions of the First Session of the Central Committee in 1951 which reminded the whole party that "our Resistance War is a long and hard struggle" and "we have mainly to rely on our own forces." The ideological remolding drives in the party and the army and the propaganda work among the people carried out on the Central Committee's instructions, basically consolidated the people's determination to wage the long Resistance War, heightened their confidence in final victory and enabled the guiding principles of long-term and self-reliant Resistance War to penetrate more deeply into the masses' consciousness.

To wage a long Resistance War, we had to highlight the spirit of *self-reliance*. During the first years of the Resistance, our people had to struggle when encircled on all sides; self-reliance was then a vital question. Our people had no other way than relying on their own forces to cope with the enemy. Highlighting the spirit of self-reliance, our troops looked for their supplies on the battlefields, capturing the enemy's weapons to arm themselves, economized in munitions, developed their endurance, overcame difficulties, strived to take part in production, supplied themselves with a part of their requirements, in order to lighten the people's contributions. Our people endeavored to build our rear, develop the economy of the Resistance to supply themselves and meet the demands of the front. We stepped up production in every aspect to supply the people with staple commodities and fought against the enemy's economic blockade. Large areas of virgin land were broken to increase the output of foodstuffs. Many arms factories were built to produce weapons for the troops. In particular, the people and troops in the Fifth Zone and in Nam Bo raised to great heights the spirit of self-reliance, scored many achievements in self-supply to perseveringly wage the Resistance War in extremely difficult and hard circumstances.

When the international situation changed to our advantage, but we were still meeting with many difficulties, there began to appear in the party and among the people the psychology of waiting and relying on foreign aid. Therefore, while continuing ideologically to prepare for a long Resistance War, attention was given by our party to rousing our self-reliance and pointing out that international sympathy and support was of importance, but only by relying on our own efforts could we insure victory for our people's struggle for liberation.

To bring the Resistance War to victory, it was not enough to have a correct strategic guiding principle; an appropriate *guiding principle of fighting* was also necessary to successfully carry out that strategic guiding principle. In general, our Resistance War was a *guerrilla war moving gradually to regular war, from guerrilla warfare to mobile warfare combined with partial entrenched camp warfare.* Basically, we had grasped that general law; hence we were successful. However, we did not thoroughly grasp it from the beginning but only after a whole process of being tested and tempered in the practice of war.

In the Resistance War, *guerrilla warfare* played an extremely important role. Guerrilla warfare is the form of fighting of the masses of people, of the people of a weak and badly equipped country who stand up against an aggressive army which possesses better equipment and technique. This is the way of fighting the revolutionary war which relies on the heroic spirit to triumph over modern weapons, avoiding the enemy when he is stronger and attacking him when he is weaker, now scattering, now regrouping one's forces, now wearing out, now exterminating the enemy, determined to fight him everywhere, so that wherever the enemy goes he would be submerged in a sea of armed people who hit back at him, thus undermining his spirit and exhausting his forces. In addition to the units which have to be scattered in order to wear out the enemy, it is necessary to regroup big armed forces in favorable conditions in order to achieve supremacy in attack at a given point and at a given time to annihilate the enemy. Successes in many small fights added together gradually wear out the enemy manpower while little by little fostering our forces. The main goal of the fighting must be destruction of enemy manpower, and ours should not be exhausted by trying to keep or occupy land, thus creating final conditions to wipe out the whole enemy force and liberate our country.

Guerrilla warfare was obviously a form of fighting in full keeping with the characteristics of our Resistance War. In the early period of the Resistance, there was not and could not be in our country regular war but only guerrilla activities. When the Resistance War started in south Vietnam, our plan was to wage guerrilla warfare, and in practice guerrilla war took shape. But when the nation-wide Resistance War broke out, the policy of mainly waging guerrilla warfare was not clearly put forth. At the beginning of Autumn-Winter 1947, the Party Central Committee put forth the task of launching and extending guerrilla activities all over the occupied areas. One part of our main force was divided into independent companies, operating separately, which penetrated deeply into the enemy's rear to carry our propaganda among the people, defend our bases and intensify guerrilla war. The policy of independent companies, concurrently with concentrated battalions, was a very successful experience in the direction of guerrilla war. As guerrilla activities were intensified and widely extended, in many places the enemy rear was turned into our frontline.

To cope with our ever expanding guerrilla activities, great efforts were made by the enemy to launch repeated mopping-up operations with ever bigger armed forces. The aim of these operations was to annihilate our guerrilla units, destroy our political bases and crops, and plunder our property, hoping to crush our resistance forces and "pacify" his rear. That is why mopping-up operations and counter-mopping-up operations became the chief forms of guerrilla war in the enemy's rear. Through the counter-mopping-up operations, our people brought to the utmost their endurance of hardships and heroic fighting spirit, creating extremely rich forms of fighting. To maintain and extend guerrilla activities in the enemy's rear, our party cleverly combined the coordination of political and economic struggle with armed struggle. The party strove hard to avail itself of the favorable opportunities to push the people forward to the armed struggle, develop our forces, annihilate and wear out the enemy forces, turn temporarily occupied zones into guerrilla zones or the latter into our bases. When meeting with a difficult situation, our party cleverly switched the movement in good time to preserve our forces and safeguard our bases. Guerrilla activities in the enemy's rear were the highest expression of the iron will and extremely courageous spirit of our people, and at the same time a proof of the talented leadership of our party.

From the strategic point of view, guerrilla warfare, causing many difficulties and losses to the enemy, wears him out. To annihilate big enemy manpower and liberate land, guerrilla warfare has to move gradually to *mobile warfare*. As our Resistance War was a long revolutionary war, guerrilla warfare not only could but had to move to mobile warfare. Through guerrilla activities, our troops were gradually formed, fighting first with small units then with bigger ones, moving from scattered fighting to more concentrated fighting. Guerrilla warfare gradually developed to mobile warfare—a form of fighting in which principles of regular warfare gradually appear and increasingly develop but still bear a guerrilla character. Mobile warfare is the fighting way of concentrated troops, of the regular army, in which relatively big forces are regrouped, operating on a relatively vast battlefield, attacking the enemy where he is relatively exposed with a view to annihilating enemy manpower, advancing very deeply, then withdrawing very swiftly, possessing to the extreme, dynamism, initiative, mobility and rapidity of decision in face of new situations. As the Resistance War went on, the strategic role of mobile warfare became more important with every passing day. Its task was to annihilate a bigger and bigger number of the enemy forces in order to develop our own, while the task of guerrilla warfare was to wear out and destroy the enemy reserves. Therefore, mobile warfare had to go side by side with annihilating warfare. Only by annihilating the enemy's manpower could we smash the enemy's big offensives, safeguard our bases and our rear, move to win the initiative in operations, wipe out more and more important enemy manpower, liberating larger and larger localities one after the other, and eventually arrive at destroying the entire enemy armed force and liberating our whole country.

Implementing the guiding principle of moving gradually from guerrilla warfare to mobile warfare, from the outset there was in our guerrilla troops, besides one part operating separately, another with concentrated activity, and this was the first seed of mobile warfare. In 1947, with the plan of independent companies operating separately and concentrated battalions, we began to move to more concentrated fighting, then to mobile warfare. In 1948, we made relatively great ambuscades and surprise attacks with one or several battalions. In 1949, we launched small campaigns not only in the North but also on other battlefronts. From 1950, we began to launch campaigns on an ever larger scale enabling mobile warfare to play the main part on the northern battlefield, while entrenched camp warfare was on the upgrade. This fact was clearly manifest in the great Dien Bien Phu campaign.

We used to say: guerrilla war must multiply. To keep itself in life and to develop, guerrilla warfare necessarily has to develop into mobile warfare. This is a general law. In the concrete conditions of our Resistance War, there could not be mobile warfare without guerrilla warfare. But unless guerrilla warfare moved to mobile warfare, not only the strategic task of annihilating the enemy manpower could not be carried out but even guerrilla activities could not be maintained and extended. To say that it is necessary to develop guerrilla warfare into mobile warfare does not mean brushing aside guerrilla warfare; on the contrary, it means that in the widely extended guerrilla activities, the units of the regular army gradually grow up and are able to wage mobile warfare and that side by side with the main force there must always be numerous guerrilla troops and guerrilla activities.

Once mobile warfare appears on the battlefront of guerrilla war, there must be close and correct coordination between these forms of fighting to be able to step up the Resistance War, wear out and annihilate bigger enemy forces and win ever greater victories. This is another general law in the conduct of the war. On the one hand, guerrilla warfare had to be extended to make full use of the new favorable conditions brought about by mobile warfare, to coordinate with mobile warfare in order to wear out and annihilate a great number of enemy troops and through these successes continue to step up mobile warfare. On the other hand, mobile warfare had to be accelerated to annihilate big enemy manpower, and concurrently create new favorable conditions for a further extension of guerrilla warfare. In the course of the development of mobile warfare, owing to the enemy's situation and ours on the battlefields, entrenched camp warfare gradually came into being. Entrenched camp warfare, which became part and parcel of mobile warfare, kept developing and occupied a more and more important position.

The conduct of the war must maintain a correct ratio between the fighting forms. At the beginning, we had to stick to guerrilla warfare and extend it. Passing to a new stage, as mobile warfare made its appearance, we had to hold firm the coordination between the two forms, the chief one being guerrilla warfare; mobile warfare was of lesser importance but was on the upgrade. Then came a new and higher stage, mobile warfare moved to the main position, at first only on one battlefield—local counter-offensive came into being—then on an ever wider scope. During this time, guerrilla warfare extended but, contrary to mobile warfare, it moved back from the main position to a lesser but still important one, first on a given battlefront then on an ever wider scope.

In the practice of the liberation war, on some battlefronts we met with numerous difficulties because we were not determined to advance guerrilla warfare to mobile warfare; on others, rashness in speeding up mobile warfare had a bad influence on guerrilla warfare, and therefore mobile warfare also met with difficulties. This manifestation was relatively widespread when the slogan "To prepare for the general counter-offensive" was put forth, but it was overcome after a certain time. In general, through tests and trials, our guidance fundamentally held firm the aforesaid ratio and was therefore successful. The Hoa Binh campaign was typical of coordination between guerrilla warfare and mobile warfare on the northern battlefront. The Dien Bien Phu campaign and Winter-Spring 1953-1954 campaign were most successful models of coordination between mobile warfare and guerrilla warfare, between the face-to-face battlefield and the theaters of operation in the enemy's rear, between the main battlefield and the coordinated battlefields all over the country.

With the forms of guerrilla fighting and mobile fighting and owing to the enemy's conditions and ours in strength, shaping up of force and topography, etc., there appeared on the battlefronts the situation of free zones interlacing with enemy-controlled areas, intersecting and encircling each other. In the enemy-controlled areas, there were also guerrilla zones and guerrilla bases, another phenomenon of interlacement, intersecting and encircling one another. The process of development of the war was that of ever widening our free zones and guerrilla areas and ever-narrowing the enemy-occupied areas, advancing toward liberating vast areas, then the whole North.

The strategy of long-term war, and the guiding principle of fighting from guerrilla war gradually moving to regular war with the forms of guerrilla warfare, were very successful experiences of our national liberation war. These were the strategy and tactics of the people's war, the art of military conduct of the people's war, of the revolutionary war in a small and backward agricultural country under the leadership of our party.

In the course of the national liberation war, *the building up of bases* for a steadfast and long resistance was an important strategic question and also a very successful experience of our party. It is absolutely necessary for us to make a profound study of and to sum up the rich experiences on this question. . . .

The sacred Resistance War of our people has continued the glorious work of the August Revolution, raising aloft the banner of national liberation against colonialism and has eloquently proved that: *"In the present international conditions, even a weak and small nation, once united to stand up under the leadership of the working class, resolutely to struggle for indepen-*

dence and democracy, will have full capacity to defeat all aggressive forces. This struggle for national liberation, in given historical conditions, can, through the form of a long armed struggle—a long resistance war—come to success."

The successful Resistance War of our people has dealt a heavy blow to the ever distintegrating colonialist system, thus contributing a part to the smashing of the imperialists' war-provoking plots, and to the struggle of the world's peoples for peace, democracy and socialism.

—*People's War, People's Army,* pp. 88–112.

4

Political and Military Forces in Revolutionary War

LE DUAN

The August Revolution, like people's revolutions in other countries, has taught the South Vietnamese revolutionaries that any revolution with a marked popular character must use both political and military forces to secure victory. Revolution being the uprising of the oppressed and exploited masses, one must adopt the revolutionary mass viewpoint to understand revolutionary violence which involves two forces—political and military forces—and two forms of struggle—political and armed struggle—and thereby to realize the offensive position of revolution when revolutionary situations are ripe.

On the contrary, if one considers revolutionary violence merely from the point of view of armed struggle, and consequently takes into account only the military force of the two sides to appraise the balance of forces between revolution and counter-revolution, mistakes will be inevitable: either one will underestimate the strength of the revolution and dare not mobilize the masses for insurrection, or, once the insurrection has been launched, one will not dare step up the offensive to push ahead the revolution, or, when the armed struggle has been unleashed, one cannot avoid falling back to a defensive strategy.

In 1959–1960, when the American imperialists and their henchmen used most barbarous fascist means to sow terror and carry out mass slaughter, the South Vietnamese revolutionaries held that the enemy had sustained a basic political defeat and could no longer rule as in the past, while the people had come to realize more and more clearly that they could no longer live under the enemy's yoke and had to rise up and wage a life-and-death struggle to liberate themselves. Under those circumstances the South Vietnamese people rose up, using mainly political struggle, broke the enemy's grip, controlled large rural areas, wrested back power, redistributed land, set up "self-management committees," made every effort to develop their forces in every field, and launched a widespread people's war to carry on their liberation struggle.

In South Vietnam, as the vast countryside has a natural economy not very dependent on the towns and an almost exclusively peasant population living on agriculture, the aggressors and their henchmen ruling in urban centers cannot establish a strict control over the rural areas. That is why, when conditions are ripe for revolution, the villages constitute the weakest spot where the puppet administration becomes shaky and sinks into a crisis, hence the possibility of most rapidly starting *local insurrections* and of destroying the enemy's power apparatus considerably.

After liberating extensive rural areas, the people gradually built up large strong armed forces, rapidly organized powerful political forces, vigorously boosted the revolutionary movement throughout the South, stepped up political and military struggle, firmly upheld their offensive position, foiled all the enemy's political and military schemes, and kept on pushing forward the South Vietnamese revolution. Since then, *the close combination of political and military struggle constitutes the basic form of revolutionary violence in South Vietnam*, the most suitable one to resist neo-colonialism. It has been used not only in the course of insurrections, but also in dealing with the American imperialists' "special warfare" and "limited warfare." This combination of political and military struggle is carried out in accordance with the balance of forces in the *three strategic rural, urban and hill-forest areas*, as well as with the general tasks of the revolution and the specific tasks of each period.

Like the national-democratic revolution all over the country in the past, the present South Vietnamese revolution has the workers and peasants as its main force and the worker-peasant alliance led by the working class as the cornerstone of the national united front. Therefore, it cannot repose exclusively on the revolutionary forces in the countryside, but has to build up revolutionary forces in the towns as well, and impel revolutionary struggle in both of these areas. In the process of the struggle the revolutionary movements in both areas have been closely coordinated, greatly influencing and vigorously impelling each other. If the revolutionary upsurge in the countryside some years ago made its impact strongly felt upon the revolutionary movement in the towns, the seething struggle of the urban masses now has created highly favorable conditions for uprisings in the countryside and the extension of the people's war.

The recent fierce political struggle of the townsfolk has restrained, sometimes slowed down or seriously upset, the military activities of the enemy on the battlefields, thus efficaciously helping the offensive of the revolutionary armed forces; conversely, the military successes on the battlefields, like the repeated attacks by the Liberation troops against the enemy's rear bases and dens in the towns and cities have accelerated the growth of the urban revolutionary movement.

In short, *the South Vietnamese revolution develops by using the revolutionary violence of the masses to launch local insurrections in the countryside, organizing revolutionary forces in both rural and urban areas—military and political forces alike—and holding firm the offensive position to attack the enemy with military and political actions and agitation among his troops in all the three strategic rural, urban and hill-forest areas so as to smash gradually all his military and political activities and win complete victory.*

> —Le Duan, *Forward Under the Glorious Banner of the October Revolution*, Foreign Languages Publishing House, Hanoi, 1967, excerpt. Le Duan is the first secretary of the Lao Dong Party (Vietnam Workers' Party).

5

"Self-Defense" Centers in a People's War

WILFRED G. BURCHETT

The conception of "self-defense" centers is one of the many original contributions the Vietnamese people have made to guerrilla warfare, inseparable from their conception of "people's war." As with many of the tactics and strategies employed by the Vietnamese, especially in their application in the South, they are either unknown abroad or misunderstood, partly because the South Vietnamese have been too busy fighting to put their experiences down on paper. "Self-defense" is largely a Vietnamese conception which to a certain extent was practiced in the anti-French Resistance War, but on nothing like the scale it has since been used in the South. As for self-defense in the cities, this is exclusively an innovation of the South. Although the stage of encirclement of the cities had been reached in the anti-French Resistance, the Geneva Agreements obviated the necessity for the actual assault on the cities. "Self-defense" in the cities is but an extension of a system already perfected in the self-defense villages.

In his book, *Revolution in the Revolution?*, Régis Debray analyzes the failures of self-defense in Columbia and Bolivia and arrives at the conclusion that "today auto-defense as a system and as a reality is liquidated." But the examples he cites, where self-defense zones were set up not only in geographical isolation from the politico-military situation inside these two countries, but in isolation from the revolutionary forces as a whole and the situation as a whole, are insufficient to draw such generalized conclusions. Self-defense as practiced in South Vietnam has been supremely successful and the resistance struggle could never have been pushed to its present stage of an assault on the cities, without the formation of self-defense units in the liberated villages and the integration of whole groups of fortified villages into self-defense zones. To discard the concept of self-defense would be to deprive revolutionary forces of a proved and tested weapon of vital importance.

The establishment of self-defense units and zones is an inevitable and logical phase in the South Vietnamese conception of people's war. The self-defense concept is inseparably linked with the political and popular aspect of the armed struggle and plays a vital supporting role of overall politico-military activities. Among other things, it mobilizes the creative initiatives of the people in developing new techniques, tactics and even weapons, initiatives which reach full fruition only when an entire nation is engaged in the struggle.

It is true that the self-defense concept has been developed in the very specific conditions of South Vietnam, including such factors as the establishment by the adversary of village "self-defense" units as an anti-guerrilla measure; the building of anti-guerrilla fortifications around the "strategic hamlets" which facilitated transforming the latter into anti-government "fortified villages," defended by at least the weapons and often part of the personnel of the original anti-guerrilla "self-defense" units. But it is also true that the basic idea of "self-defense" villages and zones had been developed during the anti-French Resistance War and presumably could be adapted anywhere people have taken to arms in a nation-wide liberation struggle. Success obviously depends on the struggle being waged not partially but on a large scale; on careful political work to lay a solid groundwork in which the widest possible unity is forged around determination to wage a resolute, long-range struggle. The self-defense zones have to be either large enough or have proper natural conditions to permit a certain mobility of the defending forces within the zone itself, or must be linked to a solid base area into which they can temporarily withdraw or maneuver.

The examples cited by Debray have nothing in common with the South Vietnamese experience—Bolivia, for instance, where the tin miners, having played a key role in overthrowing the oligarchy of the day, then set themselves up in an almost autonomous and heavily defended zone 15 kilometers long by 10 kilometers wide, separated geographically and politically from the rest of the country and against which government forces could leisurely prepare and finally, in May 1965, launch a devastating attack supported by aircraft and U.S.-trained Ranger parachutists. Debray accurately analyzes the weakness of such a concept of "auto-defense" in isolation but the conclusion is incorrect that "auto-defense therefore reduces guerrilla warfare to a tactical role and robs it of all revolutionary strategic significance" and that "even if it temporarily ensures the protection of the population it endangers it in the long run." ...

Once the self-defense forces had enough firearms for a whole group of such villages, there was never any question of them sitting around waiting for the enemy to come to their particular hamlet before they took to arms against them. The self-defense activities of hamlets were at first coordinated at village level,* and village activities were later coordinated at district level. While primarily the task of the self-defense forces was to defend their own hamlets and villages and to neutralize nearby enemy posts, in case of large-scale enemy attacks they coordinated their harassing activities, ambushes, etc. with those of the NLF [National Liberation Front of South Vietnam] regional troops and the regular NLF army as the latter gathered strength. The self-defense forces incidentally were an excellent training school for recruits for the regional troops and later for the regular army, providing a constant supply of fresh blood for the latter. They were in constant process of development; after every successful action there were more arms available. At a certain stage in the development of the regular forces, the latter turned over to the self-defense forces at first half, and then the total, of all arms captured from the enemy, except heavy machine guns and bazookas. Technique and tactics improved and also coordination between hamlets to such an extent that in some districts an elaborate network of underground tunnels linked every hamlet....

The answers to "why and for whom" were very easy for members of the self-defense units to grasp. If the task at first seemed limited to defense of their own homes and fields, the self-defense recruits soon saw the necessity of going further afield, at first to pin down the enemy night and day in nearby posts and then at an appropriate moment to take the initiative in wiping out those posts in coordinated actions which transformed a self-defense zone into a guerrilla zone, an area in which the guerrillas were complete masters at night and usually during daytime also,

---

* Most Vietnamese villages comprise 4 to 6 hamlets.

but in which locally-based enemy Saigon forces could also penetrate in daytime if they came in force. As the situation developed, it was easy to grasp that if, in coordination with other self-defense units, they could wipe out the enemy's local forces, the guerrilla zone could be transformed into a guerrilla base in which they were masters day and night and the enemy could only penetrate by using his main force units. When the call went out for recruits from the self-defense forces into the NLF regional troops to encircle enemy posts at district or even provincial level and be ready to oppose and counter-attack the enemy's mopping-up operations, there was no lack of volunteers. Concepts broadened and the necessity to engage the enemy's main force units by building up NLF main force units—especially after the direct commitment of U.S. combat troops—also became clear to everyone. Every attack by U.S. planes speeded up the flow of recruits and demands rose to go still further afield to hit the bases where the planes were stationed. Self-defense with rifles and light automatic weapons was obviously not sufficient against planes; the best defense was to attack them on the ground. The self-defense units produced natural guerrilla leaders and fighters of exceptionally high morale because every step they had taken had been so clearly right, so clearly in defense of their own interests, those of their neighbors and those of the nation.

The self-defense units are in fact the base of the pyramid on which the whole structure of the NLF armed forces rests. They are the most concrete expression of people's war. They are of the people, for the people, appointed by the people; a more democratic form of armed forces is difficult to imagine, or a more perfect form for the tasks imposed by the resistance struggle. They represent an answer to the NLF's seeming lack of mobility due to their lack of modern transport systems and to the American monopoly of air power. While the Americans have to fly their troops—and the munitions, food and even water to supply them—hundreds of kilometers on given operations, the self-defense forces are always on the spot over the entire face of South Vietnam, surrounding every U.S. base and outpost, ready for speedy concentration if necessary, with sufficient equipment on their backs to give immediate battle to the enemy's mobile forces. They can count on continuous replenishment of supplies brought them by the local population, often enough their own wives and parents among them. The self-defense units have proved capable of holding up U.S. main unit attacks, or severely slowing them down until NLF regional troops arrive to wage coordinated actions with the self-defense units, if necessary in cooperation with the Liberation Army's regular forces.

—From a book in progress by Wilfred G. Burchett, on the strategy and tactics of the National Liberation Army of South Vietnam.

6

Philippines: Hukbalahap and its Mass Base

The Huk was organized on the basis of squadrons, composed of approximately 100 men each. The squadron was subdivided into platoons and squads. On the ascending scale, two squadrons made a battalion and two battalions a regiment. In that respect, we paralleled fairly closely the ordinary army. The similarity, however, ended there.

The squadron officers were: commander, vice-commander, political instructor, supply officer, and intelligence officer. The differences between these officers and the officers in an ordinary army are stated in the opening section of the "Fundamental Spirit":*

"The People's Anti-Japanese Army should have as its fundamental spirit equality between the officers and the soldiers, friendship and unity. Why should there be equality between the officers and soldiers? Because a revolutionary army is organized by revolutionists. As their political position is the same, the officers and soldiers should not be classified as high or low, rich or poor. They join the army not to earn salary, not to obtain position, but to fight for national emancipation and social freedom. Only by actually practicing equality between the officers and soldiers can the whole army be united and carry on the fight with determination to the end."

---

* The Huk document setting forth the guiding principles which established the character of the revolutionary army.

"Why should there be friendship and unity? People with the same political will are called comrades. Comrades should be friendly to one another. Friendship brings about precious mutual help. Unity is strength. The stronger the unity, the greater will the strength be. War is a comparison of strengths. In order to defeat the enemy we must be stronger than the enemy. In order to become strong we must unite. In order to have unity we must have a common political aim under which we can be united. Therefore, our officers and soldiers should be friendly to one another, and they will be united into one body. In so doing they will become an iron-like fighting force."

The "Fundamental Spirit" stressed over and over again the necessity for comradeship. In the Huk there was no gulf between the separate members because we had nothing corresponding to "brass" and "lower rank."

"The members of the troops are all revolutionary comrades. . . . No one is allowed to say humiliating words to another, no one looks down on another, no one is coerced by another. . . . Anyone may express his opinion freely in a meeting. When there is a dispute the right opinion will be that of the majority, and will be passed and supported. . . . Everyone shares the same fortune and endures the same hardship. The leaders must set an example for the soldiers to follow. . . . Insults, coercion or deception are forbidden. . . . The officers should love and respect their subordinates. They should attend to the soldiers before themselves. They should exchange their experiences. They should criticize their mistakes. . . . The officers and the soldiers are all alike. Neither officers nor soldiers can have any individual privileges."

Another, and equally important section of the "Fundamental Spirit" dealt with the relations between our army and the people. The rules we outlined are inconceivable in an ordinary army, in which the order "Off Limits" exemplifies the barrier between the two. We stated:

"A revolutionary army should not only love and protect the people, but it should also represent the people. It should regard the fortunes of the people as its own. . . . It should struggle for the benefit of the people. It should regard the people's benefit as its own benefit in all things it does. It should help the people wherever it goes. In so doing it can have the faith and support of the people, can always receive their help, and through it can overcome the enemy."

These were no merely meaningless phrases. We concretized them in a mandatory set of rules:

"Clean the houses provided by the people. . . . Speak in a friendly tone. . . . Buy and sell things fairly. . . . Return the things we borrow. . . . Pay for the things we destroy. . . . Do not do, and even refuse to do, things which may harm the people. . . .

"All actions that may encroach upon or harm the people are forbidden. Any offender of this rule will be severely punished.

"Forcing the people to work for the army is forbidden. Coercion, beating or insulting the people are forbidden. Rape and robbery are forbidden. These are not the actions of a revolutionary army. They are criminal acts. They are absolutely forbidden in our army.

"Help the people in plowing, transplanting, harvesting or in cutting wood whenever it does not hinder the actions of the army.

"Help the people organize, and support the organizations of the people."

Finally, in all our relations with the people, when entering or leaving a place, when working with them or associating with them, we urged our soldiers to propagandize for the common cause. The Political Instructor organized and led study meetings in every squadron, and the soldiers in turn brought our message of unity and struggle into every barrio [village].

We called for a hard struggle to the end, pointing out that a revolutionary army must necessarily endure hardships and weariness:

"A revolutionary army struggles for the realization of a political aim. For example, the fight against Japan aims to defeat the Japanese and achieve national emancipation. This struggle will not stop until its aim is realized. Only by struggling and fighting to the end can the objective be reached. Even if there is only one man left the struggle must still be carried on. To sign any agreement with the enemy without victory means that we have lost faith in the revolution, and humble ourselves before the enemy. To capitulate is treachery and is a shameful crime."

The individual soldier was exhorted to exercise a self-imposed iron discipline. We said:

"An ordinary army often uses certain forms and threats of punishment to maintain its discipline. Compulsory force is used to make everyone follow the rules. If the compulsory source is weak, then the discipline of the army is poor. This is because those who have to follow the rules do not follow them willingly and voluntarily, but are forced to do so. Therefore the soldiers will often pretend to keep the rules when the officers are around, but when the officers are away they forget all about discipline. Such discipline cannot become strong and also cannot be maintained very long. We, however, can keep an iron discipline, but it is done through the self-consciousness in discipline of every member."

As an aid to self-discipline we listed the "eight requests" of the revolutionary soldier:

"1. Act with caution. 2. Act with rapidity. 3. Protect the weapons. 4. Take care of property. 5. Be on time. 6. Be tidy and neat. 7. Be clean and sanitary. 8. Be respectful."

We absolutely forbade torture, beating or scolding of soldiers. Instead, we introduced the system of making a soldier understand his duties and objectives, a collective system based on meetings and inner army organizations, giving the prerequisite leadership by example. And always we emphasized the need for drawing our strength and our determination from the masses of the people.

The "Fundamental Spirit" served as both the Articles of War and as the Constitution of the Hukbalahap.* Its revolutionary concepts of an intertwined democratic army and the people was the structure upon which we built our resistance movement, a structure which the people accepted and were willing to support, long after the Japanese were replaced by other enemies of the Filipino....

An account merely of our armed struggle against the Japanese would be only one-half the story of the Hukbalahap. The main center of the people's resistance movement came to be in the barrios, among the civilian masses.... No de facto government existed on Philippine soil. In its absence, we created one, putting the government into the hands of the people. We did this through the medium of the BUDC, the Barrio United Defense Corps....

The BUDC, or, as it was called often, the STB (*Sandatahang Tanod ng Bayan,* the people's home defense guard) was one phase

---

* Abbreviation for *Hukbo ng Bayan Laban sa Hapon,* or Army of the People Against Japan, organized in the Philippines on March 29, 1942, shortly after the Japanese invasion. The Tagalog word *hukbo* means army. In the postwar armed liberation struggle, this was changed to *Hukbong Mapagpalaya ng Bayan,* or Army of National Liberation.

of our united-front activity. Although, as its name implies, it had its military aspects, being coordinated closely with our army and having its own armed guards, the BUDC, in a deeper sense, brought a hitherto unknown phenomenon into the barrios: democratic government. After centuries of *caciquism** the people were given the opportunity to rule themselves.

A BUDC council, in a large barrio, had up to 12 members; smaller barrios had as few as five members. The size of the governing body was determined by both the size of the barrio and by its importance in our area of operations. The members included a chairman, a vice-chairman, a secretary-treasurer, and directors of recruiting, intelligence, transportation, communications, education, sanitation, agriculture, and a chief of police. Sometimes two or three of these positions were held by a single council member.

All offices in the barrio were elective. The secret ballot was extended to all residents of 18 years and over, providing they had no record of pro-Japanese activity. Disfranchisement was the penalty for acts committed against the people.

The BUDC's were created only in those areas under our influence, which became, in actuality, guerrilla areas, protected and defended by our squadrons. Elsewhere, we utilized relief associations, anti-robbery associations, all of which were really underground councils. Often we infiltrated and took over the organizations of the enemy in order to render them useless.

In those regions where the prewar peasant unions had been strong and had accustomed the people to organization and struggle, we had almost complete mass support from the beginning. However, when our squadrons entered new territory we ran into new problems. In approaching a strange barrio we first sent in contact men who sized up the people to find out whether they were pro- or anti-Japanese, if puppets and spies were present, and what kind of people the leaders of the barrio were. If the barrio was anti-Japanese, the squadron entered, called a meeting of the leading individuals, and explained the Huk and its program. This was also done with the people as a whole. Invariably such barrios were easily organized.

A different type of problem confronted us when we encountered a barrio in which puppets and spies were present or where there

---

* Local government by appointed authority, established during the Spanish colonial regime and continued under the American regime.

was pro-Japanese feelings; or when we were very mobile and had to enter a barrio where conditions were unknown. Here, too, we sent in contact men who obtained full information on who the puppets and spies were, where they lived, and about their movement. Then we surrounded the barrios with a heavy guard, permitting no one to leave and making those who entered stay. Our next step was to arrest all puppets and spies and to place them before a public meeting in the church or in the school. The people were told that we had come to arrest traitors. Our charges against those arrested were made on the basis of information we had gathered, and then the people were asked if the charges were correct, and if they had anything further to add. If the people refuted the charges, the prisoners were released. If the charges were affirmed, we next found out if the persons in question had acted under force by the enemy or willingly. Those who were avowedly traitors were punished, killed if the people thought it appropriate. Those who acted under duress were lectured on the principles of the resistance movement, and urged to remain in their positions and use them as a disguise for anti-Japanese work.

When the barrio had been thoroughly propagandized the squadron left, but after a time returned to check up. If, in the intervening time, the persons in question had aided the enemy, they were again arrested and taken with the squadron for two or three months, during which they were lectured constantly. If they changed, they were sent back to the barrio to do anti-Japanese work. Seeing such people return gave the barrio people additional confidence in Huk discipline and demolished the enemy propaganda that whoever was captured by the Huk was killed. The barrio, in the meantime, was organized along united-front lines.

This direct military approach to the barrios, however, was not the normal case. Most of the groundwork and building was done by trained mass organizers.

Before we could organize we needed organizers, just as before we could fight we needed weapons. Both militarily and politically we armed ourselves. Starting with a handful of union organizers, and of professional men who had been close to popular movements, we created our own schools to teach the technique of organization. These Mass Schools, as we called them, were held throughout the war and turned out hundreds of mass workers. They were schooled in the methods of underground work, in the ways of bringing about unity between all kinds of organizations and guerrilla groups, in the principles of democracy and of our traditions of struggle for national liberation, and in how to penetrate and combat the Neighborhood Associations, the PC and the Ganaps [Japanese control bodies]. These were the people who went into the field singly and in twos and threes and laid the basis for our expansion. Many lost their lives in lonely deaths, but live in mass remembrance....

Once fully organized under the BUDC, a barrio was a liberated island in the ocean of invaders and traitors. Within it, once spies and betrayers had been liquidated, there was absolute unity and cooperation with our armed forces, and the people practiced self-rule, hidden from the eyes of the enemy. In accordance with the demands of a people's war, the BUDC's had three main channels of activity: the most important, aid to the military struggle; second, the development of an economic program that would both supply the army and keep food products from the enemy; and third, the putting forward of new political perspectives for the people that would be a factor in a democratic Philippines at the end of the war....

Through the BUDC we were able to build mass reserves for the Huk. For every Huk soldier in the field there were two others in reserve in the barrios, where they engaged in production work or in civilian pursuits that otherwise aided the overall struggle. The BUDC director of recruiting saw to it that our reserves were drilled and schooled in tactics. Usually the man on active duty was periodically relieved in the field by one of his reserves; the soldier "rested on furlough" while the reserve became a seasoned guerrilla. In this way we were able to build an army that was very much like an iceberg in appearance, two-thirds of it being beneath the sea.

The Huk itself took particular care to avoid having encounters with the enemy in a barrio proper, or even quite close to it. This was to prevent the Japanese from taking punitive action against our masses whom they would suspect of aiding the Huk. When the vicinity of a barrio was used for an ambush, the BUDC chairman was usually contacted and the approval of the people's council obtained. Even when hard-pressed we would ask the barrio inhabitants if they objected to our use of the barrio for defense....

Between all barrios existed a network of communications, the operation of which was in the hands of the BUDC.... The communication system was very intricate and differed in various regions. Couriers were of two types, the direct and the relay. Important messages were always sent the swiftest way, by direct courier, who always traveled a definite mapped-out route; the relay system was often circuitous. The enemy, with his radio and telephone, could not keep pace with either our couriers or our other methods of communication. These functioned as in a regular signal corps, and were ordinarily carried out by the barrio police. Flashes of light or a light by an open window at night, flags, banners, or clothes hung on a line in the daytime were some of our visual signals, combinations of them translated by code. To a limited extent, we also used sounds, the cutting of bamboo with a bolo, for instance, with the number of strokes sending a message. . . .

The most significant of all the innovations made by the BUDC . . . was in the administration of justice. All cases, whether criminal or civil, were settled in the barrio, by the council. For the first time in their history, a system of jury duty and public trial was instituted among the barrio people, all of whom had the obligation of serving on the jury and, if charged with guilt, the right to choose their own defense. The party found guilty was subjected to a process of improvement instead of punishment. . . . Cases of treachery, involving informers, spies or traitors, were referred to the Military Committee, or GHQ. This was done deliberately to absolve the barrio people of later being held responsible for executions carried out in the interest of national liberation. . . .

The Harvest Struggle was carried out by the BUDC in cooperation with the army. We raised the slogans: "No Rice For The Enemy!" and "Keep The Food Of The People!" As soon as the harvest season drew near we circulated the following memorandum throughout Central Luzon:

1. All ripe palay [unmilled rice] must be harvested and threshed immediately after ripening. It must not be stored in places near towns or near roads which can be reached by the enemy.

2. Make every attempt to destroy, smash or burn the Japanese threshing machines. Give notice to all anti-Japanese proprietors owning threshing machines not to allow the enemy to use them.

3. Destroy or burn bridges, destroy trucks of the enemy. Cut his communication lines. Ask help of the nearest squadron if you cannot do it alone.

4. Establish a regular guard system around barrios day and night.

Enforce rigid discipline. No sleeping at or leaving of post. Violation of discipline punished.

5. All strangers, whether peddlers or purchasers, beggars or threshers, must be investigated well. If necessary ask help from the nearest squadron.

6. Devise ways and means of hiding palay. Use dispersal.

7. Every inhabitant of a barrio must have his own arm, whether axe, bolo, spear, or bow and arrow.

8. Create sabotage groups to steal contents of bodegas [warehouses] if food falls into hands of enemy. If it cannot be recovered, burn the bodegas. . . .

The BUDC was not perfect. Sometimes the members of the council did not function, and very often the programs that were drawn up were utopian, but for thousands of people in Central Luzon it was their first real taste of democratic rule. In any time of oppression, when the people are forced to resort to their own devices, experimentation will run side by side with practical necessity, to find the right and best way of doing things. From the experiences and the pioneering of the BUDC it was only a short step to the establishment of local people's governments, which we began to build in the last stage of the war. The people's horizons had been immeasurably expanded.

—*Born of the People*, International Publishers, 1953, pp. 67–70, 116–27. Published in the name of Luis Taruc, this book was actually written by William J. Pomeroy, compiled from interviews with numerous Huk leaders.

7

The Postwar Huk in the Philippines

JORGE MARAVILLA

Following the defeat of Japan, the Communist Party, which had led the armed struggle of the Huk movement, disbanded the guerrilla forces it had organized and adopted the tactics of legal, parliamentary struggle to help achieve a genuine independence based on national unity for democratic development. It joined with nationalist bourgeois elements to form a new political force, the Democratic Alliance, which opposed the re-establishment of colonial relations with the United States. The Democratic Alliance entered into coalition with the mildly nationalist Nacionalista Party in the pre-independence election of 1946, in an attempt to defeat the bid of the imperialist-backed Liberal Party for power. In this election, the Democratic Alliance won all the congressional seats in the Central Luzon provinces, including the election of several Communists.

Although the Liberal Party won the national election, with Manuel Roxas assuming the presidency, it failed to gain sufficient seats in the Philippine Congress to assure approval of the economic and military treaties demanded by American imperialism. Furthermore, under Communist leadership, a new strong National Peasants Union (PKM) had emerged in the areas of Huk influence and a new militant Congress of Labor Organizations (CLO) had been formed in Manila and elsewhere, both actively opposed to the neo-colonial schemes.

To ram through imperialist wishes, the reactionary Liberal Party regime launched a brutal campaign of suppression of the popular opposition. Prior to independence day, 1946,* all Democratic Alliance congressmen and a number of Nacionalistas were arbitrarily ousted from Congress without legal procedure. Once this was done, approval of the trade and "parity" agreement† was rushed through (still with a margin of only one vote). Armed terror by government troops and by private landlord-paid "civilian guards" was launched against the nationalist progressive forces, with the torture and murder of Democratic Alliance leaders, of Communists, of former Huks, and of leaders of the PKM and the CLO. The objective was to smash the mass base of anti-imperialism and anti-feudalism.

The Communist Party at this time was relatively disorganized and demoralized by the onslaught. Although the cadres and the peasant masses took up arms spontaneously, reformed the old Huk units, and fought back effectively, the leading organs of the

---

* July 4, 1946, was the date of the neo-colonial independence legislated by the US Congress. In 1964 the Philippine government formally proclaimed that independence is to be celebrated on June 12, the date of the declaration of independence by the revolutionary government of 1898.

† The US Bell Trade Act of 1944 gave US businessmen parity, or equal rights, with Filipinos in the exploitation of Philippine resources after independence, until 1974.

party were divided on whether to pursue an all-out armed struggle, to fight through legal channels in alliance with bourgeois nationalist forces, or to conduct a combination of these.

In mid-1948 a short-lived amnesty agreement was arrived at between the Huks and the Liberal government. The Communist Party sought in these negotiations to persuade the new president, Elpidio Quirino, to adopt a nationalist program as a basis for a democratic settlement of the armed conflict. Quirino, however, betrayed the amnesty agreement and turned to the United States for more military aid against the Huks. With this development, and with a re-organization of Communist Party leadership that placed advocates of a determined armed struggle to the fore, the Huk movement was re-invigorated as the *Hukbong Mapagpalaya ng Bayan* (Army of National Liberation) and embarked on an expansion policy. From its bases in Central and Southern Luzon, it expanded by means of armed expeditions that set up organized mass bases throughout the island of Luzon and across the central Vicayan Islands. This was facilitated by the growing economic crisis of neo-colonialism, by the extreme corruption of the Liberal government, and by the terror employed everywhere against the people. The program of the Huk movement at this stage was still for a democratic peace, for agrarian reform, for the abrogation of the unequal treaties with the United States, and for democratic guarantees. It continued to seek alliances with the nationalist bourgeoisie and supported candidates of the Nacionalista Party in the elections of 1947 and 1949.

Fraud and terror on a large scale were used by Quirino to keep the Liberal Party in power in the 1949 general election. Mass resentment followed among the Filipino people. In January 1950, taking cognizance of the deteriorating political and economic situation, the Communist Party decided that a revolutionary situation existed and called for an all-out armed struggle, for the armed overthrow of the imperialist-puppet regime, for the completion of the bourgeois democratic revolution under "the hegemony of the working classes" and for the establishment of a new democratic government. A period of two years was projected as "preparation for the seizure of power," during which Huk expansion would be pushed to all provinces, revolutionary committees for land distribution and for workers' control of industry would be set up in all areas, the guerrilla forces would be converted to a regular army, and a provisional revolutionary government would be organized.

The intensified armed struggle alarmed American imperialism, which responded with a variety of interventionist policies. Emergency military, economic and political missions were hurried to the Philippines. A program of import and foreign exchange controls was hastily adopted to halt the critical deterioration of the neo-colonial economy. An agreement for economic aid (the Quirino-Foster Agreement of 1950) was made, one of the provisions of which was the introduction of American "advisers" in all government departments. Most emphasis, however, was given to extensive military aid, with reorganized and greatly enlarged Philippine armed forces under the direction of an increased US "military advisory" group, with a CIA-directed intelligence force.

Finally, the imperialists undertook to replace the discredited Liberal Party government with a Nacionalista Party administration that would have a façade of reform. An obscure and pliable Liberal politician, Ramon Magsaysay, was handpicked by the JUSMAG* to be secretary of national defense in the Quirino government and promoted by skilful propaganda as an "honest man" toward national leadership.

Between 1950 and 1956, under the impact of the imperialist counter-offensive, the Huk armed struggle was defeated, the Communist Party cadres were decimated, and the movement for national liberation received a major setback.

It is important to ask and to answer the question as to why the Communist-led Huk struggle was defeated in the Philippines. The reasons lie for the most part in errors of estimate and of tactics made by the movement.

(1) In estimating that a revolutionary situation existed in 1950, the party was incorrect in concluding that the imperialists and their allies were in an irrecoverable situation and that they "could no longer rule in the old way." The party erred in thinking that the Filipino people in general at that time "could no longer endure the old rule." In truth, the imperialists had a wide range of maneuver (it was not found necessary, for instance, as in Korea and in South Vietnam, for the American troops based in the Philippines to be put into the field against the Huks), and the people were susceptible to promises of "reform."

(2) Once a revolutionary situation was declared, the party put almost all emphasis and cadres into the armed struggle, to the

---

* The Joint US Military Advisory Group, provided for under the 1947 US-Philippine Mutual Assistance Pact.

neglect of legal forms of struggle and to the neglect of allies unprepared for this sharpest of struggles. Proclaiming the principle of "the hegemony of the party over the revolution," the party failed to project and to build a united front against imperialism and to find the forms of struggle by which broader masses of the people could have been drawn into action. In the election of 1951, which prepared the way for Magsaysay to come to power, the movement declared a boycott of the election (to which the people did not respond) and turned the edge of the armed struggle against both major parties in disregard of alliances possible at all levels. The nationalist bourgeoisie was frightened and antagonized, and allied itself in 1951 and in 1953 with the rabid pro-imperialist and anti-Huk, Magsaysay. The Huk movement gradually became isolated from allies among other nationalist forces that continued in their own way to resist the neo-colonial encroachments of American imperialism.

(3) Having become over-confident in 1950, the party became careless in its security measures. The price for this was the arrest on October 1950, in the city of Manila, by the imperialist-directed Philippine intelligence agencies, of the entire party secretariat and of many other top-ranking cadres. Complete files of party documents and correspondence were captured in these raids which fully exposed the organizational and tactical preparations of the movement. With remaining leading cadres scattered on expansion assignments and unable for months to convene to re-establish a directing organ for the struggle, this blow resulted in dislocation and in loss of initiative, which was never recovered.

(4) The Philippine national liberation struggle was, in addition, physically isolated from international allies, and had to face imperialist intervention with virtually no support from anti-imperialist forces abroad.

Throughout this period the Communist Party of the Philippines conducted itself in the most heroic manner. Thousands of its cadres and members died fighting in the fields, the forests, the swamps and the streets of cities. Of the original nine members of the Political Bureau of the party in 1950, all were either killed or captured. The entire Central Committee of the party in the same period were either killed or have suffered imprisonment, with many still in prison after 15 years with the most extreme sentences.* The party was left almost without effective

---

* By 1968 their imprisonment had stretched to 18 years.

cadres to rebuild the movement after the defeat of the armed struggle.

Nevertheless, the Communist Party, firmly rooted in the Luzon peasantry and in sectors of the industrial workers, was not destroyed and has succeeded in rebuilding its organization. After 1956 a tactical shift was made from armed struggle to forms of underground and legal struggle.

—"Upsurge of the Anti-Imperialist Movement in the Philippines," *World Marxist Review*, November 1965, pp. 41–42.

8

Indonesia: Peaceful and Non-Peaceful Ways

> *The following excerpts are from two statements emanating from groups in Indonesia engaged in rebuilding the Communist Party of Indonesia [PKI] after the massacre of Communists that followed the counter-revolutionary coup in that country in October 1965. These statements, coming from different sources, analyze the reasons for the disaster that overtook the PKI and project policies for recreating the revolutionary movement.*

I

Many a classical statement has been made to defend the point of view that the revolution can be effected by violent means, i.e., an armed revolution against an armed counter-revolution. On the other hand, there is weighty proof that Marx, Engels and Lenin did not believe that the revolution should necessarily develop along military lines; they insisted that it can also be effected by peaceful means, although in their lifetime the chances for this were very slender indeed and the idea lacked practical confirmation. It would be out of place to discuss this problem *per se* in this work. It is sufficient to draw your attention to what is in concert with our consensus as laid down in the Moscow

Declaration and Statement,* which was that under present historical conditions, especially after the emergence of the world socialist system, *there are chances* for a peaceful victory of the revolution. Whether revolution can develop peacefully or not depends largely on concrete historical conditions in each individual country.

The Statute of the PKI points out in this connection that since it is we ourselves who are concerned, our way should be that of the least possible sacrifices, i.e., the way of peace. The Indonesian experience teaches us that to use this best of opportunities, i.e., to follow the peaceful way, we must *first* be sure that this peaceful way is open to us and, acting on this optimistic assumption, prepare all the conditions that will be instrumental in achieving the victory of the revolution by peaceful means; *second,* we should by no means create an illusion that there is no other opportunity, i.e., the non-peaceful way, so as not to weaken ideological, political and organizational vigilance.

In short, it is for the sake of achieving the victory of the revolution by peaceful means that we must be ready for both alternatives and do our utmost to prepare the conditions outlined above.

Later, however, this point of view underwent some changes and turned into its opposite, i.e., into the belief that the revolution could be victorious solely if effected by force of arms, while pessimism was expressed as to the peaceful way of revolutionary development.

The subjective opinion that revolution can be victorious solely if performed by force of arms had a hypnotizing effect upon us and drastically changed the course of our revolution, pushing it on to the wrong path. This revisionist leftist point of view was instrumental in paving the theoretical way for the gamble known as the September 30 Movement.†

An analysis of the facts demonstrates that the September 30 Movement was triggered off by several units of the Indonesian Republic's Armed Forces, the Army in particular, composed of the most progressive servicemen. The Movement concentrated in

---

* The Moscow Declaration of 1958, issued by 12 Communist parties of the Socialist countries, and the Statement of 81 Communist parties of 1961, both signed in Moscow, stated the position of the international Communist movement on the major contemporary questions of strategy and tactics.

† The movement led by Colonel Untung, head of President Sukarno's personal security forces, that attempted on September 30, 1965, to remove the reactionary anti-Sukarno army generals.

Djakarta. In other words, it was an action started in the center, in the hope that it would extend to all the regions of the motherland.

The following goals were pursued: 1. To foil the plot of the Generals' Council and purge the Armed Forces of the conspirators.* 2. To set up a "Revolutionary Council" as an organ of assistance to NASAKOM [the National Front] which would be a precursor of a people's democracy, a body that would consistently have to implement the five principles *(Pantja Azimat)* of the Indonesian Revolution.

It is quite clear that the September 30 Movement was a movement spearheaded against the coup, a movement that overthrew the Generals' Council and was at the same time a revolutionary movement aimed at the establishment of a state power that would be a harbinger of a people's democracy. In reality, this Movement developed into a military adventure, and was foiled.

The primary cause of the defeat of the September 30 Movement was not that the enemy confronting us was too strong, or that we lacked courage, or that our fighters lacked courage. The subjective causes lie in recklessness on the part of some leading party quarters, in the ideological, political and organizational muddleheadedness, which was the objective result of the petty-bourgeois ideology of revolutionism, an excessive revolutionary zeal, a desire to achieve a quick victory, in forcing the development of the revolution which miscarried, in gambling on the balance of forces, in indulgence in adventurist fantasies, etc. . . .

During those tense days the party, having given its support to Colonel Untung's actions, committed the following political mistakes:

(a) The organizers of and immediate participants in Untung's actions failed to take into consideration the need to draw the masses to their side in order to secure the support of the progressive forces within the country. After the successful seizure of Radio Republic of Indonesia (RRI), they did not offer the people a positive socio-economic platform, nor did they call upon the peasants and workers to watch for the danger of the conspiracy of the Generals' Council.

Instead of issuing a decree for the creation of people's armed forces, a decision was made to give a fresh boost to the military.

---

* A plot, reportedly with CIA involvement, of rightist generals, headed by General A. H. Nasution, to overthrow the government of President Sukarno.

Following all this, it was hard to count on the support of the masses for the September 30 Movement.

(b) When all the political leaders had denied their participation in the Revolutionary Council, the leadership of the party made a belated statement to the effect that it was wrong to believe that the party had taken part in the September 30 Movement. However, the party leadership did not refute allegations that it had supported the purge carried out by Untung and his followers....

The adventurism of the abortive September 30 Movement and its epilogue proved to be the inevitable result of the accumulation of the party's past mistakes, its confused ideological, political and organizational line, all of which caused the party to be punished by the objective development of history.

The alternative facing the Communist and workers' movement in Indonesia at the present time is this: whether to stick to the old erroneous positions and continue adventurist policies, failing to see the real state of affairs, and upholding organizational sectarianism, which signifies a divorce from the masses, or completely to give up pseudo-revolutionary concepts and take the right path again, to be devoted to the Statute and the Program of the party adopted at the Fifth Congress of the PKI and supplemented at the Sixth Congress, to enjoy the love and sympathies of the broad masses and to make the party play the role not just of the vanguard, but the hegemon of the revolution....

II

The PKI must be rebuilt as a Lenin-type party, a party that will be capable of fulfilling its role as the advanced detachment and the highest form of class organization of the Indonesian proletariat, a party with a historical mission of leading the masses of the Indonesian people to win victory in the anti-imperialist, anti-feudal and anti-bureaucratic-capitalist revolution, and to advance toward socialism. Such a party must fulfill the following conditions: ideologically, it is armed with the theory of Marxism-Leninism, and free from subjectivism, opportunism and modern revisionism; politically, it has a correct program which includes a revolutionary agrarian program, has a thorough understanding of the problems of the strategy and tactics of the Indonesian revolution, masters the main form of struggle, namely the armed struggle of the peasants under the leadership of the proletariat, as well as other forms of struggle, is capable of establishing a revolutionary united front of all anti-imperialist and anti-feudal classes based on the worker-peasant alliance under the leadership of the working class; organizationally, it is strong and has deep roots among the masses of the people, consists of the most trustworthy, experienced and the most steeled party members who are models in the implementation of the national tasks.

Today we are rebuilding our party under the reign of unbridled counter-revolutionary white terror which is most cruel and ferocious. The legality of the party and the basic human rights of the Communists have been wantonly violated. The party has to work under completely illegal conditions and the organizational structure of the party must, therefore, be adjusted according to the new conditions. While working in complete illegality, the party must be adept at utilizing to the full all possible opportunities to carry out legal activities according to circumstances, and to choose ways and means that are acceptable to the masses with the aim of mobilizing the masses for struggle and leading this struggle step by step to the higher stage. . . .

> —The first excerpt is from "To Brothers at Home and Comrades Abroad Fighting against Imperialism, for Independence, Peace, Democracy and Socialism, for a Second Indonesian Revolution," *Information Bulletin,* 18 (106), Prague, 1967, pp. 53–54, 59, 62. The second excerpt is from "Build the KPI along the Marxist-Leninist Line to Lead the People's Democratic Revolution in Indonesia," *Indonesian Tribune,* No. 3, January 1967, as given in *Hsinhua News,* Peking, July 7, 1967.

V. AFRICA

Although there have been proposals for a continental strategy and armed coordination in the anti-imperialist struggle in Africa, diversity is also a feature of African countries and of their conditions, and affects the nature of that coordination. Attempts were made to achieve continental unity for complete liberation through the Organization of African Unity (OAU), set up in 1963 largely on the initiative of Kwame Nkrumah of Ghana. An OAU Liberation Committee was created to give active aid to armed African liberation movements. However, the reactionary leadership in many OAU countries and the fact of imperialist-inspired military coups that liquidated progressive-inclined regimes in some countries tended to obstruct this aim.

Despite considerable differences in the development of various African countries—from the relatively industrialized South Africa to the pre-capitalist societies of the equatorial zone— there are strong reasons for forms of continental anti-imperialist unity and of regional unity. One of these is imperialist unity to resist African liberation. Portugal could not withstand the guerrilla movements in its colonies without American imperialist aid received through NATO, while a military alliance of Portugal, Rhodesia and South Africa, backed by British and American imperialists, has been operational since early in 1967. African guerrilla and other liberation forces are compelled toward continental efforts to overcome their differences in development and in leadership in order to resist imperialist moves.

One of the difficulties in this regard is the question of the vanguard party or political organization that can give revolutionary leadership. Historically-evolved conditions in most African countries do not permit the rise of a working-class party, with an absence of a proletariat and worker-peasant alliances or radicalized petty-bourgeois groups from the leadership that does come out of such conditions. This has made it necessary for other parties of a centralized revolutionary type to emerge to head the struggle against colonialism and neo-colonialism. Most of the movements of this type that have come into being have been influenced, however, to one degree or another, by Marxist-Leninist concepts, and see the need for socialist aims in national development.

In some regions unity and coordination have been well developed. A coordinating body for the guerrilla liberation movements in the Portuguese colonies of Angola, Guinea Bissau and Mozambique, the CONCP *(Conférence des Organizations Nationalistes des Colonies Portugaises)*, was set up in 1961. In 1967 an alliance of the ANC (African National Congress, of South Africa) and the ZAPU (Zimbabwe African People's Union, of Rhodesia) launched a guerrilla struggle in Rhodesia and South Africa. On another level, Algeria, since its own liberation, has provided training bases and aid for other liberation movements in Africa. Tanzania, Zambia, the two Congos, Guinea and Ghana (before the counter-revolutionary coup of February 1966) have all opened their doors to training or staging bases or transit for guerrilla forces. Since each movement has its own identity and requires its own approaches to its problems, it is still an open question as to the extent to which continental coordination can go beyond these forms of unity.

Kwame Nkrumah's *Handbook of Revolutionary Warfare* divides the continent military-wise into liberated zones, contested zones and imperialist-held zones, with the concept of armed liberation not limited to guerrilla warfare but including regular warfare as well. In actuality, a variety of forms of militant struggle have brought liberation to African countries. The revolution in Zanzibar in 1963 was an insurrection, successfully carried out. In Tunisia and in Morocco mass struggle and armed action in the main cities succeeded and made protracted guerrilla war, as occurred in Algeria, unnecessary. In the Sudan, the Communist Party seriously debated the pros and cons of armed struggle before deciding on the essentially non-violent mass struggle that overthrew the reactionary Aboud regime in 1965. In Kenya, despite the Mau Mau's suppression, the guerrilla revolt gave enough feeling of the winds of change to force Britain to relinquish its open colonial rule.

It is a long step from the isolated ill-equipped Mau Mau movement in Kenya in the 1950s to the internationally-aided and trained popular armies now in the field in southern Africa. To a considerable extent, the African continent, especially the sub-Saharan regions, has been the beneficiary of the armed liberation struggles in Asia and in Latin America. They have been provided with lessons and advisers from all the victorious movements (Vietnam, Cuba, Algeria), and at the same time have probably had more direct assistance from socialist countries (the Soviet Union, China) than movements elsewhere in the past. The careful, calculated preliminary steps toward effective liberation struggles that have resulted from this are reflected in the selections included here.

1

Algeria: Features of the Armed Struggle

The armed struggle of the Algerian people has certain characteristics that have been common in the national liberation struggles of China, Vietnam, Indonesia, Morocco and Tunisia—a war of national liberation that is conducted in an agrarian country where the masses of the peasantry are without land, in a country containing a large population of unemployed, with small merchants and artisans. But it has also certain aspects of its own:

(1) There is an Algerian proletariat that is relatively numerous, that is politically developed and has a Communist Party that has existed for 20 years, that has experience in struggle and in its composition is a cross-section of Algeria.

(2) The population of European origin is relatively more important than in other colonies and is composed in the majority of workers.

(3) The unity of nationalist forces is realized in practice. There is a single army of national liberation, the Fighters for Liberation* having integrated themselves with that army.

(4) The French expeditionary force is composed of a large number of non-mercenaries: conscripted or regular troops (200,000 out of 600,000), unlike that which occurred in Indochina, for example.

(5) The geographical situation in Algeria has certain peculiarities apart from ordinary problems of an armed struggle.

* The Communist armed groups at the outset of the liberation war.

All of these economic, social, political and geographical aspects enter into the strategy and tactics of the Algerian popular armed forces.

Military strategy is subordinated to the political objectives that one pursues. On repeated occasions, the Communist Party of Algeria has declared its political objectives: Algeria desires its national independence but it is prepared to cease fire and to negotiate on the basis of the reality of the Algerian nation. The objective of the armed struggle of the Algerian patriots does not need to be to destroy the expeditionary corps or in the immediate future to achieve a Dien Bien Phu. A correspondent of *Le Monde* in Buenos Aires asked: "Are the guerrilla fighters looking for a military victory and do they not fear a new winter campaign?"

Ferhat Abbas* answered very justly: "The guerrilla fighters have never looked for a military victory over the French army. We know that a great nation can exterminate a little people. But the guerrillas remain invincible and in existence so long as their political objectives are not reached. It can be said that they can endure many winter campaigns if necessary."

What the Algerian patriots are looking for is not so much spectacular victories but prolonged delivery of painful and repeated blows at the expeditionary force, at the colonial administration and its agents, at the ultra-colonialists. Repeated successes such as those of Palestro, Aflon, Tébessa and elsewhere have been for the purpose of rendering life impossible for the colonialists. The Spanish guerrillas forced the army of Napoleon to abandon Spain without great battles. To obtain that objective, it is clearly necessary to have to some degree an organized army, cadres, arms and ammunition, and military knowledge, but the struggle of the Algerian people is made in the manner of others who have proved that whenever a people has fought for liberty the material resources they do possess have a quality one hundred times greater than those of the army of the oppressor. The political content, the "psychological aspect," is always in favor of revolutionary wars, of just wars. The geographical situation of Algeria, which is almost that of an island, has created from the outset certain difficulties from the standpoint of replenishing arms and ammunition. But here also popular initiative has made up for that inconvenience: the people seize the arms of the enemy, they make them themselves, they resort to cold steel, etc.

---

* At that time, one of the leaders of the National Liberation Front in Algeria.

Military tactics are intimately tied up with political tactics and with the situation in our country. Politically, the Communists have always advised the anti-imperialist tactic of the unity of all the national forces: an Algerian National Democratic Front. The unification of the armed forces is a great anti-imperialist victory. Trade union unity and political unity have also been great victories. The unity of national forces permits also persistent efforts to isolate the ultra-colonialists from the important body of workers of European origin, the majority of whom consider the Algerian demands just, and some of whom, while preserving their love for their country of origin, desire nothing better than to adopt a second country.

If the armed struggle is the main feature in the Algerian political scene, it is not separated from mass action. The general strike on July 5, the street demonstration of May 1, the strike of students and school children, of merchants and artisans, the boycott of tobacco and of alcoholic drinks are some of the actions originating in the masses and helpful to the national cause. Their increase and their growth in size cannot but weaken our enemy. These are the varied and diverse forms of action discovered daily through popular initiative....

It is obvious that there is a political role for the Army of National Liberation and the armed groups in the countryside.

The *Moudjahiddines* are in general peasants connected with the masses. They are not satisfied merely to harass the enemy, to catch them in ambushes, to cause them merciless destruction, to capture their arms, etc. They are also men of the national cause, of patriotic conscience, who want to carry the struggle further in the broadest and most lofty manner together with the people.

They are propagandists, they explain to the people the character of the war, the aims of the Army of National Liberation, about who is to liberate the country and to give land to the peasants. They are at the same time the organizers who have the task of preparing the people to rule themselves, of beginning to create in the villages and rural districts the local revolutionary organs that will become the organs of local power. The popular initiative again, in this case, cannot but be of great assistance.

At the same time, the *Moudjahid* is the friend of the peasant, the one who gives him assistance in his daily problems, who aids him to the extent of his means and to the extent that military exigencies permit, in his labor, in his harvest, and in general in all the work in the fields. The *Moudjahid* knows very well that he is helpless if he arouses against himself the masses of the peasants. He knows very well that he has nothing to gain by not giving to collaborators and to others responsible for acts harmful to the national cause punishments adequate with the gravity of acts committed. Always, the good popular opinion of guerrillas and partisans has been stirred by a varied and original scale of punishments, from the black list to the ears cut off by the Spanish guerrillas, to the hair cut off the collaborator women during the liberation of France, and to the nose divided for the unrepentant collaborators in the Algerian campaign.

The *Moudjahiddines* know also that the French expeditionary force includes a large number of soldiers conscripted or regular, sent by force to Algeria, who frequently, before their departure, have raised protests, sometimes violently, against the unjust character and the uselessness of such a war for the people of France. In the history of every revolutionary struggle the people are given the task of winning to its cause the army of the oppressors and exploiters. . . .

In the cities, the tactics of the Army of National Liberation is also a tactic of harassing the enemy: the army, the police, the administration and collaborators. It is not true, as the "resident minister" Lacoste would like us to believe, that the armed struggle has been *dislodged* from the countryside to the city. It has grown in the countryside and has extended to the cities: such is the fact.

Lenin has demonstrated in regard to the insurrection in Moscow in 1905 how "the guerrilla war" in the cities progressed beyond the tactic of barricades that up to that time were employed in the armed struggle in cities: "The organization required for such tactics is that of mobile, exceedingly small units, units of ten, three or even two persons."* . . .

Thus the groups of patriots conduct the armed struggle in our Algerian cities, as those of Morocco and of Tunisia have shown. They have instinctively adopted the tactic of guerrilla groups in the cities: the army, the police, the colonial administration, and the collaborators pay a clumsy tribute to that heroic action, eminently patriotic. Each day, tens of our heroes fall obscurely in the battle of giants. Our duty is always to improve this form of struggle, to bear it always most proudly, to heighten it politically and to eliminate its defects.

---

* See V. I. Lenin, "Lessons of the Moscow Uprising," Part One of this volume.

Lenin spoke of terror exercised by the masses and he declared also that the groups did not know how to "control the mobs." That is to say, the action of armed groups must be a political-military action of the masses. In the Casbah of Algiers, in Bône, in the market-place of Tébessa, we have known in the past period of similar struggles of armed groups that have trained hundreds and thousands of persons in the struggle. The protecting of armed groups by the population of districts and of cities, the silence, the absence of informers who complain to the colonialists, are the elementary forms of participation of the masses in the armed struggle that develops and heightens.

This "terror" exercised by the masses against the tiny minority of oppressors and of colonialists demands also "to be organized and controlled." It is all the more necessary because our country is composed almost entirely of peasants and of an urban bourgeoisie (merchants, artisans) that quite naturally furnish important forces to the patriotic struggle. But in their character of "small producers," they confer upon it an ideology that expresses itself occasionally in acts of a distorted character, to the discredit of the just character of the national struggle; like the bus outrage at Diar es Saada, creating the impression of a chauvinist, racist, fanatical struggle, that does a disservice not only to Algerian social classes and ethnical groups (which does not further their cause), but also in the eyes of international opinion.

Certainly a man of good character understands the reaction of certain elements, frequently unorganized and uncontrolled, who, incensed by a bloody colonialism and its repressive atrocities, are prone to do similar acts, but he cannot justify it. Political men, conscious of their responsibilities, do not submit themselves to the *spontaneity of the masses.* Marxists say justly that a party with self-respect does not trail after the masses, but puts itself boldly at their head to guide them. This is all the more necessary since the ultra-colonialists, as they have done in Tunisia and in Morocco, try and will continue to try to attribute to the Army of National Liberation terrorist acts carried out by themselves, to discredit it at such moments as when the United Nations is about to discuss the Algerian problem. (Example: the outrage against the chapel in Darboussa Bône.) They will try, moreover, as they have done many times, to introduce into the patriotic organizations, political or military, *agents provocateurs* assigned to disorganize the struggle and to discredit it. That is why great vigilance is essential. But the best way of eliminating the defects is to raise always higher the political level of the struggle, to give political education to the innumerable masses who, each day, enter the struggle; also, to reinforce the cadres of the Army of National Liberation with proletarian elements drawn from amongst the dockers, the miners, the transport workers, the agricultural laborers, etc. The proletariat, by principle, is alien to a harmful ideology.

The Algerian Communist Party, bound tightly with the Algerian proletariat, plays a major role in that sphere. To the degree that the Communists participate actively in the struggle, they bring to it their experience and their understanding in the self-interest of the national movement and of its decisive struggle.

> —From an editorial in the Algerian Communist journal, *Réalités Algériennes et Marxisme,* No. 1, November–December 1956, as reprinted in *Réalités Algériennes et Marxisme,* editions El Hourraya, Algiers, 1962, pp. 11–20.

2

Lessons of the Algerian Liberation Struggle

BASHIR HADJ ALI

How did the armed struggle begin? What were the internal and external factors the cumulative effect of which sparked off that struggle?

The first internal factor was the upsurge of the national liberation movement on the eve of the uprising marked by organizational and political work among the masses, strikes of workers and peasants, actions in solidarity with the people of Vietnam, Tunisia, Morocco, etc., on a scale hitherto unprecedented. An important role in this struggle was played by the Communist Party.

The second internal factor was the aggravation of the contradictions between our people and French imperialism. The Algerian people as a whole realized the futility of "legal" methods and the need to find other means of putting an end to colonial dependence. This led to the appearance of the *maquis,* guerrilla detachments consisting of patriots evading the reprisals, and a semi-military secret organization founded on the insistence of the more revolutionary wing of the main nationalist party of that time, the Movement for Triumph of Democratic Freedom. This organization, despite the repressions, still had its centers in some parts of the country. Moreover, there was a considerable quantity of arms and equipment left behind, mainly in the villages, after the landing of Allied forces in North Africa in November 1942.

The political crisis of the Democratic Freedom Movement, which split into two, accelerated the growth of political consciousness among both masses and leaders. The revolutionaries who left that party sought to restore the unity of the party by passing over to a higher form of struggle, namely the armed uprising.

To these objective and subjective internal factors two external factors should be added: first, the defeat of the French at Dien Bien Phu, which showed the Algerian patriots that French imperialism could be defeated. Second, the rise of the socialist camp which exerted an enormous influence on the masses even in the most remote villages, helping them to realize the need to end the domination of the French imperialists by force of arms.

The Role of Classes and Social Strata

Algeria's population of 10 million is nearly 80 per cent peasant. Expropriation of the best lands by the colonialists had left 600,000 peasants without any land at all, while 450,000 peasants eked out a miserable existence on tiny plots.

On the eve of the armed uprising there were about one million people in the countryside without the means of subsistence, and some 500,000 unemployed in the cities. There were also about 120,000 small shopkeepers and artisans who were hard pressed by French competition. The middle bourgeoisie accounted for about 11,000 families which owned 7,000 small enterprises, none employing more than 15 workers. The European bourgeoisie owned 30,000 enterprises. The big national bourgeoisie was weak and few in number. The working class consisted of approximately 300,000 permanent and seasonal workers, mainly unskilled or low-skilled. This working class took shape in the course of the struggle against the European rather than the Algerian bourgeoisie. The majority of the workers had one foot in the village. In a country in which class differentiations were not yet clearly defined, the proletariat had not yet become a class "for itself."

Thus, it was not the big bourgeoisie that played the leading role in the revolution but the small and middle bourgeoisie, especially the former. The working class, though active and organized in the trade unions, in the Communist Party and in the Democratic Freedom Movement, played an important but not a leading role. However, as the liberation struggle developed, its political role steadily grew.

The peasants comprised the main army of the revolution. The war in Algeria was a national liberation war, a war for the land. The bulk of the people, including the women, took part in that war. All classes, all social strata participated to one or another extent, the main burden being borne by the poorest peasantry. The political alliance of all the forces of the nation, with the exception of the feudal lords, was realized within the framework and around the Front of National Liberation, the leading force of the struggle. The alliance of the armed forces was effected through the Army of National Liberation under the leadership of the FNL. Trade union unity was achieved through the General Federation of Workers. The solid support accorded the FNL by the people was manifested time and again, especially in the mass action of August 20, 1955, and in the general strike of July 5, 1956. . . .

Shortcomings and Mistakes of the Liberation Movement

No movement involving vast masses of people has ever been entirely free of mistakes. This holds true also for the FNL, whose epoch-making contributions will never be forgotten. It must be said however that the mistakes were never serious enough to endanger the successes achieved. Moreover, they were noticed in good time, and some were partly rectified in the course of the struggle. These weaknesses and errors were set forth by the Communist Party in two confidential letters to the Provisional Government in November 1958 and in the second half of 1959 (these were published after independence). . . .

On closer examination we find that the mistakes made by the movement were due chiefly to objective circumstances, i.e., to the tremendous difficulties with which the FNL had to contend in the course of the war. But there were subjective reasons as well. For example, the slogan "everything for the war, for the armed struggle," while basically correct, was applied at times too narrowly. It was not sufficiently understood for a long time that subordinating everything to the armed struggle by no means implied allowing political work to suffer. On the contrary, the armed struggle should be closely linked with political work and subordinated to the political objectives in the interests of the revolution.

Here is one example. Subsequent events showed that the Battle of Algiers in 1957 had been conceived incorrectly. In the first place, the central political leadership of the movement had its headquarters in the city. Secondly, the balance of forces did not favor the patriots: about half of the population were Europeans, most of them hostile to the national movement. The city was flooded with French troops. Moreover, Algiers served as a sort of rear supply base for the guerrillas operating in the interior of the country. From here workers and students were recruited to replenish the ranks of the Liberation Army.

The battle for the capital was started as a maneuver to divert part of the French army operating against the Liberation Army in the rural areas, notably in the Ouarsenis area, to the city and thus relieve the pressure on the Liberation Army. The Battle of Algiers lasted for about seven or eight months. The people fought valiantly against the heavily armed colonialist forces. Workers and shopkeepers staged an eight-day strike.

But since the balance of forces in the city favored the colonialists, the patriots were defeated. This cost us the lives of 7,000 young fighting men. Our Algiers organization was smashed and decapitated. The leading bodies of the FNL, left without supplies and cadres, were exposed and neutralized. The political leadership of the FNL was forced to leave the country, a fact that had serious political consequences. The strategic centralization established at the Soummam Congress in 1956 for a time ceased to exist. The FNL and the Liberation Army had no centralized leadership. From this moment on groups of the FNL and the Liberation Army began to operate independently of one another. This led to a division of the country into districts. New problems arose which were often resolved not on the basis of principle but from the standpoint of the interests of particular clans, groups, districts, etc.

It was this struggle between the clans and groupings, which began in 1957 owing to the lack of centralized leadership and the advent of several political groups, that aggravated the situation in Algeria after independence, complicated the development of the class struggle both within and outside the FNL . . . .

The root error was the failure to make a realistic assessment of the correlation of forces, the lack of sufficient information regarding the strength of the enemy on the given sector and the general conditions obtaining in the capital, and the failure to see anything but the purely military aspect of the operation at the given moment. Added to this was another failing, namely impatience. It was impatience that gave rise to the slogan "an Algerian Dien Bien Phu" advanced by some leaders, despite the fact that this was impossible under Algerian conditions. . . . Subjectivism and impatience are typical products of petty-bourgeois thinking. And combined with the underestimation of political work in that period these mistakes might have had fatal consequences had they not been corrected in time.

Underestimation of political education led to a shortage of instructors in the towns and especially in the guerrilla units, with the result that not enough attention was paid to the non-violent struggle of the masses. We for our part always stressed the need to utilize diverse forms of struggle, to be prepared for mass actions for definite economic demands. For example, we worked to establish trade unions, we supported the struggle of the women for the release of their husbands from prison, of the agricultural workers for higher wages, of the Algerian students against the OAS students. All these actions prepared the masses for bigger battles and objectively supported the armed struggle insofar as they diverted the attention of the imperialist police. . . .

The Provisional Government represented that section of the bourgeoisie which was ready to compromise. Already at that time it feared the mass movement and its social content. It was for this reason that in December 1960 the Government banned demonstrations in Algiers and other cities. We publicly criticizd this order and urged that the mass actions should go on, ending in one locality and being resumed in another. Today it is generally recognized that the mass actions of December 1960 in the big towns marked the turning point in the war of liberation. They helped to develop the social consciousness of the masses and gave powerful support to the armed struggle. . . .

Shortcomings and Errors of the Communist Party

The armed struggle took all the national parties by surprise, and the Communist Party, like the others, underestimated the significance of that struggle and its potential at first. But it did not condemn the use of armed force. It correctly appraised the causes of the struggle, and in a form dictated by the restricted freedom of speech came out (before the party was dissolved) in support of the aspirations of the people. . . .

Although the Communist Party never condemned violence or armed struggle, the warning it issued on January 13, 1955, against certain forms of individual action that might play into the hands of the colonialists was inopportune, since the best way of avoiding such actions would have been to join the armed struggle without hesitation.

Why did the Communist Party at first hesitate and underestimate the prospects of the armed struggle?

This mistake—despite our attempt to correct it as far back as 1946—sprang from a persistent tendency to underestimate the national factor and the peasantry and to overestimate the role of the European workers. The result was that the party did not give serious and timely attention to the question of armed struggle. In fact it was not until 1953, after the success of the national liberation struggles in Vietnam, Tunisia and Morocco, that the party began to make a theoretical study of this question. There is another reason for the initial underestimation of the armed actions. For a long time the party had counted too much on the possibility of a proletarian revolution in France, and this led to the belief that victory in Algeria would come through the victory of the proletariat in France.

There is still another more immediate reason for our failure correctly to assess the situation—and this applies incidentally to all other national parties—namely, a superficial approach in appraising the development of a revolutionary situation. The Communist Party believed that, if anything, the launching of the national liberation war in November 1954 was premature, because the conditions for an armed uprising, as formulated by Lenin, did not yet exist. But we forgot, on the one hand, that the conditions of which Lenin spoke applied to the capitalist countries, and on the other, that military operations and a general uprising are two different things.

Moreover, like any new form of struggle, the armed struggle was a drastic departure from the usual forms of work conducted by the national parties and organizations. Here is what Lenin had to say on this score: "Every military action in any war to a certain extent disorganizes the ranks of the fighters. But this does not mean that one must not fight. It means that one must *learn to fight.*"* ...

Some Lessons

In order to ensure the best climate for the success of an armed struggle, we believe it is necessary:

—to have a single centralized leadership and a certain degree of decentralization during the hostilities;

—to link the armed struggle closely with political mass struggle;

—to support the war by struggle in the towns, but to safeguard the towns used as rear bases for the armed struggle;

—constantly to conduct political work among the masses, in the enemy army, among the people of the country waging an unjust war, and among world public opinion;

—to advance consistent and concrete proposals for ending the war on the basis of satisfying the people's national demands, taking into account the specific demands of each section of society and linking them with the principle objective;

—to utilize the contradictions between the enemy and his allies, and to strengthen the alliance of the people with their natural allies outside the country.

These are some of the lessons that can be drawn from the war in Algeria. Naturally, we do not presume to give some sort of recipe, inasmuch as the organization and methods of waging the armed struggle are determined by the concrete conditions, the economic, social and national features of each country. However, these lessons born of the Algerian experience may perhaps be useful in other encounters with imperialism.

> —"Some Lessons of the Liberation Struggle in Algeria," *World Marxist Review,* January 1965, pp. 41, 43–46. Bashir Hadj Ali is general secretary of the Algerian Communist Party.

---

* See V. I. Lenin, "Guerrilla Warfare," in Part One of this volume.

3

National Liberation and the Social Structure

AMILCAR CABRAL

> *These are selections from an address delivered before the First Conference of the Peoples of Asia, Africa and Latin America, held in Havana, Cuba, January 3–14, 1966, by the general secretary of the* Partido Africano da Independência da Guiné e Cabo Verde (PAIGC), *which leads the national liberation struggle in the Portuguese-held colony of Guinea in West Africa. Space does not permit the inclusion of the entire address, essential parts of which have been paraphrased. It is presented as an example of the principle of careful analysis of specific conditions within a country prior to the beginning of an armed liberation struggle; in Guinea's case they were predominantly pre-capitalist conditions, which also prevail in other parts of Africa.*

Other cases may differ from ours; however, our experience teaches us that in the general framework of the daily struggle, in giving attention to the problems created by the enemy, struggle against ourselves is the most difficult, and better done in the present moment than in the future as far as our peoples are concerned. That struggle is an expression of the internal contradictions in the economic, social and cultural (and thus historical) reality of each of our countries. We are convinced that any national or social revolution that does not possess such a basic understanding of that reality runs a great risk of being unsuccessful, if not of failing.

When the African people say in their simple language that "no matter how warm the water is in the spring, it does not cook the rice," they express, with simplicity, a fundamental principle not only of physics but also of political science. We know that the unfolding of a phenomenon in motion, no matter what its external condition, depends mainly on its internal characteristics. We also know that in politics—even if the reality of others is more beautiful and attractive—our own reality is not truly transformed without concrete understanding, without our own efforts and without our own sacrifices. It is good to remind ourselves that, regardless of the similarity of appearance and identity of our enemies, national liberation and social revolution are not merchandise for export; they are—and each day further proves it—the product of local and national conditions, more or less influenced by exterior factors (favorable and unfavorable), but essentially determined and conditioned by the historical reality of each people, and consolidated by the victory or correct solution of internal contradictions between the various elements that characterize that reality. The success of the Cuban revolution, occurring within a few hundred kilometers of the strongest imperialist and anti-socialist force of all time, we think to be, in its content and in its way of developing, a practical illustration and conclusive proof of the validity of this principle.

We have acknowledged, however, that we ourselves, and the other movements of liberation in general (we refer above all to the African experience) have not given all the necessary attention to this important problem of our struggle.

The ideological shortcoming, although not the total lack of ideology, at the heart of national liberation movements—that which reveals itself basically in ignorance of the historical reality that these movements lay claim to transform—constitutes one of the greatest, if not the greatest, weaknesses of our struggle against imperialism. We believe, nevertheless, that a sufficient number of varied experiences have already been accumulated to permit the definition of a general line of thought and action in order to eliminate that deficiency. A broad discussion on the subject would be useful as a valuable contribution to strengthening the present and future action of national liberation movements. It would be a form of concrete assistance to those movements of no less importance than political and financial support or than arms.

It is with this aim that we present here our opinion on *the objective of the national liberation movement in relation to the social structure.* This opinion of ours has been shaped by our experience in the struggle and by the critical appreciation of other experiences. To those who see in it a theoretical character, we would reply that all practice engenders a theory. And that, if it is true that a revolution can miscarry, despite perfectly conceived theories, it is equally true that one cannot achieve a victorious revolution without a revolutionary theory.

> Cabral examines the generally accepted theory that the motive force of history is class struggle, and points to the difficulty of applying this theory to the situation in his own country. He inquires: "Did history commence only at the moment when the class phenomenon developed or with the consequent class struggle?" and then continues: "It would be, in that case—and we refuse to accept it—to consider that many human societies in Africa, Asia and Latin America lived without history or outside of history up to the time when they were subjected to the yoke of imperialism. It would be to consider that the populations of our countries, such as the 'Balanta' of Guinea, the 'Kouniama' of Angola and the 'Maconde' of Mozambique, have lived until today—if we disregard the slight influence of colonialism to which they were violently subjected—without history." Cabral concludes that, to understand what had happened in his country and others like it and to work for a transformation of conditions, it is better to consider that "the level of productive forces" is the motive force of history, and that imperialism, imposing itself from outside, interrupted the normal development of the productive forces of his people and thus interrupted their history. In his view, imperialism created a "pseudo-bourgeoisie" (or sham bourgeoisie) out of certain native elements, to facilitate its rule and to block popular resistance; the "pseudo-bourgeoisie" therefore does not constitute a national bourgeoisie that evolves out of the normal growth of productive forces and out of class struggle. This is an important consideration in shaping the alliances of a national liberation movement. Cabral then distinguishes between this strictly "colonial" situation and the "neo-colonial" situation in which classes and class struggle have developed.

In other words, the national liberation of people is the reconquest of the historical personality of that people, it is its return to history as a means of destroying the imperialist domination to which it has been subjected . . . only that liberty and that alone can guarantee the normalization of the historical processes of a people. Consequently, we can conclude that there is national liberation when and only when the national productive forces are completely free of foreign domination. . . . If we consider that national liberation demands for survival a transformation in the development of productive forces, we will see that the phenomenon of *national liberation* corresponds essentially to a *revolution*. It is important to be aware of the objective and subjective conditions by which that revolution is made, and to understand the forms or the form of struggle most appropriate to its realization. . . .

Although the colonial and neo-colonial situations are in essence identical, and although the principal aspect of the struggle against imperialism is the neo-colonial aspect, we believe it is important to distinguish between the practice of the two situations. In effect, the horizontal structure of the primitive society, although more or less differentiated, and the absence of a national political system, makes possible, in the colonial situation, the creation of a broad front of unity and of struggle indispensable for the success of a national liberation movement. But that possibility does not relieve us of rigorous analysis of the indigenous social structure, of tendencies of its evolution and of the adoption in practice of appropriate measures for the guarantee of a genuine national liberation. Among these measures—while admitting that each of us knows what is best in his own country—it seems to us indispensable to create a vanguard firmly united and conscious of the real meaning and of the objective of the struggle that it must direct. That necessity is proportionately more pressing when one is aware that, with rare exceptions, the colonial situation neither permits nor requires the significant existence of vanguard classes (a self-conscious working class and a rural proletariat) that can guarantee the vigilance of the popular masses in the evolution of the liberation movement. Inversely, the generally embryonic character of the laboring classes and the economic, social and cultural situation of the most important physical force of the national liberation struggle—the peasants—do not enable those two principal forces of that struggle to distinguish, by themselves, genuine national independence from artificial political independence. Only a revolutionary vanguard, generally an active minority, can be conscious, from the outset, of that difference, and can bring it, through struggle, to the understanding of the popular masses. It makes clear the fundamental political character of the national liberation struggle and gives, to a certain extent, the form of struggle the national liberation takes.

In a neo-colonial situation, the pronounced structure of the indigenous society is more or less vertical, and the existence of a political authority composed of native elements—a National State—aggravates, already, the contradictions at the heart of that society, and makes difficult, if not impossible, the creation of a united front as extensive as that in the colonial case. On the one hand, the material effects (principally a national political system and the stimulation of an economic initiative by an indigenous element, in particular in the commercial sphere) and psychological effects (arrogance from believing themselves in control over their own compatriots, exploitation of the interdependent religious and tribal order on the part of a few leaders and a fraction of the popular masses) contribute to the disorganization of a considerable part of the national forces. But, on the other hand, the necessarily repressive character of the neo-colonial state against the forces of national liberation, the aggravation of class contradictions, the permanent presence of agents and signs of a foreign domination (colonists who keep their privileges, armed forces, racial discrimination), the increasing poverty of the peasantry, and the influence more or less well-known of the external factors, contribute toward maintaining the flame of nationalism, and has progressively raised the consciousness of extensive popular sectors, and has reunited, precisely on the basis of consciousness of neo-colonial frustration, the majority of the population around the ideal of national liberation. Besides, while the leading native class progressively becomes bourgeoisified, the development of a laboring class composed of city workers and of rural proletariat, both exploited by the indirect domination of imperialism, opens new perspectives for the evolution of national liberation. This laboring class, which possesses a degree of political consciousness (if only in a limited way, as *conscious of its poverty*), is prepared, in the neo-colonial case, to constitute a genuine popular vanguard of the national liberation struggle. But it cannot realize completely its mission in the framework of that struggle (which is not finished with the conquest of independence) if it is not firmly united with the other exploited strata, the peasants in general (wage laborers, tenant farmers, small farmers, small proprietors) and the nationalist petty bourgeoisie. The realization of that alliance demands the mobilization and the organization of the nationalist forces in the framework (or through the action) of a strong and well-built political organization.

One other important distinction between the colonial and the neo-colonial situations resides in the perspectives of the struggle. In the colonial case (where the *nation class* fights against the forces of repression of the bourgeoisie of the colonizing country) it is possible to carry out, at least on the surface, a nationalist solution (a national revolution); the nation wins its independence and adopts, hypothetically, the economic structure that is most convenient. In the neo-colonial case (where the laboring classes and their allies struggle simultaneously against the imperialist bourgeoisie and the leading native class) the situation cannot be resolved by a nationalist solution; it demands the destruction of the capitalist structure implanted by imperialism in the national territory, and justly postulates a socialist solution.

That distinction derives principally from the difference in the level of productive forces in the two cases and from the consequent aggravation of class struggle. . . .

Facts show incontrovertibly that the essential instrument of imperialist domination is violence. If we accept the principle that *the struggle for liberation is a revolution* and that the latter does not come to an end when the flag is raised or the national anthem is played, we will agree that there is not nor can there be national liberation without the use of violence as a liberating factor on the part of the nationalist forces, in response to the criminal violence of the agents of imperialism. No one who knows its characteristics can doubt that imperialist domination means a permanent state of violence against nationalist forces. There are no people on earth who, previously having been subjugated to imperialist rule (colonial or neo-colonial), have won their independence (nominally or effectively) without having had victims. What is important is to determine what are the forms of violence that can be used by the national liberation forces, to reply not only to imperialist violence but to guarantee for the struggle the final victory of its cause: genuine national independence.

Experiences past and present, in the lives of certain peoples, the actual situation of the struggles for national liberation in the world—especially in Vietnam, in the Congo and in Zimbabwe [African name for Rhodesia]—as well as the contradictions and leaps caused by the situation of permanent violence in certain countries that reached independence by the path called peaceful, demonstrate to us that not only are compromises with imperialism not operative but also that the normal path of national liberation, imposed on the peoples by imperialist repression, is the *armed struggle*.

We do not believe that we shock anyone in asserting that the sole and efficacious path for the definite realization of the aspirations of peoples, of national liberation, is the armed struggle. It is the great lesson that the contemporary history of the liberation struggle indicates to all who are truly engaged in the liberation effort of their people.

It is evident as well, as far as the effectiveness of that path is concerned, that the stability of the situation after liberation depends not only on the way the struggle was organized but also on the political consciousness and morale of those who, for historical reasons, immediately inherit from colonialism or neo-colonialism. Facts demonstrate that the only social sector capable of having consciousness of the reality of imperialist domination and of leading the machinery of state inherited from it is the native petty bourgeoisie. If we keep in mind the uncertain characteristics or natural tendencies inherent in the economic situation of that strata or class, we will agree that this feature of our situation constitutes one of the weaknesses of the national liberation movement.

The colonial situation, which does not permit the indigenous development of a "pseudo-bourgeoisie" and in which the popular masses do not attain in general the necessary degree of political consciousness before the bursting forth of the phenomenon of national liberation, offers to the petty bourgeoisie the historical opportunity of leading the struggle against foreign domination, since it is, due to the objective and subjective situation (level of life superior to that of the masses, more frequent contacts with the agents of imperialism and thus with more occasions to be humiliated, degree of education, higher political culture, etc.), the strata which acquires most rapidly a consciousness of the need to be liberated from foreign domination. That historical responsibility is assumed by the sector of the petty bourgeoisie that may, in the colonial context, be called *revolutionary,* whereas its other sections preserve the doubtful characteristics of those classes that go along with colonialism, in order to defend, without illusion, their social privileges.

The neo-colonial situation, which demands the liquidation of the native "pseudo-bourgeoisie," so that national liberation can be realized, gives also to the petty bourgeoisie the opportunity to occupy a prime, and decisive, role in the struggle for liberation from foreign domination. But, in this case, by virtue of the progress attained in the social structure, the leadership of the struggle is shared (to a greater or less degree) with the sectors of the most aware of the working classes and also with the elements of the national "pseudo-bourgeoisie" imbued with patriotic sentiment. The role of the section of the petty bourgeoisie that takes part in the leadership of the struggle is again very important, as long as it is a fact that in the neo-colonial situation itself it is apt to assume this function, either because the working classes understand their economic and cultural limitations, or because of complications and limitations of an ideological nature affecting the nationalist sector of the "pseudo-bourgeoisie" that adheres to the struggle. In that case, it is important to mention that the mission that has been confided to it demands of that sector of the petty bourgeoisie a very great revolutionary consciousness, the capacity to interpret faithfully the aspirations of the masses at each phase of the struggle and to identify itself more and more with them.

But, so great must be the revolutionary consciousness of this section of the petty bourgeoisie that it must completely realize that, as a class of services (that is, not directly included in the processes of production), it cannot control the economic foundations won by the capture of power. In effect, history shows that, whatever the role, sometimes important, played by individuals coming from the petty bourgeoisie in the process of a revolution, that class has never been in possession of political power. It cannot be, because political power is based on the economic capacity of a leading class and, in the conditions of colonial and neo-colonial societies, that capacity is held by two entities: the main imperialists and the national working classes.

To maintain the power that national liberation puts in its hands, the petty bourgeoisie has only one choice: to abandon its natural tendencies to become a bourgeoisie; if it develops as a bureaucratic bourgeoisie with middleman aspects or transforms itself into a national "pseudo-bourgeoisie" it denies the revolution and necessarily rallies itself to the side of the imperialists, which is nothing more than a neo-colonial situation and a betrayal of the objectives of the national liberation. In order not to betray these objectives, the petty bourgeoisie has only one choice: to strengthen its revolutionary consciousness, to repudiate its tendencies to become bourgeois and the natural urgings of its class mentality, to identify itself with the working class, and not to oppose the normal development of the process of the revolution. This means that, to fulfill perfectly the role that falls to it in the struggle for national liberation, the revolutionary petty bourgeoisie must be capable of committing suicide as a class, to be revived as revolutionary workers, entirely identified with the most profound aspirations of the people.

That alternative—to betray the revolution or to commit suicide as a class—constitutes the dilemma of the petty bourgeoisie in the general framework of the struggle for national liberation. Its positive solution in favor of the revolution depends on that which Fidel Castro has correctly called *the development of the revolutionary conscience*. That dependence necessarily draws our attention to the capacity of the leadership of the national liberation struggle to maintain faithfully the principles and the fundamental cause of the struggle. To some extent, this shows that if the national liberation struggle is essentially a political problem, the conditions of its development impart to it certain moral features.

—From mimeographed copy of Cabral's speech in possession of the editor. Translated from the French.

4

South Africa: The Revolutionary Way

Things are coming to a head in South Africa. We are very fast coming to a big crisis in our history. The Nationalist government is tightening the screws and driving apartheid and oppression to the limits of the people's endurance. The people are fighting back. As, one after another, the government stops legal and peaceful channels of protest and resistance the oppressed masses are turning to methods that are illegal and nonpeaceful. They are looking to illegal organizations like the African National Congress and the Communist Party for leadership and liberation. Violent outbreaks of one sort or another are becoming more and more common. Sometimes, as in the operations of *Umkonto We Sizwe* [Spear of the Nation], these outbreaks are purposeful, effective and carefully planned on a nation-wide level. But very often, as hunger, persecution and police terror drive one section of the people after another to desperation, we find unplanned, spontaneous acts of resistance and retaliation taking place on a local level, and the development of bodies like "Poqo" with its outlook of blind revenge on whites.

Former leaders of the break-away Pan-Africanist Congress now living in exile, such as P. Leballo in his recent notorious Maseru speech, have attempted to claim the Poqo movement as part of their organization. This claim is made for the purpose of boosting the fallen prestige of PAC, which no longer exists as an organized force in South Africa itself. It does not bear serious examination. PAC may well have given rise to Poqo, by spreading the concept that spontaneous outbursts of people's violence are a suitable means of struggle, and by whipping up anti-white chauvinism amongst African patriots. But having produced the atmosphere in which Poqo has grown, neither PAC nor anyone else can claim to control or to lead it. For Poqo is, in essence, not an organized political movement with an ideology and long-term policy accepted by all its adherents. Outbreaks ascribed to Poqo, such as those at Paarl and the Bashee River, were not planned by PAC or any other national organization: they were semi-spontaneous reactions of men oppressed beyond endurance, inspired to action by the rudimentary political aims of the Poqo movement. . . .

Looked at from the viewpoint of the historical process, the South African regime is steadily and swiftly being driven into a position of isolation, in which the armaments, capital and other forms of material and moral support which sustain it from abroad will one after another be cut short.

Even more important, inside South Africa itself—in spite of the massive-appearing and ever-growing state machine of domination and repression—the balance of forces is steadily changing in favor of the people and their liberation forces, and against the oppressing minority.

A minority, however heavily armed, cannot prevail over the great majority of the people when the majority is organized, determined and clear in its purpose. Every new act of tyranny and oppression by the government calls forth acts of revolutionary protest and resistance by the masses. Often such acts may be unplanned, desperate and unsuccessful. They may be answered by heavy and costly reprisals. But in the process the forces of liberation are being forged. They are becoming more steeled in their determination. They are building effective and indestructible organizations. They are achieving ever greater clarity of purpose and direction.

The violent clashes which have occurred in the Cape and elsewhere are signs of the growing revolutionary upheaval in our country. The so-called Poqo operations are a reaction against unendurable oppression, and one cannot doubt the courage and patriotic feelings of those who took part in such actions as the storming of police stations. But at the same time many of these acts show negative and even harmful features. Planned badly, or not at all, they have the nature of spontaneous outbursts: acts of desperation, not acts of responsible and thoughtful revolutionaries. They reflect grave political backwardness, their only basis often being a crude, terroristic policy of hitting back and indiscriminate reprisals against the white community. Such a policy is far removed from the outlook of the advanced elements of the African people, as it has been formed in the course of a long experience of struggle for national liberation headed by the African National Congress, the trade unions and the Communist Party. At the same time, these acts of desperate retaliation have a positive side, although they cannot succeed in their objectives and although they involve heavy reprisals, setbacks and temporary defeats.

For from these defeats the people are drawing the conclusion, not that resistance is futile, but that it should be planned, purposeful and principled. The leaders of the African liberation movement have not merely taken a negative or critical attitude toward the Poqo-type outbreaks. They have acknowledged that exclusively non-violent methods are no longer of use. Indeed, it is notable that at the recent Moshi Afro-Asian Conference in Tanganyika, a spokesman of the African National Congress publicly announced support for and Congress connection with the fighting organization, *Umkonto We Sizwe*.

Such statements, and the increasing activities of *Umkonto* itself, show that the African people and their leaders are rapidly absorbing the lessons of the abortive Poqo outbreaks, that they understand the duty of experienced and responsible leaders. They do not in any way seek to dampen or discourage the revolutionary spirit abroad among the youth, the workers and peasants, and the oppressed people generally. Instead they aim to harness that spirit, not to reckless adventures, but to effective, planned action. Only such a dynamic and militant policy can avoid the repetition of fruitless acts of violence, instigated by desperate organizations of the Poqo type, or even provoked by the authorities and involving unnecessary bloodshed, reprisals and setbacks.

Another important lesson which the oppressed people are fast learning from the present crucial phase of our history is that every attempt to redress or rectify a local or partial grievance is necessarily connected with, and can only be won by, the defeat of the Nationalist government itself, and the ending of white minority rule. Where every protest and every demand is met merely by bloody suppression by the state, it becomes clear to one section of the people after another that the state itself is the obstacle to any sort of advance, and that no sort of happy or tolerable future is possible without the removal of this tyrannical state and its replacement by one which embodies the will of the majority of the people.

Does this mean that it is useless to campaign on any sort of local issue or partial grievance, and that the time has come to forget about such immediate questions and speak only in general terms of freedom? No, that would be wrong. Such a conclusion could only be reached by parlor-politicians who live in isolation from the people and their daily needs and problems. Real liberation leaders who are close to and part of the masses cannot escape their duty to take part in their everyday struggles for higher wages, against pass laws, group areas and mass evictions, against Bantu Authorities and Bantustans,* whether these struggles are on a local or a national scale.

But it does mean that in the future every local struggle more and more will tend to broaden out into a nation-wide struggle. It means that where the state and its police and military attempt to suppress strikes and demonstrations by force and violence the people more and more are going to be organized and prepared to defend themselves and strike back. It means that each campaign on a specific issue—whether it be the crucial struggle against the government's newest "Bantu" laws, the workers' demand for a living wage, the peasants' struggle for land and against the Bantustans—will inevitably develop into a struggle for state

---

* Apartheid measures of restriction and segregation of the African population in South Africa.

power, for the right of the people of our country to govern the country according to the principle of "One man, one vote." . . .

But one cannot overlook that any action anywhere is almost certain to be answered by savage reprisals from the government, the police and the military. Unless alternative proposals are adopted and prepared for, such reprisals could lead to blind rioting and to indiscriminate, Poqo-style attacks on white civilians and property. But such an outcome cannot be regarded with approval or favor by African patriots dedicated to the cause of freedom. Riots and pogroms can only lead to massive state retaliation, a serious political set-back for our cause and its prestige at home and abroad, and a crushing defeat for the people. Freedom fighters must not flirt with such ideas or remain cowardly silent in the face of them. That way lies disaster for our people and the cause of South African freedom.

Revolutionaries fight against and oppose such ideas and tactics, not because they are violent, but because they aim only to produce terror for the sake of terror. The people of this country will not be roused to struggle by such actions, which hold out no prospect of the overthrow of the state of oppression but only prospects of wide-scale blood-letting. Instead the people will be driven into inactivity.

The answer to government terror is not wild rioting, but organized and planned mass self-defense and resistance. Police and military violence against peaceful pass-burners or strikers cannot succeed if the brave and disciplined young freedom fighters are organized and prepared to stand up in defense of the homes, the lives and the security of their own people.

Today in many parts of the country, government policy is driving people into resistance to a stage where they are clamoring for action. Local leaders cannot lag behind the people, or they will cease to be leaders and the blind forces of destruction and revenge will take over. But local action must always be principled, in accordance with the established policy and general direction of the national leadership. No desperation, no adventurism, but firm, resolute and revolutionary action! That should be the watchword of the oppressed people and their leaders in the difficult days ahead. That is the policy of the Communist Party. . . .

Events in South Africa are moving toward a crisis, culminating in a direct clash between the forces of reaction, apartheid and barbarism organized by the state, and the forces of liberation.

As the struggle grows more acute, the bravest and most resolute men and women will come forward to lead the people in the path of struggle and victory. The people will organize and fight back on every front—against pass laws, Bantustans and group areas, against starvation wages, against mass evictions, against police state terrorism. They will take bold local initiative against grievances, merging every local and partial struggle into a mighty river of people's insurrection that will sweep away minority *baaskap* [master rule] and win people's rule in a free South Africa!

The Nationalist government cannot succeed in its attempts to check the awakened people of our country in their irresistible drive to freedom, they can only succeed in making that struggle more bitter and bloody. Should they persist in this course, the only effect can be that the present outbreaks of sabotage and violence will develop into full-scale civil war, beginning with guerrilla operations in various parts of the countryside and culminating in an armed insurrection of the whole oppressed people throughout the country.

It is not the Communists and it is not the oppressed non-white majority who have chosen this path, it is the ruling classes, the Nationalist Party, backed up and encouraged by the United Party, and the big capitalist interests. They are out to keep big profits, stolen land and white privileges, even at the cost of a continuous reign of terror that turns our whole country into one big concentration camp, even at the cost of many innocent lives, both non-white and white.

There is only one way out of the misery and bloodshed of Nationalist rule and white domination—the revolutionary way out. Our people will never submit to terror and intimidation; they will unite, organize and prepare to fight back. Death and sacrifices cannot deter patriots who are determined to win freedom, who have decided that it is no longer possible to live like slaves and be treated worse than dogs.

—Statement of the Central Committee of the South African Communist Party, *The African Communist,* London, April–June 1963, pp. 3–18.

5

A Political-Military Strategy for African Liberation

KWAME NKRUMAH

Africa will be liberated sooner or later against all odds. But if it is to be soon, by an accelerated revolution of the people and a total war against imperialism, then we must establish a unified continental high command here and now, to plan revolutionary war and to initiate action.

If we fail to do this, and to lead the people's revolution, we are likely to be swept away one by one by imperialism and neo-colonialism. It is no longer feasible to take a middle course. The time for reform, however, progressive, is past. For reforms cannot hold the enemy at bay, nor can they convince the silent, internal agents of neo-colonialism, eliminate the puppets, or even destroy the capitalist structure and mentality inherited from colonialism. The cancerous growths are proliferating at the very heart of our parties and territories whether they emerge under the cloak of constitutionalism, parliamentarianism, bureaucratic etiquette, an imposing civil service, officers trained in western "apolitical" tradition to maintain the bourgeois-capitalist status quo by means of military coups, or if they appear in the more obvious guise of corruption and nepotism.

The people's armed struggle, the highest form of political action, is a revolutionary catalyst in the neo-colonialist situation.

Peaceful political action to achieve liberation has been proved ineffective (a) with the accession of the majority of African states to independence and the advent of neo-colonialism on a massive scale, and (b) with the increasingly continental dimension of our struggle.

Pacific political action was, in general, potent during the national phase of the liberation movement, and mainly in sub-Saharan Africa, where independence often developed in a chain reaction. However, even then there were significant exceptions. In Kenya, for example, where recourse to peaceful political action was denied to the masses, the people's movement resorted to more direct and concentrated action in the form of Mau Mau. In Algeria, a seven-year armed liberation struggle was needed. Elsewhere, the independence movement pushed beyond the fringe of pacifism, as in Ghana and Guinea, where "positive action" was employed.

The crystallization of a more concentrated form of political action is in fact to be found in the development of almost all African independence movements. The reason for this was the need to establish a new social order after nominal independence has been achieved, and the escalation of imperialist action. The latter appeared in:

1. the corruption of independence through neo-colonialism and puppet regimes;
2. direct imperialist aggression against liberation forces, for example in the Congo;
3. increased multilateral and bilateral imperialist support to:
   (a) remaining colonial powers (Portugal, Spain)
   (b) fascist-racist regimes (Rhodesia, South Africa)
   (c) puppet regimes and local reactionaries to assist their infiltration and attempts to suppress progressive and revolutionary forces throughout the continent.

In less than three years, from 1960, the armed form of struggle became a necessity of the African anti-colonial liberation movement, and the same process may be observed in most neo-colonial situations.

From 1961 onwards, the armed form of political action reached another turning point with the creation of a united front coordinating the struggle of freedom fighters in all the "Portuguese" colonies. This organization (CONCP) links up the politico-military struggle of 12,400,000 inhabitants over an area of some two million square kilometers.

In effect, then, anti-imperialist pacifism is dying, and on a continental scale, because:

1. The political action which led to independence deviated to become the sole monopoly and privilege of a reactionary "elite" which deprives the masses of the right to political action, even in its pacific and constitutional form.
2. Neo-colonialism has created a situation whereby the masses are exploited beyond the "safe" limits of exploitation. The ensuing massive explosion of pent-up discontent can be

nothing but violent. The masses seize back their right to political action and make maximum use of it.
3. Imperialist action is escalating (a) to consolidate its positions (military *coups d'etat* in neo-colonialist states), (b) to gain ground and recapture lost initiative (reactionary *coups d'etat* in progressive states).
4. Imperialism constantly infiltrates revolutionary opposition groups with agents, "special police," and others, compelling such groups to arm even before they have attained the organizational stage of armed struggle.
5. Whenever the pseudo-democratic institutions inherited from colonial rule are not used by its inheritors to build capitalism but are gradually remodelled or suddenly re-structured toward a socialist line of development, imperialists intervene violently.
6. Violence clears the "neo-colonialist fog" and reveals the invisible enemy and the subtle methods of camouflage employed by the neo-colonialists. The issues are made clear.

As soon as the initial revolutionary units emerge, the puppet regime is doomed. A chain reaction begins. The puppets are compelled to break the promises they have made. They had survived in the teeth of opposition only because they uneasily preserved an outward appearance of progressive action. Now, they have to suppress and kill openly in order to survive. Once the first drop of patriotic blood is shed in the fight the puppet regime is irrevocably condemned. Guerrilla points spread like oil stains. Not only have the internal contradictions of neo-colonialism fully ripened but the African masses have attained such a degree of political awareness that they literally force the struggle to break out into the open.

The Need for Coordinated Revolutionary Action

The international balance of forces, and more particularly the existence of powerful socialist states, gave rise to the theory that in certain territories dominated by imperialism on our continent it was possible to take a pacific road to socialism. But such reasoning is based on the false premise that the question of co-ordinating revolutionary action in Africa and the world has already been solved and that therefore imperialism is no longer able to concentrate its forces to act decisively against the most threatening parts of the popular liberation front.

In reality, the situation is quite different:
1. Imperialists are waging an all-out struggle against the socialist states and the revolutionary liberation movements through military means, and through insidious but powerful methods of psychological warfare (propaganda).
2. Imperialists have formed an international syndicate of military and economic forces to achieve their aggressive aims.
3. Imperialists have, in recent years, assisted in the establishment of numerous puppet governments in Africa.

The historical experience of the people of Asia, Latin America and of Africa has shown that imperialism has often forcefully intervened to prevent the peaceful achievement of socialism. In the case of Ghana a coup occurred at the very time a decisive turning point in socialist development was about to be reached.

The continental scope now attained by popular insurrection in Africa is a reality. It remains for us to devise effective coordinating machinery.

Our accumulated experience has shown that only practical and planned coordination on a continental scale will prevent the enemy from concentrating its forces on isolated and therefore more vulnerable targets. In our war, isolation is one of the greatest dangers.

We have already been able to outpace the enemy in certain ways by: (1) increasing our means of production, (2) bringing a higher level of organization to the people, (3) spreading the essential features of the African people's liberation, and (4) unmasking neo-colonialism and its puppets.

We have succeeded in accumulating energy and will-power. But it is also true that we have not yet defeated either the external or the internal enemy. For victory, a politico-military organization must be established to provide the machinery for a qualitative conversion of revolutionary action in Africa.

Politico-Military Organization

The following measures should be taken: (1) The formation of an All-African People's Revolutionary Party (AAPRP) to coordinate policies and to direct action, and (2) the creation of an All-African People's Revolutionary Army (AAPRA) to unify our liberation struggle and to carry the armed struggle through to final victory.

AAPRP and the All-African Committee for Political Coordination (AACPC): The formation of a political party linking all liberated territories and struggle parties under a common ideology will smooth the way for eventual continental unity, and will, at the same time, greatly assist the prosecution of the All-African people's war. To assist the process of its formation, an All-African Committee for Political Co-ordination (AACPC) should be established to act as a liaison between all parties which recognize the urgent necessity of conducting and organizing a unified struggle against colonialism and neo-colonialism. This committee would be created at the level of the central committees of the ruling parties and struggling parties, and would constitute their integrated political consciousness.

The AACPC as the political arm of the AAPRA (All-African People's Revolutionary Army) would fulfill the following functions:

1. Ensure co-operation between the ruling parties of the liberated territories building socialism, and enable them to support each other in the fight against the internal enemy.
2. Promote widespread and collective ideological training for the cadres of parties teaching the theory of anti-colonialist and anti-neo-colonialist struggle, the case for African unity and for the building of socialism. This would be done in AACPC schools or in political training camps throughout liberated territories.
3. Co-ordinate and harmonize all political effort and assistance given to the revolutionary movements in colonized or apartheid areas, and to the progressive forces in all the neocolonized areas.
4. Provide an organic link with the peoples of Africa, Asia and Latin America who are struggling against imperialism (Organization of Solidarity with the Peoples of Africa, Asia and Latin America, OSPAAL).
5. Ensure permanent relations with the socialist states of the world.
6. Maintain and create links with all workers' movements in the capitalist-imperialist states.

Thus the AACPC would emerge as the organizational instrument of a united struggle, and a centralizing and disciplinary organ providing permanent contact with the masses and with the scattered centers of their revolutionary activities. Such coordination would unify revolutionary action of the vanguard

African territories and would enable them to exert decisive influence on the revolutionary liberation movement by allowing them to participate actively in it.

Members of AAPRA will be the armed representatives of the African people's socialist parties struggling against colonialism and neo-colonialism. They will be the direct product of the African revolutionary liberation movement. . . .

These revolutionary armed forces will be under the direction of a high command made up of the military leaders (AAPRA) of the various revolutionary movements in Africa. This in its turn will come under the AACPC, which represents the political leadership of the entire revolutionary movement. Thus the military, i.e., the armed forces, will always be subordinate to, and under the control of, the political leadership.

—Kwame Nkrumah, *Handbook of Revolutionary Warfare: A Guide to the Armed Phase of the African Revolution,* Panaf, London, 1968, pp. 51–58.

VI. LATIN AMERICA

As in Asia, guerrilla warfare is not a new form of struggle for Latin America. In the 1920s and 1930s, Sandino in Nicaragua and Luis Carlos Prestes at the head of the "Prestes Column" in Brazil had legendary stature as guerrilla leaders, and they followed the earlier fame of Pancho Villa and Zapata during the Mexican revolution and of Charlemagne Péraulte in Haiti when US marines intervened on the island in 1915. Earlier still, by over a century, was the epic guerrilla struggle in Haiti against the French, led by Toussaint L'Ouverture.

Attention has been drawn to Latin American guerrilla movements by the victory of the Cuban revolution early in 1959, but long before the impact of that event Communists in several Latin American countries had organized and supported guerrilla movements and other popular forms of armed struggle: in Colombia from 1946 onwards (a period known as *La Violencia*, with 200,000 people slain by reactionaries to suppress it), in Paraguay during civil war in 1947 and in widespread guerrilla war in 1958–60, in Venezuela in 1928 and in 1958, in Bolivia during repeated armed defense action by tin miners in the 1950s, in Guatemala in resistance to imperialist counter-revolution in 1954.

The Cuban 26th of July Movement, therefore, did not initiate guerrilla tactics in Latin America. It carried out a *form of* guerrilla warfare that proved suitable to Cuban conditions. However, the fact that it was led by radicalized petty-bourgeois elements in alliance with workers and peasants revealed a new revolutionary potential in Latin America. It set an example of what could be accomplished by determined revolutionary struggle, and it precipitated a continent-wide debate over strategy and tactics of the anti-imperialist struggle.

This controversy in Latin America is *not* one between those who advocate armed struggle and those who advocate peaceful struggle. The ardent admirers of the type of struggle conducted and later elaborated into a theory by Che Guevara and Fidel Castro have sometimes interpreted it as such. Also, at times, the nature of the new anti-imperialist forces set in motion in Latin America has given rise to criticism along this line of the older Marxist-Leninists in the Latin American Communist parties. In actuality, however, none of the Latin American Communist parties reject armed struggle, guerrilla or otherwise, and many of them are engaged in carrying it out or in organizational preparations for it. In point of fact, the debate, which has had value in forcing an examination of revolutionary theory and practice, has really been over *when* armed struggle should be employed and over *how* it should be used when the time has come for it.

The following selections have been made with the intention of illustrating the various positions of those involved in the debate. In general, selections have been limited to statements from those movements that have been actively engaged in guerrilla or other forms of armed struggle in Latin America, but Communists from parties not actively engaged in armed struggle also helped to formulate the OLAS Declaration included here.

A central question in Latin America in recent years has been the relation of guerrilla struggle to a revolutionary situation. It can be asserted that in no country on the continent where guerrilla struggle has occurred since 1959 (i.e., since the Cuban victory) has a revolutionary situation actually existed. It was Che Guevara's belief that the guerrilla struggle can create the revolutionary situation. On the other hand, it has been the belief of others that guerrilla activity is but one aspect of the working out of the revolutionary process.

This issue was paramount in Peru in 1964–66, when a guerrilla movement developed among the peasants in the Andamarca region, led by the non-Communist Left Revolutionary Movement. During its course, the Peruvian Communist Party, in pointing to the limitations of the guerrilla struggle while supporting it, defined it as "a new form of the peasants' unceasing struggle for the land," but contended that, "the peasants' struggle for the land cannot succeed unless it is part of the struggle of the people for a democratic and nationalist transformation of the country. . . . To be able to develop, the guerrilla movement needs not only the sympathy but also the solidarity and support of the movement of the urban masses."

Asserting that "the guerrilla movement alone cannot generate a revolutionary situation," the Peruvian Communists said that "we consider that although certain objective factors favor the guerrilla movement at present, it could have been developed much more successfully from the very outset had its leaders borne in mind the importance of: (a) choosing a political situation most suitable for launching it, and (b) ensuring, in good time, maximum coordination of actions with all the revolutionary forces pursuing the same objectives."* This resolution of the Peruvian party was adopted in October 1965. In 1966 the guerrilla movement in Peru was crushed by US-directed military suppression operations.

The first major test of the guerrilla theory of Che Guevara, occurring in Bolivia, resulted in the defeat of the guerrillas and in the tragic death of Guevara in October 1967. Guevara was reported to have admitted that the Bolivian peasants were not being won to the support of the guerrillas as had occurred under Cuban conditions.

In the view of leaders of the Bolivian Communist Party, "The guerrillas began [their action] without an adequate evaluation having been given to political and social factors indispensable for their development, and they came into existence prematurely." The setback in Bolivia, as the Bolivian Communists stated, however, did not invalidate the concept of guerrilla struggle itself,† nor did the similar setback in Peru. Increasing emphasis, in fact, has been given to preparations for armed struggle by all Latin American Communist parties in countries where conditions point to it.

This outlook has been balanced, as discussions at the 1967 OLAS Conference in Havana showed, by the position of Communists in certain countries where non-violent forms of struggle can conceivably lead to the formation of anti-imperialist popular governments able to effect serious economic, social and political changes. Chile is considered to be such a country, although the danger of imperialist intervention through Chilean military "gorilla" elements is recognized. The OLAS Conference was but the first of efforts that should lead to common approaches and understandings among the revolutionary forces in Latin America.

* Resolution of the 21st meeting of the Central Committee, Peruvian Communist Party, *Unidad,* October 7, 1965.

† Interview with Jorge Kolle, member of the Secretariat, Bolivian Communist Party, by Eduardo Labarca, editor of the Chilean Communist newspaper, *El Siglo,* as printed in *Morning Star,* London, November 27, 1967.

A selection has been included here from a book by Régis Debray, a French writer who reflects the radical petty-bourgeois viewpoint in Latin America and who was imprisoned in Bolivia for his association with the ill-fated guerrilla group organized in that country by Che Guevara. Although Debray does not speak for a Latin American movement, his writings have been circulated on the continent and elsewhere to enhance one side in the general debate. His rather dogmatic formulations need to be contrasted with statements by Cuban leaders in whose behalf he is often thought to speak. "In our struggling world," wrote Che Guevara, for example, "all discrepencies regarding tactics and methods of action for the attainment of limited objectives should be analyzed with the respect that the opinions of others deserve. Regarding our great strategic objective, the total destruction of imperialism via armed struggle, we should be uncompromising."*

To Debray's critics, his ideas on tactics in the struggle are contradictory to the Marxist-Leninist position, particularly his theory, without regard to the diversity of specific conditions in Latin American countries, that a Latin American model of guerrilla warfare patterned after the Cuban 26th of July Movement should be adopted on the whole continent.

Among the main features of such a model in the Debray theses are: the precedence of military over political considerations in the struggle, with the guerrilla force (or *foco*) playing the vanguard role, as "the party in embryo," superseding or replacing established political parties (in effect, an attitude of hostility toward the Latin American Communist parties); a tendency to think in terms solely of the importance of the guerrilla force, to the point of avoiding organized links with the people and of distrusting them in the name of "security" for the guerrillas; the downgrading of urban working class movements and giving full emphasis to guerrilla warfare in the countryside; an emphasis on the biological factor of youth and physical fitness for guerrilla life as a reason for rejecting older participants in the struggle (the implication being that older revolutionaries are too accustomed to forms of struggle other than armed).

Of the Latin American Communists who have spoken in refutation of Debray and his supporters, it is worthwhile to quote

---

* Message to Tricontinental, *Granma*, Havana, April 23, 1967.

the Communist Party of Colombia which has led armed struggles for two decades:

"The historical and revolutionary unity of Latin America is undeniable, and it demands of us, above all, coordination and solidarity of the movements in our countries. But it does not imply that everyone must follow one and the same strategy. The real principle of the continental revolution should be conceived as a series of common factors in the struggle and in its perspectives. However, this struggle must not be equated to the war of independence from Spain, for in the century and a half of economic and political development that has passed since then the Latin American nations have taken shape and acquired characteristics of their own."*

In regard to the argument that the guerrilla force should fulfill the political tasks of the revolution, the Colombian party has said: "There is clearly a gulf between this concept and the Communist concept. In effect, this concept, as well as the tendency to deny the role of the working class in the revolutionary movement, expresses the point of view of revolutionary elements whose ideological and political views are diametrically opposed to those of the proletariat. . . . In our country, the CP represents the proletarian, Marxist-Leninist view on the revolution and its development. There are other forces, likewise revolutionary, progressive and democratic, which share these ideas fully or partly and are fighting for them. This is why the revolutionary struggle should be carried forward through alliance and understanding, and first of all through unity of action between Communists and other, non-proletarian forces. This is what we call a patriotic front. We must not rule out the possibility of even merging with these forces eventually. It may also be that the revolutionary movement will win and will build the new society with both the CP and other parties which will exist without merging. This will be determined by the struggle itself, by the stance of each force at this or that juncture."†

The Communist Party of San Salvador, which made known its position at the OLAS conference in Havana in August 1967, has agreed that it is perfectly feasible to work out theses for a strategic revolutionary concept for all Latin America, because of

---

* "Reply to Comrade Montana, by CEC of the Communist Party of Colombia," *Information Bulletin*, No. 2 (114), Prague, 1968, p. 34.
† *Ibid.*, pp. 28–29.

certain common features (a common imperialist enemy, a common tendency of capitalist development, a relatively simultaneous ebb and flow of mass revolutionary activity), but it has pointed out the danger of oversimplifying this situation:

"Despite the acuteness of the contradiction between US imperialism and the peoples of Latin America *the revolution on our continent is, first and foremost, an 'internal' process, stemming from the development of the class struggle.* Failure to take this into account has led to the assumption that the Latin American revolution is an 'absolutely uniform' process originating not on the basis of the 'internal' class struggle, but simply as a result of the peoples' collision with imperialism, that the objective prerequisites for this collision exist permanently whereas the subjective prerequisites have to be created by the armed struggle started by a group of revolutionaries. This strategic concept is bound to lead to mistakes of both a military and a political nature."

While taking issue with such an assumption, the San Salvador Communists at the same time have urged unity of all those struggling against imperialism: "The task is to find the *practical forms* for our theoretical work that would help to enlist in the common effort other revolutionary forces, above all those professing to be socialist, even Marxist-Leninist. Instead of questioning their right to proclaim allegiance to Marxism-Leninism, we should enlist them not only in joint actions (which is regularly done), but also in joint theoretical work."*

---

* Schafik Handal, "Reflections on Continental Strategy for Latin American Revolutionaries," *World Marxist Review*, Vol. 11, No. 4, April 1968, pp. 23, 25.

1
Lessons of the Cuban Revolution

ERNESTO CHE GUEVARA

The armed victory of the Cuban people over the Batista dictatorship was not only the triumph of heroism as reported by the newspapers of the world; it also forced a change in the old dogmas concerning the conduct of the popular masses of Latin America. It showed plainly the capacity of the people to free themselves by means of guerrilla warfare from a government that oppresses them.

We consider that the Cuban Revolution contributed three fundamental lessons to the conduct of revolutionary movements in America. They are:

(1) Popular forces can win a war against the army.
(2) It is not necessary to wait until all conditions for making revolution exist; the insurrection can create them.
(3) In underdeveloped America the countryside is the basic area for armed fighting.

Of these three propositions, the first two contradict the defeatist attitude of revolutionaries or pseudo-revolutionaries who remain inactive and take refuge in the pretext that against a professional army nothing can be done, who sit down to wait until in some mechanical way all necessary objective and subjective conditions are given without working to accelerate them. As these problems were formerly a subject of discussion in Cuba, until facts settled the question, they are probably still much discussed in America.

Naturally, it is not to be thought that all conditions for revolution are going to be created through the impulse given to them by guerrilla activity. It must always be kept in mind that there is a necessary minimum without which the establishment and consolidation of the first center is not practicable. People must see clearly the futility of maintaining the fight for social goals within the framework of civil debate. When the forces of oppression come to maintain themselves in power against established law, peace is considered already broken.

In these conditions popular discontent expresses itself in more active forms. An attitude of resistance finally crystallizes in an outbreak of fighting, provoked initially by the conduct of the authorities.

Where a government has come into power through some form of popular vote, fraudulent or not, and maintains at least an appearance of constitutional legality, the guerrilla outbreak cannot be promoted, since the possibilities of peaceful struggle have not yet been exhausted.

The third proposition is a fundamental of strategy. It ought to be noted by those who maintain dogmatically that the struggle of the masses is centered in city movements, entirely forgetting the immense participation of the country people in the life of all the underdeveloped parts of America. Of course, the struggles of the city masses of organized workers should not be underrated, but their real possibilities of engaging in armed struggle must be carefully analyzed where the guarantees which customarily adorn our constitutions are suspended or ignored. In these conditions the illegal workers' movements face enormous dangers. They must function secretly without arms. The situation in the open country is not so difficult. There, in places beyond the reach of the repressive forces, the inhabitants can be supported by the armed guerrillas.

—Ernesto Che Guevara, *Guerrilla Warfare,* Monthly Review Press, New York, 1961, pp. 1–2.

2

What Is a Guerrilla?

ERNESTO CHE GUEVARA

The guerrilla is a liberation fighter *par excellence:* elected of the people, vanguard combatant in their struggle for liberation. Guerrilla warfare is not, as often thought, a small-scale war, a war conducted by a minority grouping against a powerful army. No, guerrilla warfare is war by the entire people against the reigning oppression. The guerrilla movement is their armed vanguard; the guerrilla army comprises all the people of a region or a country. That is the reason for its strength and for its eventual victory over whatsoever power tries to crush it; that is, the base and grounding of the guerrilla is the people.

One cannot imagine small armed groups, no matter how mobile and familiar with the terrain, surviving the organized persecution of a well-equipped army without this powerful assistance. The test is that all bandits, all brigand gangs, eventually succumb to the central power—and one must bear in mind that for the inhabitants of a region these bandits often appear as more than mere brigandage: they appear as a liberation struggle, though the sheerest caricature of one.

Each member of the guerrilla army, the people's army *par excellence,* must embody the qualities of the best of the world's soldiers. The army must observe strict discipline. The fact that the formalities of orthodox military life do not correspond to the guerrilla movement, the fact that there is no heel-clicking or snappy saluting, no kow-towing explanations to superior officers, does not, by any stretch of the imagination, mean that there is no discipline. Guerrilla discipline is within the individual, born of his profound conviction, of the need to obey his superior, not only so as to maintain the effectiveness of the armed group of which he is a part, but also to defend his own life. Any slight carelessness by a soldier in a regular army is controlled by his nearest comrade. In guerrilla warfare, in which each soldier in a unit within himself, an error is fatal. No one can be careless. No one can commit even the smallest slip, as his life and those of his comrades are at stake.

This informal discipline is often not apparent. For the uninformed, the regular soldier, with a whole complex system for showing recognition of superior officers, seems far more disciplined than a guerrilla, any guerrilla, following his chief's instructions with simple and stirring respect. Moreover, the liberation army is a pure army with no room for even the smallest of man's weaknesses; it has no repressive apparatus, no intelligence service to prevent individuals from falling victim to temptation. Self-control is the operative force. Rigid awareness of duty and discipline.

Besides being a disciplined soldier, the guerrilla is very agile, physically and mentally.

One cannot conceive of static guerrilla warfare. Night is the setting. Depending on his knowledge of the terrain, the guerrilla moves at night, takes position, attacks the enemy and withdraws. That does not mean that he must withdraw very far from the theater of operations; only that the withdrawal must be swift.

The enemy will immediately concentrate all its repressive forces at the point attacked. It will begin aerial bombardment, send in tactical units to surround the area, send in soldiers to take up a delusive position.

The guerrillas need only present a front to the enemy. By withdrawing a short distance, waiting for the enemy, attacking and withdrawing again they have accomplished their specific mission. Thus, the army can be exhausted over a period of hours or even days.

The people's soldier attacks from ambush at the propitious moment. There are other basic axioms in guerrilla tactics. Knowledge of the terrain is a must. The guerrilla must be familiar with the place of attack, and he must also know all the paths of retreat as well as all means of access and those that are closed, the homes of those who are friends or enemies, the safest places, those where a wounded comrade may be hidden, those where a temporary camp may be set up—in other words, he must know the theater of operations like the palm of his hand. And this is possible because the people, the great nucleus of the guerrilla army, are behind each action.

The inhabitants of the area are porters, informants, nurses, the source of new recruits—in short, they constitute the highly important assistants of their armed vanguard.

But in view of all these things, in view of the guerrilla's myriad tactical needs, one may ask, "Why fight?" The resounding answer is: "The guerrilla is a social reformer. The guerrilla takes up weapons as the wrathful protest of the people against their oppressors; the guerrilla fights to change the social system that subjects his unarmed brothers to approbrium and poverty. He acts against the special conditions of the Establishment at a given moment. And he is determined to smash the Establishment's patterns, with all the force that circumstances permit."

—As printed in *Granma* (English edition), Havana, December 3, 1967.

3

OLAS: General Declaration

This Conference, after a deep and exhaustive analysis of the conditions existing on the continent and after having ideologically clarified the essential problems of the revolutionary movements, has arrived at the following conclusions:

Latin America exists in conditions of convulsion, characterized by the presence of a weak bourgeoisie which, in indissoluble union with the landholders, constitutes the controlling oligarchy of our countries. Increased submission and almost absolute dependence of this oligarchy on imperialism has caused the intense polarization of forces on the continent, consisting of the oligarchic imperialist alliance on one side and the peoples on the other. The peoples have a tremendous revolutionary power which is only waiting to be channeled by a correct leadership, by a revolutionary vanguard, in order to develop or to initiate the fight.

That power is the power of the proletarian masses, of city and rural workers, of a poor and highly exploited peasantry, of the young intellectuals, of students with a great tradition of struggle, and of the middle strata, all joined together by the common denominator of the exploitation to which they are subjected.

In the face of the crisis of the whole structure of the economic, social and political system throughout the continent, and the growing rebelliousness of the peoples, imperialism has designed and developed a continental strategy of repression which proposes vainly to detain the course of history. The survival of the colonial and neo-colonial systems of exploitation and domination are the aims of US imperialism.

This situation determines and demands that revolutionary violence be unleashed and developed in response to reactionary violence.

Revolutionary violence as the highest expression of the peoples' struggle is not only the path, but it is the most concrete and the most direct potential for the defeat of imperialism.

The peoples as well as the revolutionaries have confirmed this reality and consequently realize the need to initiate, develop and bring armed struggle to its culmination in order to destroy the bureaucratic-military apparatus of the oligarchies and the power of imperialism.

In many countries the special conditions prevailing in the countryside, the favorable topography and a potentially revolutionary social base, in addition to the special adaptation of technical methods and professional armies to repress the people in the cities (which, moreover, are ill-adapted to an irregular war), mean that guerrilla warfare is the fundamental expression of armed struggle, the best school for revolutionaries and their indisputable vanguard.

The revolution, already underway in some countries, an imperative necessity in others and a future prospect in the rest, has a well defined anti-imperialist character within its anti-oligarchic aims.

The principal objective of the peoples' revolution on the continent is the seizure of power by means of the destruction of the bureaucratic-military apparatus of the state and its replacement by the people in arms in order to change the existing economic and social regime. This objective can be achieved only through armed struggle.

The development and the organization of the struggle depend on choosing the right site on which to carry it out and the most adequate methods of organization.

The lesson of the Cuban Revolution, the experiences accumulated by the revolutionary movement in recent years throughout the world, and the presence in Bolivia, Venezuela, Colombia and Guatemala of an ever-growing armed revolutionary movement show that guerrilla warfare as a genuine expression of the peoples' armed struggle is the most effective method and the most adequate form for waging and developing revolutionary warfare in most of our countries and, consequently, on a continental scale.

In this particular situation the unity of the peoples, the identity of their aims, the unity of their views and their disposition to unite in carrying out the struggle are the elements characterizing the common strategy that must be opposed to that which imperialism is developing on a continental scale.

This strategy requires a precise and clear expression of solidarity, whose most effective characteristic is the revolutionary struggle itself, which extends across the continent and whose vanguard detachments are the guerrillas and liberation armies.

We, the representatives of the peoples of our America, conscious of the conditions which prevail on the continent, aware of the existence of a common counter-revolutionary strategy directed by US imperialism,

PROCLAIM:

1. That making the Revolution is a right and a duty of the peoples of Latin America;
2. That the Revolution in Latin America has its deepest historical roots in the liberation movement against European colonialism of the 19th century and against imperialism of this century. The epic struggle of the peoples of America and the great class battles that our people have carried out against imperialism in earlier decades, constitute the source of historical inspiration for the Latin American revolutionary movement;
3. That the essential content of the Revolution in Latin America is to be found in its confrontation with imperialism and the bourgeois and landowning oligarchies. Consequently, the character of the Revolution is the struggle for national independence, for emancipation from the oligarchies, and for taking the socialist road to complete economic and social development;
4. That the principles of Marxism-Leninism guide the revolutionary movement of Latin America;
5. That armed revolutionary struggle constitutes the fundamental course of the Revolution in Latin America;
6. That all other forms of struggle must serve to advance and not to retard the development of this fundamental course, which is armed struggle;
7. That, for the majority of the countries of the continent, the problems of organizing, initiating, developing and completing the armed struggle now constitute the immediate and fundamental task of the revolutionary movement;
8. That those countries where this task is not included in immediate planning must nevertheless inevitably consider this as a future probability in the development of their revolutionary struggle;
9. That the historic responsibility of furthering revolution in each country belongs to the people and their revolutionary vanguards;

10. That in most of our countries the guerrillas are the embryo of liberation armies and constitute the most efficient way of initiating and carrying out revolutionary struggle;

11. That the leadership of the revolution requires, as an organizing principle, the existence of a unified political and military command in order to guarantee success;

12. That the most effective type of solidarity that the revolutionary movements can offer each other lies precisely in the development and culmination of their own struggle within their own countries;

13. That solidarity with Cuba and cooperation and collaboration with the armed revolutionary movement are imperative duties of an international nature, the duties of all the anti-imperialist organizations of this continent;

14. That the Cuban Revolution, as a symbol of the triumph of the armed revolutionary movement, constitutes the vanguard in the anti-imperialist movement of Latin America. Those peoples that carry out armed struggle will also place themselves in the vanguard as they advance along the road of armed struggle;

15. That the peoples directly colonized by European powers— or subjected to the direct colonial domination of the United States—who are now on the road to liberation must maintain, as their immediate and fundamental objective, their struggle for independence and their close ties with the general struggle on this continent, since this is the only way of preventing their being absorbed into the neo-colonial system of the United States;

16. That the Second Declaration of Havana, a résumé of the great and glorious revolutionary tradition of the past 150 years of Latin American history, serves as a guiding document for the Latin American Revolution, and has been upheld, widened, enriched and made even more radical by the peoples of this continent during the past five years;

17. That the peoples of Latin America harbor no antagonisms toward any peoples of the world and extend their hand of brotherly friendship to the people of the United States itself, encouraging them to fight on against the oppressive policy of imperialist monopolies;

18. That the struggle in Latin America is strengthening its bonds of solidarity with the peoples of Asia and Africa and the socialist countries, especially with the Negroes of the United States, who suffer from class exploitation, poverty, unemployment, racial discrimination and the denial of the most basic

human rights and who constitute a force of considerable importance within the revolutionary struggle;

19. That the heroic struggle of the people of Vietnam aids all revolutionary peoples fighting against imperialism to an inestimable degree and constitutes an inspiring example for the people of Latin America;

20. That we have approved the Statutes and created a Permanent Committee with its seat in Havana for the Latin American Organization of Solidarity, which constitutes the true representation of the peoples of Latin America.

We, the revolutionaries of our America, the America lying south of the Rio Bravo, successors of those men who won our first independence, armed with an irrevocable will to struggle and a revolutionary scientific orientation and with nothing to lose but the chains which bind us,

ASSERT:

That our struggle constitutes a decisive contribution to the historic struggle of humanity to liberate itself from slavery and exploitation.
The Duty of Every Revolutionary is to Make the Revolution!

—Documents, First Conference of the Latin American Organization of Solidarity (OLAS), Havana, July–August 1967.

4

Speech to the OLAS Conference

FIDEL CASTRO

The importance of the guerrilla, the vanguard role of the guerrilla—much could be said about the guerrilla, but it is not possible to do so in a meeting like this. But guerrilla experiences on this continent have taught us many things, among them the terrible mistake, the absurd concept that the guerrilla movement could be directed from the cities.

This is the reason for the thesis that political and military commands must be united. This the reason for our conviction that it is not only a stupidity but also a crime to want to direct the guerrillas from the city. And we have had the opportunity to appreciate the consequences of this absurdity many times. It is necessary that these ideas be overcome, and this is why we consider the resolution of this Conference of great importance. The guerrilla is bound to be the nucleus of the revolutionary movement. This does not mean that the guerrilla movement can rise without any previous work; it does not mean that the guerrilla movement is something that can exist without political direction. No! We do not deny the role of the leading organizations, we do not deny the role of the political organizations. The guerrilla is organized by a political movement, by a political organization. What we believe incompatible with correct ideas of guerrilla struggle is the idea of directing the guerrilla from the cities. And in the conditions of our continent it will be very difficult to suppress the role of the guerrilla. . . .

This does not imply the negation of forms of struggle. When someone writes a manifesto in a newspaper, attends a demonstration, holds a rally or propagates an idea, he may be using the so-called famous legal means. We must do away with the differentiation between legal and illegal means; methods should be classified as revolutionary or non-revolutionary.

The revolutionary employs various methods to achieve his ideal and his revolutionary aim. The essence of the question is whether the masses will be led to believe that the revolutionary movement, that socialism, can come to power without a struggle, that it can come to power peacefully. And that is a lie! And any persons in Latin America who assert that they will come to power peacefully are deceiving the masses.

We are talking about conditions in Latin America. We don't want to involve ourselves in other problems which are already large enough—those of the revolutionary organizations of other countries, such as in Europe. We are addressing Latin America. . . . We are absolutely convinced that, in the long run, there is only one solution, as expressed in the Resolution: guerrilla warfare in Latin America.

Does this mean that if a garrison rises in rebellion because there are revolutionaries in it we should not support the rebellion because it is not a guerrilla struggle? No! It is stupid to think, as one organization did, that the Revolution would be made with the rebellion of garrisons only. It is no less stupid to have a rebellion in a garrison and afterwards let it be crushed by overpowering forces. New situations are arising; new situations may arise—we do not deny that. For example, in Santo Domingo a typical case came up: a military uprising that began to take on a revolutionary character.

But, of course, this doesn't mean that the revolutionary movement has to wait around for what may come up, for what may take place. Nobody was able to foresee, nobody was able to estimate the form, the character that the revolutionary movement would take on, especially as a result of imperialist intervention.

In other words, by stressing the role of the guerrilla as an immediate task in all those countries where true conditions exist, we do not discard other forms of revolutionary armed struggle.

The revolutionary movement must be ready to take advantage of, and support, any expression of struggle that may arise, that may develop or that may strengthen the position of the revolutionaries. What I do not believe is that anybody who considers himself a revolutionary can wait around for a garrison to rebel in order to carry out revolution, that any revolutionary can dream of making a revolution through the rebellion of garrisons. The uprising of military units may constitute a factor—one of those unforeseeable factors that may arise—but no really serious revolutionary movement would base itself on those eventualities. Guerrilla warfare is the main form of struggle, but it does not exclude any other expressions of armed struggle that may arise.

—From speech on closing day of the Conference, August 10, 1967.

5

Revolution in the Revolution?

RÉGIS DEBRAY

The impact of the Cuban Revolution has been experienced and pondered, principally in Latin America, by methods and schemas already catalogued, enthroned, and consecrated by history. This is why, in spite of all the commotion it has provoked, the shock has been softened. Today the tumult has died down; Cuba's real significance and the scope of its lessons, which had been overlooked before, are being discovered. A new conception of guerrilla warfare is coming to light.

Among other things, Cuba remembered from the beginning that the socialist revolution is the result of an armed struggle against the armed power of the bourgeois state. This old historic law, of a strategic nature if you like, was at first given a known tactical content. One began by identifying the guerrilla struggle with insurrection because the archetype—1917—had taken this form, and because Lenin and later Stalin had developed several theoretical formulas based on it—formulas which have nothing to do with the present situation and which are periodically debated in vain, such as those which refer to conditions for the outbreak of an insurrection, meaning an immediate assault on the central power. But this disparity soon became evident. American guerrilla warfare was next virtually identified with Asian guerrilla warfare, since both are "irregular" wars of encirclement of cities from the countryside. This confusion is even more dangerous than the first.

The armed revolutionary struggle encounters specific conditions on each continent, in each country, but these are neither "natural" nor obvious. So true is this that in each case years of sacrifice are necessary in order to discover and acquire an awareness of them. The Russian Social-Democrats instinctively thought in terms of repeating the Paris Commune in Petrograd; the Chinese Communists in terms of repeating the Russian October in the Canton of the twenties and the Vietnamese comrades, a year after the foundation of their party, in terms of organizing insurrections of peasant soviets in the northern part of their country. It is now clear to us today that soviet-type insurrections could not triumph in prewar colonial Asia, but it was precisely here that the most genuine Communist activists had to begin their apprenticeship for victory. . . .

One may well consider it a stroke of good luck that Fidel had not read the military writings of Mao Tse-tung before disembarking on the coast of Oriente: he could thus invent, on the spot, and out of his own experience, principles of a military doctrine in conformity with the terrain. It was only at the end of the war, when their tactics were already defined, that the rebels discovered the writings of Mao. But once again in Latin America, militants are reading Fidel's speeches and Che Guevara's writings with eyes that have already read Mao on the anti-Japanese war, Giap, and certain texts of Lenin—and they thnk they recognize the latter in the former. Classical visual superimposition, but dangerous since the Latin American revolutionary war possesses highly special and profoundly distinct conditions of development, which can only be discovered through a particular experience. In that sense, all the theoretical works on people's war do as much harm as good. They have been called the grammer books of the war. But a foreign language is learned faster in a country where it must be spoken than at home studying a language manual. In time of war questions of speed are vital, especially in the early stages when an unarmed and inexperienced guerrilla band must confront a well-armed and knowledgeable enemy . . . .

All decisive revolutionary processes must begin and have begun with certain missteps for the reason that we have mentioned: because the existing points of departure are those left by the preceding historical period, and they are used, even if unconsciously. Of all these false starts, the Latin American is the most innocuous. In each case it has been a matter of adjusting the pace without changing the direction of movement, of correcting tactics without renouncing correct strategies or principles. At such a time profound differences between two camps come to the surface . . . .

In Latin America today, a political line which, in terms of its consequences, is not susceptible to expression as a precise and consistent military line, cannot be considered revolutionary. Any line that claims to be revolutionary must give a concrete answer to the question: How to overthrow the power of the capitalist state? In other words, how to break its backbone, the army, continuously reinforced by North American military missions? The Cuban Revolution offers an answer to fraternal Latin American countries which has still to be studied in its historical details: by means of the more or less slow building up, through guerrilla warfare carried out in suitably chosen rural zones, of a *mobile strategic force,* nucleus of a people's army and of a future socialist state....

The revolutionary guerrilla force is clandestine. It is born and develops secretly. The fighters themselves use pseudonyms. At the beginning they keep out of sight, and when they allow themselves to be seen it is at a time and place chosen by their chief. The guerrilla force is independent of the civilian population, in action as well as in military organization; consequently it need not assume the direct defense of the peasant population. The protection of the population depends on the progressive destruction of the enemy's military potential. It is relative to the overall balance of forces: the populace will be completely safe when the opposing forces are completely defeated. If the principal objective of a revolutionary guerrilla force is the destruction of the enemy's military potential, it cannot wait for the enemy to approach before taking the initiative and going over to the attack. In every case this objective requires that the guerrilla *foco* be independent of the families residing within the zone of operations.

First, to protect the population against the repressive army. Faced with elusive *guerrilleros,* the army takes vengeance on the peasants whom it suspects of being in contact with them. If it finds one among them who has withheld information it will kill him, declaring in its report to headquarters that he was a *guerrillero,* in this way giving evidence of its own heroism. Mobility, the special advantage of guerrilla forces over the civilian population, imposes a special responsibility on them with respect to the peasants, who are exposed day and night to repressive measures—eternal victims-by-substitution. The guerrilla force is thus clandestine for two reasons; it is concerned as much with the peasants' safety as with that of its own fighters. After all, the safety of the one is the safety of the other....

Second, to protect the safety of the guerrilla force itself: "Constant vigilance, constant mistrust, constant mobility"—the three golden rules. All three are concerned with security. Various considerations of common sense necessitate wariness toward the civilian population and the maintenance of a certain aloofness. By their very situation civilians are exposed to repression and the constant presence and pressure of the enemy, who will attempt to buy them, corrupt them, or to extort from them by violence what cannot be bought. Not having undergone a process of selection or technical training, as have the guerrilla fighters, the civilians in a given zone of operations are more vulnerable to infiltration or moral corruption by the enemy. Therefore peasants, even those who collaborate with the guerrillas, are generally not permitted to go to the encampments, nor are they informed of the whereabouts of arms dumps, or of the destination or real objectives of the guerrilla patrols whose passage they may observe....

One cannot see how a political leadership, in the Latin America of today, can remain aloof from technical problems of war; it is equally inconceivable that there can be political cadres who are not simultaneously military cadres. It is the situation itself, present and future, that requires this: "the cadres" of the mass armed struggle will be those who participate in it and who, in the field, prove their ability as its leaders. But how many political leaders prefer to concern themselves, day after day, with world trade unionism or to involve themselves in the mechanisms of a thousand and one "international democratic organizations" dedicated to their own survival rather than devote themselves to a serious and concrete study of military questions related to the war of their people? .... It has been proved that for the training of revolutionary cadres, the people's war is more decisive than political activity without guerrilla experience. Leaders of vision in Latin America today are young, lacking in long political experience prior to joining up with the guerrillas. It is ridiculous to continue to oppose "political cadres" to "military cadres," "political leadership" to "military leadership." Pure "politicians"—who want to remain pure—cannot lead the armed struggle of the people; pure "military men" can do so, and by the experience acquired in leading a guerrilla group, they become "politicians" as well. The experiences of Cuba and, more recently, of Venezuela, Guatemala, and other countries demonstrate that people—even petty bourgeois or peasants—are more quickly and more completely molded by the experience of guerrilla warfare than by an equal amount of time spent in a training school for cadres—a consequence, as far as men are concerned, of the essentially and totally political character of guerrilla warfare. There is a double advantage over "traditional" political training, whether within the party, in trade union struggle, or in a national or international school for cadres: in such a political *cursus honorum* it is certain that no one will receive military training (except for details), and it is not certain that the political training received will be the best. . . .

We are witnessing today, here and there, strange reversals. Che Guevara wrote that the guerrilla movement is not an end in itself, nor is it a glorious adventure; it is merely a means to an end: the conquest of political power. But, lo and behold, guerrilla forces were serving many other purposes: a form of pressure on bourgeois governments; a factor in political horse-trading; a trump card to be played in case of need—such were the objectives with which certain leaderships were attempting to saddle their military instrumentalities. The revolutionary method was being utilized for reformist ends. Then, after a period of marking time, the guerrillas turned away from and rejected these goals imposed from outside and assumed their own political leadership. To become reconciled with itself, the guerrilla force set itself up as a political leadership, which was the only way to resolve the contradictions and to develop militarily. Let it be noted that no part of the guerrilla movement has attempted to organize a new party; it seeks rather to wipe out doctrinal or party divisions among its own combatants. The unifying factors are the war and its immediate political objectives. The guerrilla movement begins by creating unity within itself around the most urgent military tasks, which have already become political tasks, a unity of non-party elements and of all the parties represented among the *guerrilleros*. The most decisive political choice is membership in the guerrilla forces, in the Armed Forces of Liberation. Thus gradually this small army creates rank-and-file unity among all parties, as it grows and wins its first victories. Eventually, the future People's Army will beget the party of which it is to be, theoretically, the instrument: essentially the party is the army.

Did not the Cuban Revolution experience this same paradox? It has been said with dismay that the party, the usual instrument for the seizure of power, was developed *after* the conquest of power. But no, it already existed in embryo—in the form of the Rebel Army. Fidel, its commander-in-chief, was already an official party leader by early 1959. A foreign journalist in Cuba was astonished one day to see many Communist leaders in battle-dress; he had thought that battle-dress and pistols belonged to the folklore of the Revolution, that they were really a kind of martial affectation. Poor man! It was not an affectation, it was the history of the Revolution itself appearing before his eyes, and most certainly the future history of America. Just as the name of socialism was formally applied to the revolution after a year of socialist practice, the name of the party came into use three years after the proletarian party had begun to exist in uniform. In Cuba it was not the party that was the directive nucleus of the popular army, as it had been in Vietnam, according to Giap; the Rebel Army was the leading nucleus of the party, the nucleus that created it. The first party leaders were created on July 26, 1953, at Moncada.* The party is the same age as the revolution; it will be 14 on July 26, 1967. Moncada was the nucleus of the Rebel Army, which was in turn the nucleus of the party. Around this nucleus, and only because it already had its own political-military leadership, other political forces have been able to assemble and unite, forming what is today the Communist Party of Cuba, of which both the base and the head continue to be made up of comrades from the guerrilla army.

The Latin American revolution and its vanguard, the Cuban Revolution, have thus made a decisive contribution to international revolutionary experience and to Marxism-Leninism.

Under certain conditions, the political and the military are not separate, but form one organic whole, consisting of the people's army, whose nucleus is the guerrilla army. The vanguard party can exist in the form of the guerrilla foco itself. The guerrilla force is the party in embryo.

This is the staggering novelty introduced by the Cuban Revolution....

Thus ends a divorce of several decades' duration between Marxist theory and revolutionary practice. As tentative and tenuous as the reconciliation may appear, it is the guerrilla movement—master of its own political leadership—that embodies it.... The guerrilla force, if it genuinely seeks total political warfare cannot in the long run tolerate any fundamental duality of functions or powers. Che Guevara carries the idea of unity so far that he proposes that the military and political leaders who lead insurrectional struggles in America "be united, if pos-

---

* The Moncada Barracks, in Santiago de Cuba, scene of the first, abortive, insurrection led by Fidel Castro.

sible, in one person." But whether it is an individual, as with Fidel, or collective, the important thing is that the leadership be homogeneous, political and military simultaneously.

—Régis Debray, *Revolution in the Revolution?*, Monthly Review Press, 1967, pp. 19–24, 41–44, 89–90, 105–06, 115–16.

6

Venezuela: The Non-Peaceful Path

JUAN RODRÍGUEZ

In 1962 a revolutionary situation matured in the country which, it is true, did not develop into a victorious revolution, despite the armed actions in Carupano and Puerto Cabello (unsuccessful because the party had not yet mastered the art of insurrection). That same year a guerrilla movement started in which four groups, military and civil, participated. At one period the movement spread to half the states of Venezuela.

However, beginning with 1963, the political and economic pattern of the struggle began to change. The economy was gradually put on its feet. The ruling classes, despite the armed frontal opposition of the revolutionary forces, staged new elections in December 1963. The outcome of these elections was that Betancourt handed over the presidency to his confederate Leoni. The revolutionary forces were isolated.

The Central Committee meeting [1967] drew the conclusion that the party "failed to make the maximum use of the election campaign," that "we should have taken part in the elections —temporarily suspending the armed operations—and put the accent on a policy of a broad alliance with a view to regrouping the democratic opposition; this would have made it possible to defeat Betancourtism at the polls and, at any rate, to create a broad Left mass movement . . . .

"After the 1963 elections the change in the correlation of forces became evident and the conditions for insurrection—which had deteriorated as a result of the aforementioned errors—became even more unfavorable, ending ultimately in the situation confronting us today."

In its critical assessment of the situation, the Central Committee paid particular attention to the question of armed struggle. It noted that the decision to meet the violence of the Betancourt gorillas with violence, "the decision to uphold the gains of January 23* by using all forms of struggle, including armed action, to overthrow Betancourt, was absolutely correct." By fighting in the front ranks of this struggle the party and the Communist youth showed themselves to be truly revolutionary organizations.

However, mistakes were made in this struggle, and the meeting noted the following:

(a) "We assessed as a 'revolutionary war for national liberation' a movement which had not yet acquired such a character and which was directed chiefly at overthrowing the government. . . .";

(b) "The party did not take the necessary action, using all its forces, to carry out an armed uprising when the conditions for this existed";

(c) "Subjectivism in applying the different forms of struggle; a tendency toward adventurism . . . manifestations of sectarianism";

(d) "Mass work was not adequately geared to our general line; we underestimated the role of various sectors of this work," especially in the trade unions;

(e) From the aforesaid it follows that the problem of combining the different forms of struggle "was raised in a very inconsistent and desultory manner." This was evident in the fact that "we were unable at the time to chart a correct and substantiated military line, one based on the political exigencies and on the basic features of national reality."

While not rejecting the experience of guerrilla warfare as a specific form of armed struggle, and while not taking the view that it has outlived its purpose in our country ("the party holds that guerrilla warfare in our country, waged in keeping with the specific features of our revolution, will play a significant role"), the CC meeting noted at the same time that, in the present conditions, to regard guerrilla warfare in the rural areas as the

---

* January 23, 1958, date of the overthrow of the previous military dictatorship.

main form of revolutionary struggle would be mechanically to transfer an experience which, while successful in other countries, does not correspond to the peculiarities of national reality.

We proceed from the fact that nearly three-fourths of our population are urbanized, that the radicalized masses and the main motive forces of the revolution are concentrated in the towns. We also proceed from the fact that the foreign monopolies—which dominate our economy—and native capital have their principal industrial centers in the towns and in the adjacent areas. Furthermore, Venezuela's history since the turn of the century shows that as a rule it was in the cities and towns that the main political conflicts erupted and were resolved. Revolutionary armed actions were therefore mostly in the form of *urban insurrections* in which patriotic military men participated with civilians. This was particularly the case after the events of January 1958.

In other words, the CC meeting held that the guerrilla movement is an auxiliary form of struggle in Venezuela and for Venezuela. The concrete conditions of our life and the course of events completely disprove the view that the guerrilla unit is "the embryo of a real Communist Party" which is counterposed to the existing Communist Party, disprove the claim that the guerrilla movement is the decisive strategic force of *any* national-revolutionary struggle.

Critical discussion of this problem helps the collective thinking which aims at defining the party's strategic line, and contrasts sharply with the attitude of the factionalists who persist in the old errors. As the CC meeting noted, "the deviationists, by exaggerating the importance and possibilities of the guerrilla movement, are steering it toward defeat, which we are witnessing today." Furthermore, this deviation with its "underestimation of work in the towns, weakens revolutionary activity in general."

The aforesaid does not signify in any way complete or partial rejection of the concept or the general line charted six years ago. "The Central Committee confirms the Third Congress thesis on the non-peaceful character of the Venezuelan way to national liberation and socialism." Hence its call to the party and to the youth "to raise the level of preparation in all spheres . . . . to master . . . all forms of struggle, to learn to combine them correctly and flexibly, and to be prepared in all contingencies to fulfill their revolutionary mission and to win power for the working people."

These points, in our view, are of enormous significance not only because they confirm the soundness of our strategic line, but also because they bring us a step closer toward elaborating the all-important question of the aims of the Venezuelan revolution today.

As we look back over the ten years of revolutionary battle in Venezuela, we recall Lenin's words when summarizing the results of the first Russian revolution: "The correctness of revolutionary Social-Democratic tactics . . . is confirmed by the experience of the mass struggle in 1905–07. The defeat of the revolution resulting from this first campaign revealed, not that the tasks were wrong, not that the immediate aims were 'utopian,' not that the methods and means were mistaken, but that the forces were insufficiently prepared, that the revolutionary crisis was insufficiently wide and deep."*

The struggle to achieve the ultimate aim of the revolution must therefore be continued, bearing in mind that "the great wars in history, the great problems of revolutions, were solved only by the advanced classes returning to the attack, again and again—and they achieved victory after having learned the lessons of defeat. . . . In new forms and by other ways, sometimes much more slowly than we would wish, the revolutionary crisis is approaching, coming to a head again. We must carry on with the lengthy work of preparing larger masses for that crisis; this preparation must be more serious, taking account of higher and more concrete tasks; and the more successfully we do this work, the more certain will be our victory in the new struggle."† That is the essence, spirit and meaning of the resolutions of the recent meeting of the Central Committee.

—"The New in the Political Line of the Communist Party of Venezuela," *World Marxist Review,* September 1967, pp. 42–43. This article by a leading Venezuelan Communist summarizes the conclusions of the Central Committee of the Communist Party of Venezuela.

---

* V. I. Lenin, "On the Road," *Selected Works,* New York, 1967, Vol. 1, p. 587.
† *Ibid.,* pp. 587–8.

7

Colombia: Theses on the Guerrilla Movement

> This is a section of the main report endorsed by the Tenth Congress of the Communist Party of Colombia, held illegally in January 1966 and attended by party leaders and functionaries from all parts of the country, including participants in the guerrilla and self-defense movement. These theses, endorsing the guerrilla struggle waged by the peasants, sum up the experience of many years of struggle and chart the further development of armed action parallel with other forms of revolutionary mass struggle.

The new stage in the guerrilla movement in Colombia ushered in particularly by the splendid resistance put up by the peasants of Marquetalia, has demonstrated the following:

1. The armed resistance to the aggression in Marquetalia, El Pato, Guyabero, Riochiquito, Southern Tolima and elsewhere shows that a guerrilla movement which springs from the masses, which expresses their demands and is guided by Marxism-Leninism is invincible, however strong the forces of the enemy and even when the conditions in the country are not yet ripe for armed action to become everywhere the main form of struggle.

2. Armed struggle in Colombia began and is developing as guerrilla warfare at a time when a revolutionary situation does not yet exist throughout the country. It would be disastrous for the Colombian revolutionary movement passively to allow the peasant organizations to be destroyed on the plea that it is necessary to wait until the revolutionary situation has fully matured before taking armed action. To the armed aggression of the enemy it is necessary to counterpose in the villages guerrilla resistance and armed struggle and, when the conditions are ripe for it, the question of armed struggle must be posed also in the towns and working-class centers.

3. There is no contradiction between mass struggle and armed guerrilla struggle. Guerrilla warfare is one of the higher forms of mass struggle, and it can make headway only when it assumes a *mass character,* when it originates from the midst of the people and when it is a faithful expression of their immediate and historical interests. The experience of revolutionaries who have sought in recent years to spark off armed struggle without enjoying the support of the peasant masses, without the backing of their resolve and activity, shows that such idealistic undertakings only spell easy victory for the army, police or hired bandits in the service of the authorities and the latifundists.

4. The policy of mass self-defense proclaimed by our party was and remains basically correct. But it was not carried out consistently in some areas, and in others it was frustrated by more ingenious methods of repression and political and military forms of struggle employed by the enemy.

The transformation of mass self-defense into a powerful guerrilla movement, in the face of a systematic wide-scale offensive waged by the army against the peasant areas, represents the logical development of the entire concept of revolutionary struggle in the specific conditions of Colombia. At the same time, combination of all methods of struggle and emphasis on the particular method which accords with the concrete situation in each given locality is not only a correct interpretation of the Marxist-Leninist teaching but also its correct application to the social process in our country.

5. In the areas subjected to attack in fulfillment of the plans of the US military mission, guerrilla action has become the principal form of mass struggle. In these areas all other forms of struggle become auxiliary to the main form, armed struggle, on which all other forms of mass action and the defense of the people's organizations should hinge. On the other hand, the concentration of government forces in the areas subjected to attack creates favorable conditions for taking the initiative.

6. The guerrilla movement is being consolidated and expanded in a number of peasant areas even though the vast majority of the Colombian people are continuing ever broader resolute mass actions of other types as the main form of struggle. These mass actions include militant students' strikes, hard-fought workers' strikes, enlistment of government employees in the strike movement, and other major strike actions. Our people engage also in forms of struggle which cannot be called "peace-

ful," but which nevertheless are not yet armed struggle. Of these forms, special mention should be made of the seizure of vacant lots in urban centers by homeless city people for the purpose of building homes in defiance of the authorities and police repression. Such mass actions, although they nearly always are of an economic nature, are bound increasingly to raise the level of the slogans advanced by the masses and the methods they employ to a higher plane as the guerrilla struggle of the peasants is increasingly combined with the mass struggles of the workers, students and other urban sections.

7. Although in the course of this process the peasants' guerrilla struggle is not yet the main form of struggle, it acquires growing importance as the most effective reply by the people to the policy of terror pursued by the regime subordinated to US imperialism, and develops into a new revolutionary factor which has a tremendous appeal to the masses. Having begun with peasant guerrilla actions, armed struggle has become inevitable in Colombia owing to the resumption on a wide scale of a policy of violence against the people on the part of the oligarchic government.

8. The growing guerrilla movement of today is of a more definitive and more advanced nature than the guerrilla struggle which developed at the preceding stages, not only because this movement has accumulated rich experience but also, and mainly, because it has a clearly defined revolutionary anti-imperialist content and because its chief aim is to win power for the people. This new Colombian guerrilla movement is a patriotic reply to the growing military intervention of US imperialism against our people with the objective of implementing the Laso Plan and the principles of the so-called "preventive" war. The US imperialist intervention is expressed also in the growing interference of the US military mission in the armed forces, in the direct financing by the US government of military operations against the peasant areas and in the "lending" of all kinds of arms, planes and squadrons of helicopters to be used to wage war against the working people of Colombia. In this way, to the old causes of terroristic violence in Colombia, chief of which was and remains the greed of the latifundists, there is added as a decisive factor the US imperialist policy of intervention.

—*Colombia, An Embattled Land,* Peace and Socialism Publishers, Prague, 1966, pp. 76–78.

8
Criteria of Revolutionary Armed Struggle in Colombia

ALBERTO GOMEZ

It is now more imperative than ever for all groups and sections objectively interested in the overthrow of the present regime to find their place in the revolutionary process. Our point of departure is the class criterion set forth in our program, which declares that the Colombian revolution will be led by the working class in close alliance with the peasantry, and in unity with the students, intellectuals and salaried workers. All sections of the working population have a contribution to make to the revolutionary struggle, and the magnitude of the contributions will be determined in the process of this struggle.

We proceed from the reality, not from pre-conceived notions. Our guide is the Marxist-Leninist precept concerning the need to build the alliance of the working class and the peasantry. The absence of this alliance in the past enabled the reactionaries to paralyze popular actions in the earlier phases of the armed struggle (1949-53 and 1954-57). One of the shortcomings of the past was the weakness of the revolutionary movement in the cities. The ruling classes took advantage of this, and when the military dictatorship of Rojas Pinilla fell on May 10, 1957, the fruits of the popular struggle were reaped by the bourgeoisie, which put a "national front" government in the saddle.

But it would be an act of sheer desperation if, because of this, we were to anathematize the towns and surrender them to the class enemy, It should be borne in mind, first, that 52 per cent of the population live in towns (moreover, there are 17 cities with more than 100,000 inhabitants each). Second, there is the example of the spontaneous uprising of the urban masses which began on April 9, 1948, when the Liberal leader Jorge Eliecer Gaitan was murdered. Some towns were in the hands of the workers for several days. And we know how important a role the mobilization of the urban masses played on May 10, 1957, when the dictatorship was overthrown. In recent years there have been numerous strikes of workers and students, and major actions have been undertaken by teachers and clerical workers. Hence the importance we attach to work in the towns. This work is a component of our policy of combining diverse forms of struggle.

The guerrilla movement is well aware that it *alone* cannot carry out the revolution. Guerrillas know from experience what it means to act in isolation. A victorious revolution calls for the unity of the people, and already there are signs that this unity is growing. Every action by workers, students or teachers helps the guerrilla movement. As the headquarters of FARC* have declared on repeated occasions, every action taken by the working people is inseparably linked with the struggle waged by the guerrillas.

Leading Role of the Communist Party in the Guerrilla Movement

No claimants to political leadership of any movement can expect to succeed unless they throw themselves into the thick of the struggle. No group can really take the lead merely by declaring itself to be the vanguard. We Communists have always made it clear that we do not consider ourselves to be the only revolutionaries. On the contrary, we have always extended a fraternal hand to all those outside our ranks also fighting against imperialism.

Colombia is the scene of a life-and-death struggle. In the center of this struggle is the guerrilla movement headed by the FARC and its headquarters. The united military-political leadership of the FARC follows the line of the Communist Party as set forth in the decisions of its central bodies. To meet the requirements of the revolutionary process in our country, the Tenth Congress of our party [January 1966] centralized the leadership of armed action in the rural localities. The leading positions in the headquarters of FARC are held by such tried and tested fighters as Manuel Marulanda Velez, Ciro Trujillo, Jacobo Arenas and Isauro Yosa, all members of the Central Committee of our party. Our combat training, based on the decisions of the inaugural

---

* *Fuerzas Armadas Revolucionarias de Colombia*, Revolutionary Armed Forces of Colombia.

conference of FARC, takes cognizance of both the concrete situation and the general situation in our country. It is not by chance that 48 per cent of the delegates to the Tenth Congress were peasants, some of whom have been waging armed struggle since 1950. It can be said that the revolutionary armed struggle in our country is largely the result of the work done by the Communists.

Playing its part in the thick of the armed struggle, forging ahead from success to success—and committing inevitable mistakes as well—our party has consistently charted the basic course of this struggle. It evolved the tactics of mass self-defense which led on to guerrilla action. We created the FARC, which first emerged at the time of the aggression against Marquetalia and crystallized thanks to the experience accumulated by the Guerrilla Bloc of the South. FARC is destined to develop into a people's army and play a decisive role in winning power for the people.

The party and the guerrilla detachments are at one, they interweave and are interdependent. By strengthening the party we strengthen the guerrilla movement. And when the guerrilla detachments gain in influence, so does the party. All party organizations throughout the Cordillera help the armed units solve the problems confronting them. Every Communist in the zone of hostilities is a guerrilla behind the enemy's lines. Whenever a detachment moves into a new locality, provided the conditions are ripe, it lays the groundwork for a new party organization. Conversely, in areas where guerrilla action has not yet begun but the political base exists, the party paves the way for the guerrillas to move in. Every zonal, municipal or district committee in the theater of hostilities works to strengthen the guerrilla movement. Party organizations are as necessary to the guerrillas as the air they breathe; they are a pre-condition of successful operations. *The "secret" of the indivisible unity of the Communist Party and the guerrilla detachments is that the party and its leadership are in the center of the armed struggle.*

Some leftists at one time insisted on beginning armed action everywhere. But when it actually began and the peasants were in greater need than ever of support and concrete aid, these people were not available. Their exhortations were not matched by deeds. Some of them now consort with the bourgeoisie. Others unconditionally support all the economic and repressive measures of the government, repudiating the very demands they once put forward. This happened because politics can rest only on realities, not on myths. The merits of each are measured by his concrete participation in the revolutionary process.

One hardly finds anyone today who believes that because the guerrilla movement is headed by Communists it will lose popular support. Experience has shown that the guerrilla movement led by our party has extended its radius of action and penetrated into zones where Liberal and Conservative influences used to predominate, and also into areas where there formerly were neither self-defense organizations nor any sign of Communist influence. The guerrilla movement is developing into a factor uniting the democratic forces. By working to build a united front of all groups carrying on the armed revolutionary struggle, FARC is helping to translate into reality the party's call for a patriotic national liberation front. Only such a policy can ensure the victory of the revolutionary movement.

The Tenth Congress of our party pointed out that a specific type of revolutionary way *combining all forms of struggle* is opening up before Colombia, and stressed that in the overall context of this way *popular armed action will develop into the main form of struggle against imperialism,* to win power. FARC is paving the way to a people's army. We Communists are working to realize this perspective. We are fighting for an independent, sovereign Colombia based on socialism.

—"The Revolutionary Armed Forces of Colombia and Their Perspectives," *World Marxist Review,* April 1967, pp. 34–35. Alberto Gomez is a member of the Political Bureau of the Communist Party of Colombia.

9

Revolutionary Tactics in Guatemala

JOSÉ MANUEL FORTUNY

The Workers' Party [Communist] considers the present situation extremely unstable. Class conflicts and their aggravation as a result of the structural crisis gripping Guatemala will most likely impel the army in the immediate rather than the more distant future to pursue one of two lines of action: either it will resort to force to overthrow the government in case the latter lifts the restrictions on the actions of the masses (though this is not very likely), or will force the government to adopt a tough line typical of any camarilla of "gorillas." In the latter case the government would be turned into a civilian variant of the military regime that preceded it; it could then rightfully be called the "fourth counter-revolutionary government." Clearly, if the conditions which gave rise to armed revolutionary struggle remain, this struggle, too, will continue.

Some people feel that the present political situation affords grounds for changing the line of the party, for turning to the peaceful way as the only possible alternative to the present line. Those who think so confuse, at best, the *forms of struggle* and the *overall course of the revolution,* or, at worst, reduce the question of the party line to a purely tactical matter.

The party has already made its stand clear, but it will not be amiss to repeat once again: we hold that defining the course of the revolution is a question of *strategy,* while the choice of the form of struggle is one of *tactics.* The question of recharting the overall course can rise objectively only as result of radical qualitative changes in the situation which only a victory of the popular, anti-imperialist revolution can bring about. Our party holds that in the present conditions such a revolution can be carried out only by adhering to the strategy of armed action. Those who fail to see this will find themselves caught in a vicious circle. The form of the struggle is another matter. This is a tactical issue which depends on the arena of struggle and the concrete circumstances, in other words, on transient, non-qualitative factors. This indeed is the situation in Guatemala, where the change of government has not altered the nature of forces in the saddle.

Lenin, as Marx before him, said: *"Never play* with insurrection, but when beginning it realize firmly that you must *go all the way."* We believe that we are not taking a mechanical approach if we apply this basic rule to the revolutionary people's war (since it is a variant of insurrection) to which the Guatemalan Communists have had recourse because of the specific conditions of the country. If, as Marx said, *"insurrection is an art quite as much as war,"* the conclusion suggests itself that like any art it requires systematic preparation. And thoroughly prepared use of force is not only a matter of tactics. . . .

It should be borne in mind that both the election of Montenegro and the pressure exerted by Washington on Peralta Azurdia to make him yield the presidency to the former were basically the result of the armed struggle waged by the revolutionaries. Paradoxical though it may sound, the armed struggle was indeed the main factor in the peaceful change of government. For the Revolutionary Party, besides the usual promises of a social and political order, made a point of stressing in its election campaign that if the election were to be faked and an official military candidate imposed on the country, the armed struggle would inevitably be stepped up and eventually end in the victory of the guerrillas.

US imperialism is no champion of democracy. The same applies to Peralta Azurdia, who ruthlessly trampled on the elementary rights of the people. His first action after seizing power was to suspend the Constitution, and he ruled by means of naked terror. If a man like this and US imperialism found it necessary to allow Montenegro to take over, the sole reason was the fear that the revolutionary armed struggle and popular discontent would make Guatemala another Dominican Republic.

"The facts thus show," the Central Committee of the Workers' Party declared in its resolution of June 10, 1966, "that the main enemy—North American imperialism—is changing its tactics. Formerly it openly supported the extreme reaction in order to rule the country through the army. Now it is drawing new forces into the administration and using the army to control the government." From this the party concluded that it was necessary, without changing the general line of its policy and firmly adhering to the strategy of armed action, to "define the concrete tactics in the present political situation." The basic aspects of these tactics are the following:

1. Despite the meanderings of Montenegro's Revolutionary Party, it should not be confused with the parties of reaction. Because of its class composition and policy, it plays a specific role, basically seeking to deceive the masses and to win them over by using reformism as a decoy. Moreover, the Revolutionary Party is not a homogeneous entity; it is rent by antagonisms between the leading clique, the middle-echelon leaders and the rank and file. It is neither a combination of three different currents nor a united party, but consists of three different groupings. The immediate task is to combat the reactionary top stratum, to neutralize the opportunists in the middle group, and to win over the rank and file to Left positions.

2. Since the government is clearly seeking to pursue a policy different from that which the army would like to impose on it, the Communist tactics toward the two differ. The Communists expose the repressive policy of the military and seek to bring home to the government that high-ranking army officers are plotting and preparing a coup. One of the party's objects is to make it clear to the government that at the given moment its direct adversary is not the Rebel Armed Forces but the official army. The above-mentioned Central Committee resolution points out that if the army will continue its "anti-guerrilla and repressive operations, the Rebel Armed Forces will reply with a military offensive, taking the initiative in order not to be caught unawares." But in the event of the army discontinuing operations, the resolution stresses, the Rebel Armed Forces will confine themselves to "retaliatory action in the event of repression against the masses or the arrest or torture of our comrades."

3. Faced with the constant danger of a coup (witness the activities of some officers and the outrages committed by reactionary gangs), revolutionary tactics consist in alerting the masses and the government to this danger; and, in the event of a coup being essayed, in complementary action by the Rebel Armed Forces and rallying the masses to repel the putschists; and, in the event of the latter succeeding in seizing power, to wage resolute armed struggle and to build up a broad front to repel the direct intervention which the US imperialists may undertake.

4. The change of government was merely a reshuffling of the forces in the saddle. Real power remains in the hands of the US imperialists, who combine the repressions and violence employed by the army with some insignificant reforms and concessions implemented through the agency of the government. The official propaganda claim that the reforms and concessions have introduced a new element in the country's political life are, of course, true up to a point. As the party sees it, this new element "consists in the imminent new upswing in the political struggle which will make it possible to combine to a greater extent than before diverse forms of struggle and organizational activity, for new opportunities are opening for mass actions and for open, legal organizations of the masses to the greatest possible extent in order to win economic, social and political concessions for the workers, peasants and other sections of the population. Armed struggle waged in conformity with the political situation will support the mass actions, and should be carried further in order to build up our strength to meet the new situation."

The party sees its main task in all-round utilization of the possibilities afforded by the present situation for improving the organization of the revolutionary struggle in the three basic areas—the masses, the Rebel Armed Forces and the party itself. But work in this direction and the steady development of revolutionary action (in particular, the opening of new guerrilla fronts) in no way detracts from the party's efforts to build alliances or to achieve unity of action with the remainder of the Left and with all groups and organizations having influence among the masses. In particular, the Workers' Party is determined not to allow the Revolutionary Party to capitalize on our sectarian mistakes to win support among these groups and to isolate the Communists in the Rebel Armed Forces. "The best reply to the enemy's tactics," our Central Committee pointed out, "is in the final analysis the proper combination of political, armed, economic and social struggle. But for this it is necessary for the revolutionary forces always to be guided by the aspirations and the demands of the masses, for the Communists always to apply Marxism-Leninism creatively and to be guided by it."

—"Guatemala: the Political Situation and Revolutionary Tactics," *World Marxist Review,* February 1967, pp. 32–33. José Manuel Fortuny is a secretary of the Workers' Party of Guatemala.

10

A Dominican View of the Latin American Revolution

JOSÉ CUELLO and ASDRUBAL DOMÍNGUEZ

The October Revolution affected practically all the sociopolitical processes of the century. Now all revolutions against exploitation and oppression contain elements determined by the socialist content of the times, although their immediate aspects, the objective and subjective motivations of the class forces engaged in the revolution, the program, the stages and the forms of struggle and of the state structures born of revolution differ widely and are not always of a directly socialist character. The revolutionary ways to socialism, as Lenin predicted, are becoming ever more varied.

One aspect of this process is the growing participation of non-proletarian strata and groups in the revolutionary anti-capitalist struggle. These highly diverse strata and groups, at present our allies in the world proletarian revolution, have already contributed—and will contribute in still greater degree—their own features to the socialist revolution and the building of socialism both in economically undeveloped regions and developed capitalist countries. At the same time, this process is, at the moment, generating certain difficulties in the fight for the unity of the Communist movement and the revolutionary forces on a world scale.

Ever since the Cuban Revolution the entry of new social strata and groups into the revolutionary movement has assumed a mass and dynamic character in the Latin American countries.

The role played by forward-looking intellectuals and students in the revolutionary struggles of the past decade is generally known. We think that the features of the given stage of the struggle in Latin America demand of us close attention to the processes now observed among army officers, the clergy, etc.

The example of the Venezuelan military men who participated in the Carupano and Puerto Cabello rebellions; of Turcios Lima, Yon Sosa and the November 13 Movement in Guatemala; of Francisco Caamano, Ramon Manuel Montes Arache, Hector Lachapelle Diaz and hundreds of other participants in the April 1965 events in the Dominican Republic,* shows that when a revolutionary crisis breaks out many officers and men will join in the fight for genuine independence, for national dignity.

We see from the example of Camilo Torres and his followers that among the Latin American clergy, too, revolutionary, anti-imperialist sentiment is on the rise. Christian humanism is its subjective basis and form.

We think that these processes, eminently positive, have not always been correctly interpreted by Marxists on our continent. True, the radical petty bourgeoisie, and in the first place its

---

* Date of the popular uprising by the Dominican people that shattered the former pro-imperialist military dictatorship and was followed by massive American imperialist intervention with 42,000 marines.

intellectual elite, tries at times to play the leading role in the revolutionary process which in the other continents is played by the working class; at times, it is true, this bourgeoisie tries to oust the Marxist parties, and it does so where the organized working class becomes captive to erroneous tactics, sectarianism or dogmatism. But, while combating the "vanguardism" of these sections of the petty bourgeoisie, which can be an objective danger to the revolution, we always bear in mind Lenin's words, so topical today for the Communist movement in the continent: "It is not enough to call ourselves 'the vanguard', the advanced contingent; we must act in such a way that all the other contingents recognize and are obliged to admit that we are marching in the vanguard."

Differing political and social groups, some of which gravitate toward Marxism while others do not, are and will be taking part in the continental revolutionary process. In order really to lead this conglomerate of forces, some of which lay claim to the leading role in the movement, we must assimilate Marxism creatively, apply flexible and bold tactics, and display capacity for struggle and work greater than that of the other revolutionary contingents. Only the dialectical combination of revolutionary unity and ideological struggle within the framework of this unity can lead to the genuine hegemony of the party of the working class in the anti-imperialist front, especially at those times when the growing sharpness and rapidity of the objective process greatly exceed the level of the organized consciousness of the working class.

Where Communists are in the minority in the united front, ideological struggle helps ensure a correct orientation of the movement as a whole, helps to win the majority; if we are the principal force of the front, ideological struggle leads to unity through persuasion and not through mechanical imposition of our will upon others.

The policy of joint action by the different social and political forces against a common enemy requires a very serious approach to, and theoretical clarity in, the *methodology* of the struggle. Further proof of this is the debate on this question now already under way in the Latin American revolutionary movement, a debate which at times assumes sharpness impermissible from the standpoint of the revolution presaging a split in the movement.

Our approach to this is based on categorical rejection of concepts which presuppose antagonism between "armed struggle" and "mass struggle"; we regard this posing of the issue as senseless, unwarranted and utterly contrary to the realities of our country (and, we think, of the entire continent).

If *methods* are understood as the totality of means enabling the working class and its allies to win power, then the problem of methods is, as we said, transferred to the realm of strategy, with the result that the polemic becomes mixed up with the debate on the *nature of the transition* from capitalism to socialism.

Our party knows from the bitter experience of April 1965 that we cannot regard ourselves as the vanguard if we do not prepare for the eventuality of the revolution taking the way of armed struggle. If at the moment the bourgeoisie and imperialism set in motion the machinery of armed counter-revolution the Communist Party fails to adapt its policy to the concrete demands of revolutionary war, the masses will turn away from it. And leadership of the movement, by virtue of the very dynamics of the revolutionary process, might be seized by the non-proletarian groups (in this case the alternative is the immediate defeat of the revolution or of the national liberation struggle).

In the continental discussion on the methods, forms and ways of revolutionary struggle few deny the need for propaganda and agitation, for strikes and peasant actions, for tireless work to organize the working class. What in our view is really debatable, is whether the bourgeoisie will reconcile itself to expropriation, and imperialism to the loss of a territory it regards as vitally important, or whether internal and external reaction will at the decisive moment offer "total" resistance, utilizing *all* the possibilities of the machinery of state, *all* the technical means at its disposal, including the entire arsenal of modern weapons.

It is not enough, in our view, to proclaim "the need to master all methods of struggle," for this extremely loose formula does not orient the revolutionaries of the particular country on a consistent policy aimed at winning power, and at times prevents them from concentrating attention and forces on *real* mastery of those forms of struggle that are *really necessary,* i.e., those in keeping with the long-term trends of development.

As Engels pointed out, the ruling classes, by perfecting their weapons and training their armies in new methods of warfare, determine the level of armed violence which the revolutionary parties must overcome if they want victory.

In the phase of street demonstrations, meetings and strikes the oligarchy, the bourgeoisie and imperialism can defend the existing socio-economic system with the help of police and riot squads, water cannon and truncheons. But the moment the revolutionary masses overrun this "first trench" of the reactionaries' defense, they will be met by the army with its guns and tanks. And when the tanks burst into flames and the guns captured by the people are turned against the last bastions of reaction, there will appear on the horizon the warships and troop-carrying planes of the United States—the last and most powerful line of defense of the exploiting classes in any country of the hemisphere.

That, at any rate, is what we experienced three years ago.

And so Dominican Communists, holding that the revolution remains on the order of the day, are actively preparing for armed struggle at all levels. For the same reason, we consider it important to conduct systematic preparation of the masses, because the party's readiness for armed struggle does not signify yet that the masses will go over to it at the decisive moment. Lenin regarded psychological preparation of the masses for revolutionary violence as a duty of the Communist Party. History has yet to prove him wrong.

We think that the barbaric actions of counter-revolution in Vietnam, the Middle East, Africa and Latin America confront us, the revolutionaries in these regions, with an alternative; either paralysis from fear and from realization of one's own impotence, or a redoubling of the energy of the revolution, which will win only if the working class and its party do not allow themselves to be caught unawares and study well the methods of the enemy. It would be a crime against the working class if its organized political detachment were paralyzed because it was unprepared for armed struggle and came belatedly and hesitantly to the barricades spontaneously erected by the revolutionary masses.

Should the situation so change that the working class and its party do not need to take up arms, so much the better; but all-around preparation for the struggle is never superfluous.

Now for another issue in the current debate. In principle, an armed revolutionary movement can start wherever the class struggle reaches the level of armed violence. However, in view of imperialism's interference in the internal affairs of our countries, it becomes necessary for Communists not only to lead the struggle born of a spontaneous aggravation of the social and political contradictions, but also to organize this struggle on their own initiative where, given proper preparation, a military organization of the masses can be created. Therefore, systematic preparation for irregular struggle in rural areas is so important for the Communists of our country and for the majority of countries on our continent.

The connection between the threat of intervention and the imperative guerrilla struggle is, to us, self-evident. More often than not, irregular wars in rural areas have been waged by the people against the technically superior forces of a foreign invader, against his occupation forces. Such was the war waged by the North Americans for independence from Britain; the nations of Europe fought against fascism; the Communist Party of the Soviet Union directed the guerrilla war in the rear of the Hitler invaders; a guerrilla war was waged in China against the Japanese. Its role and effectiveness have been tested in Vietnam, the Philippines, Algeria and in many other parts of the world.

The thing is not only that rural terrain is most favorable for irregular war (specifically, against an invader), but also that a war of this kind makes it possible to draw into active revolutionary struggle the peasants, rural semi-proletarians and agricultural laborers suffering from inhuman exploitation and misery.

Those who hope to accomplish the revolution in our countries without the rural masses will never secure its victory. But after a large-scale penetration by the "green berets" into the mountains of America it would be irresponsible, in our view, to try to win the masses for revolution solely through trade union or craft union methods of organization and education. (The effectiveness of other methods of revolutionary organization and education of the peasantry is evident in the experience of the Colombian Communists.) The US military presence in our mountains is an admission of the danger (to the enemy) and of the possibilities (for the revolution) inherent in the revolutionary struggle of the peasantry. But it is also a reminder of a serious weakness of the liberation movement—slow progress in drawing the exploited rural masses into the democratic and anti-imperialist struggle.

The need to involve the masses in this protracted action becomes increasingly clear, the action that can have the character of resistance to the invader (or putschists) until conditions are created for a military-political offensive along the entire front of the revolution.

—"The Dominican Republic: Two Years After," *World Marxist Review*, March 1968, pp. 38–39. The authors are leading members of the Dominican Communist Party.

11

Anti-Imperialist Alliance in Latin America

LUIS CORVALAN

The Latin American wars of independence in the past century were continental wars. When Bolivar, Sucre, San Martin and O'Higgins fought for the independence of their countries, they were striving also for the freedom of other American peoples. No national states and no geographical frontiers existed on our continent in those days. The borders of the various colonial possessions were rather indistinct, and the independence armies fighting for the liberation of their people counted in their ranks officers and soldiers from other colonies.

It was not until independence was won and capitalism began to develop that the national states came into existence. But, as before, the peoples of Latin America had a common destiny, common problems and common enemies. Still, they could not and did not escape the effects of the law of uneven development of capitalism and capitalist society. Against the present general setting of backwardness, there are appreciable disparities between the countries in levels of economic, political and social development. This gives the revolutions a national complexion and conditions their variety in form and discrepancy in time.

For this reason, the present situation differs from that of the past century. However, Washington is pursuing its policy of aggression and intervention throughout the continent, which, as the Cuban Communist Party stressed in its statement of May 18 [1967], "internationalizes aggressive wars, in which soldiers of different nationalities are engaged, as in the Korean War and now in South Vietnam where North American, South Korean,

Thai, Filipino, New Zealand and Australian troops have been committed, and as in Santo Domingo where soldiers were shipped from Brazil, Costa Rica, Honduras, Nicaragua and Paraguay; furthermore, imperialism is trying through the OAS [Organization of American States] to build up an international armed force for use against Cuba and the liberation movements on the continent."

This necessitates joint action by the Latin American peoples and imparts an all-continental complexion of outstanding international importance to their struggle.

Working hand in hand with the local oligarchies, imperialism spurns the principle of non-interference and the sovereignty and frontiers of the Latin American countries. It espouses the so-called doctrine of ideological frontiers, which revolutionaries have to counter with the utmost solidarity. Among other things, this presupposes direct participation in the liberation struggles of fraternal peoples wherever this is warranted by necessity, provided it is done under their leadership.

In some cases, as in the anti-fascist war in Spain, revolutionaries of different nationalities may participate in large numbers, with marked political and historical effect. However, the most important contribution revolutionaries can make to liberation and working-class victory on a world scale is struggle in their own countries and their moral and material support to revolutionary battles in other countries.

In the *Communist Manifesto*, Marx and Engels, the founders of Marxism and of proletarian internationalism, stressed that "though not in substance, yet in form, the struggle of the proletariat with the bourgeoisie is at first a national struggle. The proletariat of each country must, of course, first of all settle matters with its own bourgeoisie."

In this national struggle it is the revolutionaries in each country who determine the various aspects and concrete tasks of the revolution. They know the home situation better than anybody else and are in a far better position to define the aims and the methods of attaining them. They may err, but are less likely to do so than others. In any case, revolutionaries in their respective countries are best equipped to assume full responsibility for working out the right course of action after a preliminary review of their own experience, their successes and setbacks. Needless to say, this does not rule out exchanges of opinion and, in some cases, fraternal counsel.

The Cuban Revolution is proof of the fact that reality plays havoc with preconceived assumptions, serving as a reminder of the folly of generalizing the singular features of this or that experience. This is not to say, however, that the specific features of one revolution, say that of the Cuban, will not recur elsewhere (at least in a somewhat different form). We believe, therefore, that in some Latin American countries revolution may be sparked off by a guerrilla movement, as was the case in Cuba.

For this to happen the courage and determination of a group of revolutionaries, though an important, sometimes even decisive factor, is not enough. Much more essential are favorable general conditions. To be sure, we hold that they need be neither absolutely favorable nor completely mature, but they must be in the process of maturing with a clear prospect of becoming fully ripe.

Certainly, it is not easy to define the place and the exact time for guerrilla or some other form of armed action. Lenin warned against reckless ventures which, as a rule, cause a senseless waste of lives and end in retreat. On the other hand, Leninism has always been creatively bold, infused with the desire to advance the revolutionary cause. It would be wrong therefore to reject out of hand or blindly accept any specific form of struggle. The main thing is to embark squarely on the path of struggle, size up the situation to the best of one's ability and decide on the most propitious course of action. The revolutionary must be ready to take the offensive at any moment, to retreat when necessary, and to perceive situations favorable for the revolution.

—"Alliance of the Anti-Imperialist Forces in Latin America," *World Marxist Review,* July 1967, pp. 25–27. Luis Corvalan is general secretary of the Communist Party of Chile.

VII. THE UNITED STATES

In the United States, the question of armed action has arisen in connection with the black ghetto revolts which have occurred with increasing frequency and intensity since the outburst in Harlem (New York City) in 1964. Coinciding with the contemporary American imperialist policies of intervention and aggression on a world scale, these spontaneous revolts have been met with the same violence and repression at home. As a consequence, some black Americans, inspired by the national liberation struggles in Africa, Asia and Latin America, have visualized their liberation also in terms of armed struggle, such as guerrilla-type actions in the cities. In the following selection, Henry Winston, chairman of the Communist Party, USA, presents the position of his party on this question.

Revolutionary Struggle for Afro-American Freedom

HENRY WINSTON

The stubborn refusal of the ruling class of our country, and the Johnson administration in particular, to permit anything but token changes in the unbearable conditions faced by black Americans, especially in the ghettos, despite the massive peaceful demonstrations of recent years, has led to a growing lack of confidence in the possibility to achieve meaningful change through the democratic process.

The meaning of the mass rebellions of 1967 in the black ghettos should be clear: millions of black Americans will no longer live under the conditions of the depression '30s while the United States boasts of the "affluence" of the '60s.

The failure of most white Americans, including large sections of the liberal and progressive forces, to understand the desperate nature of the crisis in the ghettos, their failure to ally themselves with the black people in their struggle for necessary radical changes to resolve the crisis, has resulted in an increasing lack of confidence in the ability of white masses to overcome racism and in their readiness to join with black people in the fight for meaningful solutions.

The repeated failure of the Federal government, as well as the cities and states, to take decisive action against the racists who murder and maim black people has aroused a new awareness of the need for greater reliance on determined self-defense, including armed defense.

The Minutemen, the Birchites, Ku Klux Klan, White Citizens Council, National Riflemen's Association and American Nazi groups, are openly inciting and organizing racial violence with impunity. Alabama's former Governor Wallace is not only given free rein to spread the plague of racist violence, but is rallying racist and fascist-like forces all over the United States.

Black people, with good cause, smell the stench of the gas chamber in these menacing developments. They have rightly served notice that they have no intention to play the role of passive victims of genocide.

Moreover, an alternative program to violence, radical enough to solve the problems of the ghettos and possible of achievement, has not been put forward with any conviction.

Furthermore, there is a lack of class consciousness and of an understanding of revolutionary tactics, geared to specific US conditions—and not borrowed from other countries—in the ranks of the leadership of the Negro freedom movement. The world liberation struggle of recent years in Africa, Asia and Latin America has inspired the determination to fight for full freedom in the United States.

All of these factors have given rise to a new emphasis, on the part of some, on the need for armed struggle, particularly in the black ghettos.

Courage is the banner of the fight for black freedom. Communists join all militant black freedom fighters in bearing this banner high. The ghetto uprisings, and countless heroic battles, have made it amply clear that black people are prepared to fight to win full freedom *Now*. The task, especially of Negro leaders, is jointly and skillfully to seek the ways to make the best use of our heroic people's militancy. The task is to prevent the power structure, by its provocations, from misusing this militancy and turning it against the black people.

The task ahead is to make the most effective use of every position gained, to exert the utmost skill in rallying allies to our struggle and in isolating our enemies. It is for this reason we stress courage and clarity of purpose. It is in this spirit that the question of armed struggle should be soberly considered.

Communists believe in the use of violence to achieve political change only when reaction has closed off the channels whereby a majority of the people can realize their objectives by peaceful means. As we see it today, the overwhelming majority of the American people, including black people, are not yet convinced that the system must be changed, much less that it is necessary to do so by armed force.

Armed uprisings for such objectives cannot be undertaken successfully by the black communities alone, no matter how courageously they struggle. They require powerful allies in the ranks of the working class—white and black. Therefore, we reject the organizing of armed uprisings in the black communities today. However, it is necessary to issue the warning that there are extremely dangerous pressures to close the channels of the democratic process; in many areas, they have been virtually closed. Should this continue, it would leave the black people no alternative to violent struggle.

We believe that conspiratorial, terroristic actions which are not based upon a program aimed at improving the conditions of life for the masses, and which do not receive the support of the people, are adventurous, provocative and politically irresponsible, inviting reprisals against the black community. They should, therefore, be rejected.

We also believe that terrorism within the Negro community, directed against so-called Uncle Toms or others who refuse to go along with such tactics, is entirely out of place, divisive and harmful to the struggle for full freedom. It, too, should be rejected.

Although we do not advocate a policy of looting and arson, it is clear that ghetto uprisings, while unable to end the unbearable condition against which the spontaneous revolts were directed, did achieve certain positive results. These militant actions forcefully exposed to the nation and the entire world the urgent nature of the crisis in the ghettos. They made it painfully clear to many white Americans that life in our great cities will be unbearable for all unless it is made bearable for the people of the black community.

Moreover, these militant actions have intensified and deepened the mass resistance to the unjust war in Vietnam and inspired to greater militancy the struggle to end it. They greatly stimulated the struggle for Negro representation, spurred the Negro communities to the highest levels of political unity, and contributed to convincing larger sections of the white communities to work for, and accept, black municipal leaders. They have compelled the administration to respond to the pressure for additional black representation on all levels. Every advance that has been made in Negro representation in the recent period owes much to the message contained in the explosions in the black ghettos in 1967.

However, those who conclude that the task now is to give an organized character to spontaneous uprisings in the black ghettos, gravely misjudge both the mood of the black communities and the relationship of forces such organized armed uprisings would have to contend with. The strength of the 1967 uprisings lay in their spontaneity. It was this quality of the rebellions which rallied the sympathy and support of black communities and jolted large numbers of white Americans into an understanding of the depth of the crisis in the ghettos.

It would be quite a different matter, under present conditions, to win support in the black communities, let alone in the white neighborhoods, for an organized armed uprising. Nor can there be any comparison between the repressive measures employed in the suppression of the spontaneous uprisings, harsh as they were, and the unlimited force that would be used by the ruling class and its government against an organized uprising.

Black communities, of course, have the right to take necessary measures to defend themselves from invasion and assault by armed forces. But the real task at hand is to rally nation-wide support of all truly democratic white Americans, especially white workers, to stop the annual "summer slaughter" and to aid the struggle for survival of black Americans....

There is an urgent need for organized, militant and united struggle in every black community in the United States. Its arsenal of tactical weapons should include any and all forms of struggle that will most effectively and most speedily advance the fight for full freedom: mass marches, demonstrations, massive militant civic disobedience, boycotts and strikes. It should include sit-ins and sit-outs, and armed defense when necessary. It should include black community mass marches to the polls to elect Negro mayors, US Senators and Congressmen, and Negro public officials on every level.

The door should be wide open to any new and effective forms of struggle forged in the fires of the freedom fight. The only test for tactical weapons of the freedom struggle should be: Will they advance or set back the struggle? Will they unite or divide the mass of the black people? Will they aid in winning allies or in isolating us?

Militancy, the indispensable ingredient for all effective struggles, has to meet the test. The courage of brave individuals has played, and can play, a significant role in today's freedom struggle. But the real value of individual militancy lies in the ability to inspire *mass* militancy. It can never be a substitute for it. Individual courage, therefore, must be synchronized with those forms of struggle to which the mass of black people are ready to respond at any given stage of the struggle.

—"Unity and Militancy for Freedom and Equality," *Political Affairs,* New York, February 1968, pp. 3–7.

Index

ABBAS, FERHAT, 250
Abd-el-Krim, 28
Adventurism, 25, 175f, 182, 245, 273
African Liberation Committee, 29
African National Congress, 42, 43, 248, 269, 271
Afro-Asian Conference, Moshi, 271
Agrarian revolution, 181f, 213
Algeria, 29, 30f, 36, 38, 40; Communists, 37, 249; National Liberation Front, 37, 256ff
Algerian War of Liberation (1951–62), 10, 37, 248, 249ff, 254ff, 276, 323
Algiers, battle of, 257
American War of Independence, 1776, 10, 59, 65, 323
American Civil War, 59
Anarchists, 13, 87ff, 101
Angola, 40, 248, 263
Apartheid, 272, 274
Armed propaganda, 203f, 207
Austria, 22, 135

BARRICADE FIGHTING, 13, 16, 68ff, 74, 78ff, 86, 99f, 136ff
Base areas, 26, 179, 181, 183ff, 197, 212, 221, 229ff
Bashir Hadj Ali, 254
Batista, F., 38, 287
Belgium, 135
Bernstein, Eduard, 109
Betancourt, 304, 305
Black Hundreds, 86ff
Blanqui, Louis A., 88n, 94
Blanquism, 88ff, 109f
Boer War, 10
Bolivar, 324
Bolivia, 31, 225, 226, 281, 283f, 292
Bolsheviks, 16, 17, 18, 111, 113, 116
Bonaparte, Louis, 72n

Bourgeois nationalism, 119
Brazil, 281, 325
Brunei, 202
BUDC, 232ff
Bulgaria, 135
Burchett, Wilfred, 225
Burma, 31, 200, 202

CAAMANO, FRANCISCO, 319
Cabral, Amilcar, 41, 261
Cameroons, 102
Canton Commune, 27
Castro, Fidel, 37, 38, 39, 269, 281, 295, 299, 304
Chernov, Victor, 111f
Chiang Kai-shek, 175n, 178f, 209f
Chile, 283
China, 26, 29f, 34, 36, 40, 108f, 117, 167ff, 249, 323; anti-Japanese National United Front, 190f; Communists, 26, 177, 179f, 195, 299; Revolution of 1924–27, 179f
CIA (U.S.), 244n
Cities, encirclement of, 26, 198, 212, 225
Cities, struggle in, 16, 20, 22, 24, 35, 45, 103, 136ff, 224, 252, 260, 306, 308, 310, 311f, 322; see barricade fighting
Clausewitz, 59
Colombia, 225, 281, 292, 308ff; Communists, 285, 323
Communist International, 25, 30, 108, 118
Communist League, 12
Communist Manifesto, 13, 325
CONCP, 41n, 248, 276
Congo (Brazzaville), 30, 248
Congo (Leopoldville), 31, 248, 276
Congress of Labor Organizations (P. I.), 238

INDEX

Connally, James, 136
Continental revolution, Africa, 275*ff;* Latin America, 285*f*, 292*f*, 324*ff*
Corvalan, Luis, 324
Costa Rica, 325
Coup, role of, 17*f*, 103
Cuba, Catholic Church, 38; Communists, 303, 324; Popular Socialist Party, 38*f;* 26th of July Movement, 37, 281, 284
Cuban Revolution, 31, 37*f*, 40, 249, 262, 281, 287*ff*, 292, 294, 298, 300*f*, 303, 319, 325*f*
Cuella, José, 318
Cyprus, 30
Czechoslovakia, 28, 135

Danton, 53
Debray, Régis, 225*ff*, 284, 298
December uprising, *see* Moscow uprising
Democratic Alliance (P.I.), 238
Democratic Army (Greece), 165*f*
Democratic Conference (Russia), 112*ff*
Denmark, 135
Dictatorship of proletariat, 194
Dien Bien Phu, 215, 219, 221, 250, 255, 258
Dimitrov, Georgi, 22*f*
Dominican Republic, 297, 316, 318, 319, 325
Domínguez, Asdrubal, 318
Dubasov, Gen., 78, 80, 81

EAM (Greece), 158*ff*, 163, 166
Egypt, 30
ELAS (Greece), 135, 159, 160, 165
Engels, Frederick, 9, 11, 12*f* 16, 23, 48, 53, 57, 63, 68, 82, 242, 321, 325

Fadayev, Alexander, 123
FARC (Colombia), 312*ff*
FARP (Guinea Bissau), 41
Forms of struggle, 85*ff*, 92, 97, 99, 144*f*, 205, 241, 258, 293, 296*f*, 305, 309, 314*f*, 318, 320*f*, 330

Fortuny, José Manuel, 314
France, 23, 135, 154*ff*
Franco, 140*ff*
Franco-Prussian War, 57, 66, 67, 138
FREMLINO (Mozambique), 29, 41
FTP (France), 154*ff*
"Fundamental Spirit" (Huk), 229*ff*
Fyodorov, A., 127, 133

Gaitan, Jorge E., 311
General strike and uprising, 78*f*
Geneva Agreements (Vietnam), 225
Ghana, 30, 247*f*, 276, 278
Giap, Vo Nguyen, 203*n*, 204, 208, 299, 303
Gneisenau, 59
Gomez, Alberto, 311
Great French Revolution, 65, 68, 72, 94*f*, 108
Greece, 24, 31, 135, 158*ff;* Civil War, 161*ff;* Communists, 158, 161*ff*
Grenier, Fernand, 154
Guerrilla (*foco*) center, 145, 284, 300, 303
Guatemala, 281, 292, 301, 314*ff;* Nov. 13 Movement, 319; Revolutionary Party, 316*f*
"Guerrillaism," 19, 26, 182
Guevara, Ernesto Che, 38, 39, 281*ff*, 287*f*, 302
Guinea, 30, 248, 276
Guinea Bissau, 40, 248, 261, 263

Haiti, 281
Hitler, 139, 145
Ho Chi Minh, 203, 207, 211
Honduras, 325
Hungary, 135
Huk, 32, 35, 201, 229*ff*, 237*ff*

India, 109, 117, 202
Indochina, 27, 200; *see* Vietnam
Indonesia, 29*f*, 200*f*, 242*ff*, 249; Communists, 28, 203*f*, 206*f*, 212, 216*f*, 242*ff;* September 30 Movement, 243*ff*

Insurrection, art of, 21, 53, 109*ff*
International Brigades, 135
International Working Men's Association, 61, 95
Irish National Congress, U.S., 103
Irish Rebellion of 1916, 102*ff*, 135*f*
Irish Republican Army, 22, 136, 139
Italy, 23, 135

JENA, BATTLE, 60
Joannides, E., 158
Johnson, J. B., 327
Junius Pamphlet, 107*ff*

KATIPUNAN, 201
Kautsky, Karl, 82, 85*f*, 93, 98*f*
Kautskyites, 105*f*
Kenya, 30, 248, 276
Kerensky, Alexander, 17, 111, 112*n*
Khrushchev, Nikita, 128
Kolchak, Admiral, 19, 115, 126*f*
Kolle, Jorge, 283*n*
Kornilov, General, 17, 110*n*, 111*f*
Korea, 28, 48, 240, 324
Kugelmann, L., 61
Kuomintang, 27, 171, 175, 177*f*, 180*f*
Kuomintang-Communist United Front, 167, 180*n*
Kuomintang, Vietnamese, 209*f*

LANDWEHR SYSTEM, 66*f*
Lao Dong Party, 224
Laos, 202
Leballo, P., 270
Le Duan, 222
Lenin, V. I., 9, 16*ff*, 73, 77, 84, 94, 97, 102, 107, 109, 115, .123*f*, 164, 177, 195, 206, 242, 253, 259, 298*f*, 307, 315, 320, 322, 326
Leoni, 304
Lettish Territories, 83, 88*f*
Liberal Party (P.I.), 238*f*
Lin Piao, 29, 168, 194
Lister, Enrique, 139
Lumpen-proletarians, 168

MAGSAYSAY, RAMON, 34, 240*f*
Malakhov, Gen., 81
Malaya, 31*f*, 34, 200*f*; Communists, 33; People's Liberation Army (MPLA), 32*f*, 35, 200
Malaysia, 202
Mali, 30
Mao Tse-tung, 26, 29, 168, 177, 183, 194*ff*, 299
Maravilla, Jorge, 237
Marquetalia, 308, 313
Marx, Karl, 9, 11*f*, 16, 22*f*, 48, 53, 61, 81, 95, 100, 113, 195, 242, 315, 325
Mau Mau, 248, 276
Mensheviks, 97, 111*f*
Metaxas, Gen., 158*f*
Minz, I., 124
Mobile warfare, 218*ff*
Moncada Barracks, 303
Mondlane, Eduardo, 41
Morocco, 28, 30, 37, 248*f*, 252*f*, 259
Mozambique, 40*f*, 248, 263
Moscow Declaration, 1958, 243
Moscow uprising (1905), 77*ff*, 87, 96*f*, 137
Moudjahid, 251*f*
Mussolini, 139, 145

NAPOLEON I, 54, 59, 65, 72*n*, 108, 250
Nasution, Gen. Abdul, 202, 244*n*
National bourgeoisie, 39, 199, 241, 263*ff*
Nationalista Party (P.I.), 238*f*
National liberation, 31, 34, 262*ff*
National Liberation Front, South Vietnam (NLF), 37, 136, 227*f*
National liberation wars, 23, 37, 102*ff*, 107*ff* 115*ff*, 186, 324
National Peasants Union (P.I.), 238
NATO, 247
Navarre, Gen., 214
Negro people, U.S., 31, 45, 294, 327*ff*
Neo-colonialism, 264*ff*, 275*ff*
Netherlands, 135
Nicaragua, 27, 281, 325

INDEX

Nigeria, 30
Nkrumah, Kwame, 247f, 275
Norway, 135

OAS (Algeria), 258
OAS, Latin America, 325
October Revolution, 20, 27, 194, 199, 299, 318; *see* Soviet Union
OLAS, 282f, 285, 291ff
OSPAAL, 279
Organization of African Unity, 29, 246

PAIGC, 40f, 261
Pan-Africanist Congress, 270
"Paper tigers," 196f
Paraguay, 281, 325
Paris Commune, 27, 61ff, 72n, 94ff, 298
Party, and armed forces, 151ff, 169, 171, 174ff, 302f, 312ff
Peaceful coexistence, 123
Peaceful road, 242ff, 277, 315
Peasantry, 198, 212, 256, 265, 287f, 309, 323
Péraulte, Charlemagne, 281
Persia, 108, 117
Peru, 31; Communists, 282f
Petlyura, Simon, 19
Petty bourgeoisie, 39, 103f, 199, 244, 247, 257f, 265ff, 280, 284, 319f
Philippines, 10, 28, 31f, 34f, 46, 200f, 229ff, 323; Communists, 33, 46f, 237ff; Sakdals, 28; *see Huk*
Pinilla, Rojas, 311
Plekhanov, 79, 99f
Poland, 89, 101, 135; Socialists, 101
Pomeroy, William, 237
Poqo, 270ff
Political and armed struggle, 205f, 222ff, 226, 230ff, 250f, 257, 260, 275ff, 288ff, 294, 301
Portugal, 41, 247
Potemkin, 73f
Praetorianism, 56f
Prestes, Luis Carlos, 281

Proletariat, 23, 36, 91, 212, 224, 247, 256, 265, 268f, 284f, 311, 320
Proudhonist theories, 95
Putsch, *see* coup

QUIRINO, ELPIDIO, 239f
Quirino-Foster Agreement, 240

RACISM, U.S., 327ff
Radek, Karl, 103
Ramos, Benigno, 28
Rashidov, Sharaf, 123
Red Army (China), 27, 35, 168, 170ff
Red Army (Soviet Union), 19f, 24ff, 115, 124ff, 132, 135
Resistance, anti-Nazi, 135ff, 323
Revolutions of 1848, Europe, 12f, 53, 62, 69f, 94, 137
Rhodesia, 40, 247, 276; *see* Zimbabwe
Riff War, 28
Rodríguez, Juan, 304
Roving insurgents, 183f
Roxas, Manuel, 238
Rumania, 135
Russian Revolution of 1905, 13, 16f, 73ff, 86ff, 97ff, 104, 307
Russian Revolution of 1917, 17, 118; Provisional Government, 17, 110f; *see* October Revolution
Russian Social-Democrat Labor Party, 16, 298
Russo-Japanese War, 74, 83

SALAZAR, A. O., 41
Sandino, 27, 281
San Salvador, 285f
Santo Domingo, *see* Dominican Republic
Sarawak, 202
Scharnhorst, 59, 60
Sedan, battle of, 61
Self-defense, 207, 225ff, 273, 309, 313, 328
Self-determination, 102f
Smith, Ian, 43
Socialist-Revolutionaries, 111f, 114

Socialists, right wing, 13, 22f, 105
Socialist world and national liberation struggles, 28f, 40, 123, 249
Soummam Congress, 257
South Africa, 40, 42f, 247, 269ff, 276; Communists, 42, 269ff
South African Indian Congress, 42
Soviet Union, 18, 29, 40, 142, 147, 161, 249; Civil War (1918–21), 18, 116f, 124ff, 177, 180; Communists, 125; Great Patriotic War (1941–45), 18, 20, 23, 127ff, 323
Soviet of Workers' Deputies (1905), 77, 96
Spain, 24; Civil War (1935–39), 22, 135, 325; Communists, 24, 139, 142; guerrilla war (1939–51), 139ff; war against Napoleon, 54ff
Stalin, Joseph, 130, 177, 298
Statement of 81 Communist Parties (1961), 243
Sudan, 248
Sukarno, President, 243n, 244n

TAMBO, OLIVER, 43
Tanzania, 30, 248
Taruc, Luis, 237
Thailand, 202
Thiers, 61f
Tito, Josip Broz, 146, 151
Torres, Camilo, 319
Tricontinental Conference, 123, 261
Trung Chinh, 215
Tsereteli, Iraky, 111
Tunisia, 30, 37, 248f, 252f, 259
Turcios Lima, 319
Turkey, 108, 117

UGANDA, 30
Umkonto We Sizwe (Spear of the Nation), 42f, 270f
United Nations, 253
United States, guerrillas in, 44f, 327ff
U.S. intervention, 198; in Africa, 247; Colombia, 310; Dominican Republic, 319, 323, 325; Guatemala, 281, 316; Indonesia, 244; Latin America, 322ff, 291; Peru, 283; Philippines, 200f, 238ff; Spain, 140; Vietnam, 37, 201, 223, 226f
United Socialist Party, Catalonia, 142
Utung, Col., 243n, 245

VENEZUELA, 281, 292, 301, 304ff
Vienna uprising (1934), 22
Vietnam, 28ff, 36, 40, 48, 102, 123, 200ff, 240, 249, 259, 266, 295, 299, 303, 322f, 330; anti-French war, 208ff, 225ff; anti-U.S. war, 223ff; August Revolution (1945), 36, 204ff, 209, 211f, 221f
Viet Minh, 36, 41, 205, 207
Villa, Pancho, 281
Vinoy, 62
Vorster, John, 43

WALLACE, GEORGE, 328
Wagram, battle, 72
Waterloo, battle, 72
Winston, Henry, 45
Winter Palace, Petrograd, 17
Worker-peasant alliance, 17, 20, 27, 194, 224, 247, 311
World War I, 102, 107
World War II, 23, 140, 142, 201, 208, 213f

YON SOSA, 319
Yugoslavia, 24, 135, 146ff

ZACHARIADES, N., 163
Zambia, 30, 248
Zanzibar, 248
Zapata, Emilio, 281
ZAPU, 43, 248
Zimbabwe, 43, 248, 266
Zografos, Zizis, 161

SOUTHEASTERN MASSACHUSETTS UNIVERSITY
U240.P62
Guerrilla warfare and Marxism

3 2922 00166 618 6

WITHDRAWN